英語における聖書の言葉
―英語学習者のために―

Bible Words in Everyday English

"Cast your bread upon the waters …" Ecclesiastes 11:1

Jim D. Batten・Harris G. Ives・髙橋 教雄・上野 尚美

はしがき

　まずはじめにみなさんにお伝えしたいのは、この本の主たる読者として対象にしているのは、次のいずれかの方であるということです。

　(1) 日頃、聖書に触れる機会のない方
　(2) 聖書を通して英語の勉強をしたい方

(1) のような方のために、聖書について簡単な解説と、日常生活で使っている会話表現がいかに聖書から影響を受けているか、そして、映画、小説、スピーチ等にいかに聖書の言葉が使われているかについて紹介しています。(2) のような方のために、英語を多めに使い、日本語の要約（第1章と第3章）や英語についての解説（第2章と第3章）を加えています。
　この本にある聖書からの引用は、基本的に

　　英語訳　　　New International Version（以下 NIV と略記）(1973、他)
　　日本語訳　　『聖書 新共同訳』（日本聖書協会：1999）

を使用しています。ただし、必要に応じて、英語訳は King James Version (Authorized Version)（以下、KJV と略記）(1611) も用いています。KJV からの引用については、語形や文法に関する注を付けています。
　また、聖書を宗教書とは別の角度から見ていますので、もしかするとご存知なかった情報も含まれている可能性もあり、クリスチャンとして聖書に慣れ親しんでいる方々にも、きっと楽しく読んでいただけるものと思っています。
　さらに、この本に書かれている内容に触れて、みなさんの人生の味わいが深くなると感じていただければ、幸いに思います。
　最後に、この本は、茨城キリスト教大学の助成を受けて出版されました。また、塚田幸子さん（表紙と第2章）と金村美穂さん（第1章と第3章）にはイラスト作成にご協力をいただきました。それぞれに、感謝の意を表したいと思います。

　　　　　　　　　　　　　　　　　　　　　　　　　　2015年1月　著者一同

Table of Contents
（目次）

Preface（はしがき）... iii

Chapter I: A Simple Introduction to the Bible（聖書について）...................... 1

    The Book of Books（書物の中の書物、聖書）... 2
    The Story of the Old Testament（旧約聖書の物語）..................................... 3
    The Story of Jesus（イエスの物語）... 9
    The Parables of Jesus（イエスの寓話）... 11
    The Story of the Believers (the Church): Acts & Letters（使徒言行録、手紙）.... 14
    The End of Time and Heaven: Revelation（黙示録）.................................. 14

Chapter II: Idioms from the Bible（聖書由来のイディオム）.......................... 15

1. The King James Version: A Monument in English
（英語における記念碑「欽定訳聖書」）.. 15

2. KJV Idioms in Modern Conversations
（現代の会話に見られる「欽定訳聖書」からのイディオム）............................ 16

    1. An eye for an eye（目には目を）.. 17
    2. As you sow, so shall you reap（自分の蒔いたものは自分で刈り取る）........ 18
    3. Broken heart（失意／失恋）.. 19
    4. Eat, drink and be merry（食らえ、飲め、（明日は死ぬのだから））............ 21
    5. It is better to give than to receive（受けるよりは与える方が幸いである）.... 22
    6. Salt of the earth（地の塩）.. 23
    7. Good Samaritan（善きサマリア人）... 24
    8. Labor of love（愛の働き）... 26
    9. More than I can bear（わたしには負いきれない）................................ 27
    10. Prodigal son（放蕩息子）.. 28
    11. Scapegoat（贖罪の山羊）.. 29
    12. See eye to eye（目の当たりに見る）... 30
    13. The blind leading the blind:（盲人の道案内をする盲人）..................... 32
    14. The handwriting on the wall（壁に書かれた文字）............................ 33
    15. The second mile（二ミリオン）... 35
    16. There is nothing new under the sun（太陽の下、新しいものは何ひとつない）... 36
    17. Wit's end（途方に暮れて）... 37
    18. Wolves in sheep's clothing（羊の皮を身にまとった狼）....................... 38
    19. You can't take it with you（世を去るときは何も持って行くことができない）... 39

20.	A drop in the bucket（革袋からこぼれる一滴のしずく）	40
21.	Bite [Lick] the dust（塵をなめる）	42
22.	Cast the first stone（最初の石を投げる）	43
23.	Doubting Thomas（疑い深いトマス）	44
24.	Fall from grace（堕落する、神の恩寵を失う）	45
25.	Get your feet wet（足を水際に浸す）	47
26.	Man after my own heart（御心に適う人）	48
27.	To everything there is a season（何事にも時がある）	50
28.	A baptism of fire（火のバプテスマ）（聖霊による霊的洗礼）	51
29.	A fig leaf（いちじくの葉）	52
30.	A little bird told me（翼あるものがその言葉を告げる）	53
31.	A two-edged sword（両刃の剣）	54
32.	An upright man:（まっすぐな人）	55
33.	Apple of the [his] eye（御自分のひとみ）	56
34.	By the skin of our teeth（命からがら、辛うじて）	58
35.	Fight the good fight（戦いを立派に戦い抜く）	59
36.	Kiss of death（死の接吻）	60
37.	Man does not live by bread alone（人はパンだけで生きるものではない）	61
38.	A fly in the ointment（香料の中の蠅）	63
39.	Fall on his own sword（自分の剣の上に倒れ伏す）	64
40.	How the mighty have fallen（勇士らは戦いのさなかに倒れた）	66
41.	Strait [Straight] and narrow（狭い門から入りなさい）	67
42.	The spirit is willing, but the flesh is weak（心は燃えても、肉体は弱い）	69
43.	By the sweat of his brow（額に汗して）	70
44.	Feet of clay（陶土の足）	71
45.	Laughingstock（物笑いの種）	72
46.	My cup runneth over（わたしの杯を溢れさせてくださる）	73
47.	Stumblingblock（障害物）	75
48.	The bitter cup（苦いものを混ぜたぶどう酒）	76
49.	Written in stone/Nothing is written in stone （神の指で）記された石の板／何も記されていない石の板	77
50.	A prophet is without honor in his own country （預言者が敬われないのは、その故郷、家族の間だけである）	78
51.	Old as Methuselah（メトシェラのように長生きをした）	79
52.	Two are better than one（ひとりよりもふたりが良い）	80
53.	A flood of biblical proportions（聖書の規模の洪水）	81
54.	Fire and brimstone（火と硫黄）	83
55.	Manna from heaven（天の恵み／天からのマナ）	84
56.	Old wives' tale（愚にもつかない作り話）	85
57.	Out of the mouth of babes and sucklings:（幼子、乳飲み子の口から）	87
58.	Thorn in the flesh（わたしの身に一つのとげ（が与えられた））	88
59.	Your number is up!（あなたの治世は終わった）	90
60.	Jot and tittle（一点一画）	91

Chapter III: The Bible and Popular Culture（聖書と大衆文化） 93

Scripture in Political Speeches（政治演説で使われる聖書の言葉） 93
Scripture in Cities（市民が使う聖書の言葉） 95
Scripture in Hollywood（ハリウッド映画と聖書） 99

- *Footloose, 2011*（『フットルース 2011』）... 100
- *Snow White and the Seven Dwarfs*（『白雪姫と七人のこびと』）.................... 105
- *Les Miserables* (The Musical)（『レ・ミゼラブル』）...................................... 109
- *Places in the Heart*（『心の中』）.. 113
- *Simon Birch*（『サイモン・バーチ』）.. 117
- *Blind Side*（『しあわせの隠れ場所』）.. 122

Scripture in World Literature（文学作品と聖書）... 126

- *The Chosen*（『選ばれし者』）.. 127
- *I Know This Much Is True*（『ここまでは真実であると知っている』）................. 130
- *The Life of Pi*（『ライフ・オブ・パイ／トラと漂流した 227 日』）........................ 134
- *A Prayer for Owen Meany*（『オーウェン・ミーニーのための祈り』）................. 137
- *The Martyr*（『殉教者』）.. 141
- *The Old Man and the Sea*（『老人と海』）... 143
- *Anne of Green Gables*（『赤毛のアン』）... 147
- *The Sun Also Rises*（『陽はまた昇る』）... 152
- *Today Is Friday*（『今日は金曜日』）... 156
- *The Grapes of Wrath*（『怒りの葡萄』）... 158
- *A Tale of Two Cities*（『二都物語』）.. 163

Appendix 167

Chapter 1
★
A Simple Introduction to the Bible
（聖書について）

The Christian Bible is a very unique book. The Bible is actually a collection of many books over a period of more than 1,500 years (see Appendix for a list of the books included). It is the most published book in history. Translated into a very large percentage of the world's languages, the Bible is the all-time bestseller. In many countries of the world, it would be difficult to find a home that doesn't have a Bible. Missionaries have even gone into pre-literate communities, listened to the language, and transcribed that language into an alphabet and into a written form. Then they arranged for printing Bibles so that those people would have access to the grand ideas of "The Holy Bible." That is precisely what happened when missionaries went to New Zealand in the 1800s and developed a written form of the Maori language so that the people would have "The Word of God" among them. More will be said about English translations in the next chapter.

（キリスト教の聖書は、1500年以上にわたって記された「書」の集合であり、人類史上最も多く刊行されている書である。大多数の言語に翻訳されている聖書は、世界のベストセラーとなっている。伝道者たちは文字を持たない社会にまで出かけ、現地の言語を記述し、その言語を使って聖書を刊行してきた。1800年代に、マオリ族の言語で聖書を著し、「神の言葉」を伝えたのはその一例である。）

Why has the Bible been so widely published for so long? Of course, one reason is there are many Christians who want to have their own copy, and give copies to their friends and relatives who are not Christians. There are also many non-Christians who buy Bibles, for many different reasons. Since the Bible is so widely read in many societies, a basic knowledge of the Bible is very helpful in understanding those societies. One reason the English Bible has been a top seller is because many people want to learn English while at the same time learn about the history, communication patterns, ethics and morals of those English speaking cultures.

(聖書が長年にわたって広く出版されている理由は、自分自身のため、また、友人などのために購入するキリスト教徒に加え、キリスト教圏の文化などを理解しようと努める非キリスト教徒も購入しているからである。)

Many idioms, phrases, stories and parables used in English speaking cultures come from the Bible, even though people who use them may not know their origin. We will be looking at many of those idioms, phrases, stories and parables in the succeeding chapters.

(英語圏で使われているイディオムや逸話などには聖書に由来するものが多く見られる。)

The Book of Books

(書物の中の書物、聖書)

The English word 'Bible' is a transliteration of the Greek (τὰ βιβία, tà biblía), which means "the Books". There are 66 books that are divided into the "Old Testament" and the "New Testament". The Jewish holy writings have the same content as the Old Testament, but the books are arranged differently. The Old Testament is made up of 39 books. The first five are called the "Books of Moses" or "Books of the Law". They begin with the story of creation and give the history of the Hebrew people. There are also history, literature and poetry books. Among these, Psalms (songs) and Proverbs (sayings) are two of the most popular books. For example, the 23rd Psalm is a song which compares the love of God for humanity to the love a good shepherd has for his sheep. Many sayings in Proverbs are so common in English (e.g.: 22:1 "A good name is more desirable than great riches …") that people don't even know these words are from the Bible. In the last chapter of Proverbs the ideal wife is described in very picturesque language.

(英語の「Bible（聖書）」は、『書』を意味するギリシャ語の「τὰ βιβία, tà biblía」を訳したものである。聖書は39の書から成る『旧約聖書』と、27の書から成る『新約聖書』に分けられる。『旧約聖書』はユダヤ教の聖典と内容が一致している。『旧約聖書』の最初の5書は、『モーセの書』あるいは『律法の書』と呼ばれ、天地創造とヘブライ人の歴史が描かれている。『詩編』と『箴言』はよく知られた書である。)

The remainder of the Old Testament is a compilation of writings of the prophets (rcpresentatives or spokesmen for God). Throughout the Old Testament there are numerous prophecies (forecasts) about a coming messiah, or savior. One could say that the overall message of the Old Testament is summed up in the words "Someone Is Coming".

(『旧約聖書』の後半は、預言者の言葉で、来るべき救い主について書かれている。『旧約聖書』全体は「ある人がやって来る」という言葉で要約することができる。)

The New Testament is a collection of Christian documents. The first four books are called the "gospels" (good news) and give us the story of the birth, life, death and resurrection of Jesus. They affirm that Jesus is the one that prophets of the Old Testament pointed to. The book of Acts is a record of the first 30 years of the history of the "Church," the group of believers in Jesus as the Christ. Following Acts are the letters to churches and individuals from Jesus' apostles. These books could be summed up with the words "Someone Has Come".

(『新約聖書』の最初の4書は、「福音書」と呼ばれ、イエスの生涯、死、復活について書かれている。イエスこそが、『旧約聖書』で預言されている救い主であることを示している。イエスを信じる者の『使徒言行録』と使徒たちの手紙が続き、『新約聖書』は「ある人がやって来た」という言葉で要約することができる。)

The last book is the Revelation of John, a highly figurative letter written to the believers as they faced persecution from the Roman Empire. It encourages believers to continue to live lives of love and hope, even in a difficult situation. It also tells them (and us) about the future paradise, heaven. This book can be summed up with the words "Someone Is Coming Again".

(最後の書はヨハネによる『黙示録』で、ローマ帝国において迫害されていた信者たちを勇気づける象徴的な手紙である。この書は、「ある人が再びやって来る」という言葉で要約することができる。)

The Story of the Old Testament

(旧約聖書の物語)

How did the world begin? Where did man come from? What is his purpose or reason for existence? What is his duty/responsibility? Philosophers have argued these questions for ages. The Bible gives us the answers.

(哲学者たちが長年議論してきた「人間とは」という問に対して、聖書が回答を与えてくれる。)

The Beginnings (すべての初まり)

THE first book of the Bible, Genesis, is a book of beginnings. Genesis, the word, means beginning. The first sentence of the Bible is simple in structure but very deep in meaning. "In the beginning God created the heavens and the earth." God existed before the beginning of what we know now as the universe. Many times in the first chapter of Genesis we read, "God said … and it was so." God spoke all things into existence. On the 6th day of creation, God made man (Adam) "in His own image." He said, "It is not good for man to be alone …" so he created a woman (Eve). He gave humans the ability to reason, to choose, and to be creative in ways no other creature can. But man is a creation, God the creator. Throughout the rest of the Bible, God is teaching man to accept his role as a created being with responsibilities as well as privileges.

（『創世記』は「初めに、神は天地を創造された。」という言葉で始まる。神は宇宙が存在する以前に存在し、「神は言われた。…そのようになった。」が繰り返し見られる。天地創造の６日目に、「神は御自分にかたどって人を創造された。」聖書を通して、神は人間が被造物としての役割を受け入れるよう教えている。）

At first, God placed Adam and Eve in the Garden of Eden, a paradise. They had a good relationship with God. They totally trusted Him and obeyed Him. God provided all they needed and they in turn were able to be with God. He gave them freedom to eat from every tree of the garden except for one—the tree of knowledge of good and evil. They were told not to eat the fruit from this tree. Man had free choice, the ability to follow God or go against Him. With that freedom came responsibility. If they chose to disobey, humans would suffer separation from God, and eventually death.

（最初神はアダムとイヴをエデンの園に置かれた。二人は神に従順で、神は二人が必要とするものを全て与えられた。〈善と悪を知る木〉を除き、どの木の実でも食べる自由を与えられた。人には選択の自由が与えられたが、それには責任が伴う。人が神に対する不従順を選ぶならば、神から離れ、死を受けることになる。）

Satan (the devil) had already rebelled from God. He tempted Eve to eat from the forbidden tree. She ate the fruit and also shared it with Adam. As a result, their relationship with God changed. They had not followed what God said, and they tried to blame others and rationalize their actions rather than admit their disobedience. As a consequence God put Adam and Eve out of the garden. They were no longer able to eat of the tree of life, so they would, in time, die. By their sin (disobedience) they were separated from God, separated from each other, separated from the perfect natural garden, and separated from their own complete, ideal selves. Since that time man has had to work hard to secure food, and woman has suffered in childbirth. We now live in a broken world.

（サタンはすでに神に背き、禁断の木の実を食べるよう、イヴを誘惑した。イヴはその実を食べ、アダムにも食べさせた。二人は神への不従順を認めようとせず、自分の行動を正当化しようとした。そのた

め、男は食べ物を得るために労働しなければならなくなり、女は出産の苦しみを受けなければならなくなった。）

Adam and Eve were the first couple. For many generations the father of the family was the leader in God's plan, so this was called the "Patriarchal Era" (in Latin patriarch = father). Adam and Eve had children. Cain, their eldest, killed his brother, Abel, because of jealousy. This was the first murder. After that, their descendants became more and more rebellious and finally God decided to destroy all he had made with a great flood. However, one man, Noah, was a very good man who sought to do what God wanted. God told Noah to build a large ship, the ark, in order to save himself and his family, a total of 8 people, along with the animals. This is known as the great flood. We cannot be sure that there is a direct connection, but it is interesting that the old Chinese character for a large boat（船）is comprised of 舟 "boat" and 八口 "eight people".

（アダムとイヴは最初の夫婦となり、男が主導権を持つ父権社会であった。二人には二人の息子がおり、兄のカインは、嫉妬のために弟のアベルを殺してしまった。その後、人はますます反抗的になり、神は創造された全てのものを破壊する決意を固めるが、神に従順であるノアとその家族、および全ての種類の動物を救うためにノアに箱舟を造るよう命じられた。）

The Tower of Babel （バベルの塔）

EVEN after the flood, people continued to disobey God. Some decided to build a tower that would reach into the heavens ... perhaps an effort to prove their supremacy. God came to the tower and confused their language. Another beginning. Until that time they had all spoken one language, but from this point there were different languages, making communication more difficult ... talk was just "babble" (a word now commonly used for incomprehensible talk ... probably a reference to the Tower of Babel). They were scattered abroad and developed into various cultures.

（ノアの大洪水の後でも人は神に不従順であり、天に届く塔を建設しようとする者も現れた。それにお怒りになった神は塔の建設に関わった人の言葉を乱し、共同作業に必要なコミュニケーションが不可能になり、人々は各地へ散って行った。）

Abram—Abraham （アブラム－アブラハム）

ABRAM was a deeply dedicated man. God saw his faith and obedience, and gave him a promise.

I will make you a great nation, and I will bless you, and make your name great, so that you will be a blessing. I will bless those who bless you, and him who curses you I will curse; and by you all the families of the earth shall bless themselves. (Genesis 12:3)

Abram's name (exalted father) was changed to Abraham, "father of a multitude". God blessed him and his family. In the New Testament we learn that the phrase "all the families of the earth shall bless themselves," is a prophecy of Jesus Christ.

(敬虔なアブラムに忠誠心と従順さを見出した神は彼を祝福し、父祖アブラハムとした。
3 あなたを祝福する人をわたしは祝福し　あなたを呪う者をわたしは呪う。地上の氏族はすべて　あなたによって祝福に入る。
「地上の氏族はすべてあなたによって祝福に入る」とは、イエス・キリストの啓示である。)

Abraham's son, Isaac, also received the same promise. Isaac had two sons, Esau and Jacob (whose name was changed to Israel). Jacob had 12 sons, fathers of the 12 tribes of Israel. Jacob also received the same promise as his father and grandfather. Jacob was partial to one of his younger sons, Joseph. Joseph's 10 older brothers became jealous of him, and sold him to some slave traders who were passing through on their way to Egypt.

(アブラハムの息子イサクも人々の長となることを約束された。イサクの息子ヤコブは、後にイスラエルと名を改め、イスラエル 12 部族の始祖となる。ヤコブの息子ヨゼフは、兄弟の嫉妬心から奴隷商人に売られ、エジプトに連れて行かれた。)

The life of Joseph in Egypt was full of ups and downs, but because of God's guidance and Joseph's wisdom and ability to interpret dreams, he was able to survive. Pharaoh had a dream. Joseph interpreted the dream as a prophecy of seven years of plentiful harvests followed by seven years of famine. Pharaoh appointed Joseph to build barns and store up grain during the seven good years. He was successful, and made Pharaoh very happy. Eventually, during the seven years of famine, Jacob and the rest of the family moved to Egypt to be with Joseph. They lived happily in the area called Goshen for many years. After the death of Joseph, a new Pharaoh was afraid the Israelites might desert him, so he made them into slaves. This lasted for four hundred years.

(エジプトでのヨゼフの生活には浮き沈みがあったが、神の導きと自身の知恵と能力によって生き延びることができた。ファラオの夢を「7 年の豊作の後に 7 年の飢饉がやってくることが予言されている」と解釈したヨゼフは、豊作の間に穀物蔵を建てて準備するようにファラオに命じられた。ファラオの命に首尾よく対応したヨゼフのもとに、ヤコブとその家族が飢饉を逃れるためにやってきた。ヨゼフの死後、イスラエルの民がエジプトを見捨ててしまうのではないかと恐れた新ファラオは、イスラエルの民を奴隷とし、その状態が 400 年も続いた。)

Moses and the 10 Commandments（モーゼと十戒）

THE people of Israel cried out to God and he sent Moses to deliver the people from bondage. Moses was born into a Jewish (Levite) family in Egypt, but was raised by the daughter of Pharaoh. He would have been killed by the army of Pharaoh because of a decree against all male children of Israel, but his mother put him in a basket and floated him on the Nile River near where the Pharaoh's daughter was bathing. She found the child and took him as her own son. After he grew up he realized his true ancestry and tried to help his Hebrew (Jewish) brothers. He killed an Egyptian guard who was beating the Hebrew slaves, and was forced to run away and live in the wilderness. After 40 years of living as a shepherd, he was called by God to return to Egypt and lead Israel out of bondage. Pharaoh was not willing to let the people go, and God sent 10 different plagues on Egypt in order to convince Pharaoh to let them go. The tenth plague was the death of every firstborn son. In order to show this was from God, the Hebrew people were told to sacrifice to God and paint the blood of the sheep on the doorpost so that the plague would "pass over" them. This was the beginning of the Passover feast, a yearly Jewish holiday to commemorate their being freed from Egyptian slavery.

（イスラエルの民を奴隷の境遇から救うために、神はモーゼを遣わされた。モーゼはユダヤの家に生まれ、ファラオの娘の手で育てられた。成長したモーゼは、自分の素性を知り、同朋を救うために立ち上がった。ヘブライ人の奴隷を鞭打つエジプトの兵士を殺したモーゼは、40年間荒野で羊飼いとして暮らしていた。神のおぼし召しにより、エジプトに戻ったモーゼは、イスラエルの民の解放を目指した。ファラオが渋ったため、神は疫病を送って決断を迫った。その疫病から逃れられるよう、ヘブライ人は門前に羊の血で印をつけるように命じられた。その印を見て、疫病は〈過ぎ越す〉ことになっていた。これがユダヤ教の「過越の祭り」の起源である。）

Once delivered from Egypt, the Hebrews started on their journey to the "promised" land, Canaan. They disobeyed Moses and caused many problems along the journey, but finally came to the holy mountain where God gave Moses the Law … the Ten Commandments. You can find these in the second book of Moses: Exodus 20:1–18. This started the era known as the Mosaic era, the era of the Law of Moses. This law is the basis of Jewish culture. The first four laws tell how man should relate to God, and the latter six are the moral basis for man's relation to his fellowmen.

（エジプトを脱出したヘブライ人は、「約束の地」カナンに向かった。人々はモーゼに反抗し、様々な問題を引き起こしたが、シナイ山にたどり着いたとき、神はモーゼに〈十戒〉を授けられた。）

Joshua and the Judges （ヨシュアと士師記）

THE story of the first five books of the Bible ends with the transition from Moses to Joshua as leader of Israel, and the preparation for entering The Promised Land. The books of Joshua and Judges tell of Israel's entering and settling the land promised to Abraham. They had a good life as long as they followed God, but when they drifted away from His teachings, God would allow them to be beaten by some enemy until they repented and came back to Him. He would then send another leader, a judge or a prophet, to bring them back and to defeat their enemy. The cycle repeated many, many times.

（〈モーゼの五書〉は、モーゼからヨシュアへとリーダーが替り、アブラハムに約束された地に入る準備を整える話で終わっている。）

The Kingdom of Israel—Saul, David, Solomon
（イスラエル王国―サウル、ダビデ、ソロモン）

THE people of Israel finally decided they wanted to be like the other countries around them and have a king. Until that time the prophets or judges had led them, teaching them that God was their King, but they wanted an earthly King. Samuel, the prophet at that time, tried to reason with them, but they demanded an earthly King. Finally Saul was selected as King of Israel. At first he was a good King, but later his pride and greed caused many problems. After Saul, David was made King. The Bible says he was "a man after God's own heart" but he, too, had many problems. His successor was his son, Solomon. Solomon was the wisest, most famous King of Israel. However, he did not teach his children well. At his death the kingdom was divided by two of his sons into Israel and Judah.

（イスラエルの民は、周辺諸国と同様、王を望んだ。それまでは預言者や士師が民を導いてきたが、現世的王を望んだのである。最初に王に選ばれたのはサウルであった。次に王になったのは「神の御心にかなう」ダヴィデであり、その息子ソロモンがその跡を継いだ。ソロモンは賢明な王であったが、死後王国はイスラエルとユダに分割された。）

The Divided Kingdom—Israel & Judah （分断された王国―イスラエルとユダ）

THE rest of the story of the Old Testament is about the many problems of Israel and Judah. Israel, the largest part of the nation, quickly fell into idolatry and never really regained its strength. Judah also had many problems, but it lasted longer than Israel. The last portion of the Old Testament, the prophets, is a collection of writings of many prophets for Israel and for Judah who tried to bring the Hebrews back to their God. There are many references in these writings to a messiah, a savior, who would one day bring people back to God and redeem them. We learn in the New Testament that many of these references were prophecies about Jesus.

(イスラエルは偶像崇拝に陥り、その力を取り戻すことはなかった。『旧約聖書』の後半は、ヘブライ人を神の下に戻そうとする預言者たちが書き記したものである。そこには、人々を再び神の下に導く救い主が現れることが予言されている。『新約聖書』において、この救い主がイエスを指していることが描かれている。)

The Story of Jesus

(イエスの物語)

THE life story of Jesus is told in the first four books of the New Testament. These are called the "Gospels" (Good News). They give accounts of the birth of Jesus, his life and ministry, his teachings, and his death on a Roman cross and his resurrection.

(イエスの生涯については、福音書と呼ばれる『新約聖書』の最初の4書に記されている。)

Although we are not told a specific birthday in the Bible, the birth of Jesus has been celebrated for many years in Western culture on December 25. The name "Christmas" is made up of "Christ + Mass (worship)". The tradition of giving gifts is related to God giving His Son to the world. Santa Claus is not from the Bible story; it comes from the story of Saint Nicholas, a Christian man of the 4th century who was always giving to the poor and needy. The Bible does tell us Jesus was born in Nazareth to Mary, who had traveled there with her fiancé, Joseph. They had never had sexual relations. An angel had appeared to Mary and told her that God would give her a child whose name would be Jesus. The child was the Son of God. Some of the Old Testament prophets had foretold this, hundreds of years before.

(イエスの誕生日については特定されていないが、西洋では伝統的に12月25日に生誕を祝っている。「クリスマス」の語源は、Christ（キリスト）＋ Mass（礼拝）である。聖書にしるされていることによると、イエスはマリアとヨセフの子どもとされている。マリアとヨセフは交わりを持ってはいなかったが、神の使いによって、マリアは神の子を宿すことを伝えられた。)

We don't know much of Jesus' young life. He was born in Bethlehem, then God told Joseph in a dream to take his family and move to Egypt for a while, then back to Nazareth. His youth is summed up in this sentence: "Jesus increased in wisdom and in stature, and in favor with God and man." (Luke 2:52) Everyone needs to grow in these four ways: intellectual, physical, spiritual and social.

（イエスの幼年期のことについてはあまり知られていない。イエスはベツレヘムで生まれ、神の命によってヨゼフはマリアとイエスを連れてエジプトに行き、しばらくしてナザレに戻った。その青年期は、「イエスは知恵が増し、背丈も伸び、神と人とに愛された」という言葉に要約される。人は皆、知的にも、肉体的にも、精神的にも、社会的にも成長することが求められる。）

Jesus started his earthly ministry when he was around 30 years old. Many of his actions and teachings are recorded in the first four books of the biographies of Matthew, Mark, Luke and John. Jesus was always doing things to help others. He healed many who had physical problems. He encouraged the weak.

（イエスは30歳のころに伝道生活を始めた。イエスの行動や教えは、福音書に記されている。）

His social/moral teachings could be summarized in what he called the two greatest commandments.

"'Love the Lord your God with all your heart and with all your soul and with all your mind.' This is the first and greatest commandment. And the second is like it: 'Love your neighbor as yourself.' All the Law and the Prophets hang on these two commandments." (Matthew 22:37–40)

In another place Jesus gives what is now known as 'The Golden Rule'

"Do to others as you would have them do to you." (Luke 6:31)

If everyone followed these commandments our world would be a place of love and understanding.

（イエスの社会的、道徳的教えは、「心を尽くして主なる神を愛しなさい」そして「自分自身を愛するごとく隣人を愛しなさい」という言葉に要約される。イエスはまた別のところで、「あなたが人にしてもらいたいように、相手にもしてあげなさい」という黄金律も述べている。）

Jesus also taught about God. According to Jesus, God is our Father. He created us, He sustains us, and He loves and cares for us. In this broken world we sometimes cannot see God's love for all the horrible results of hatred and other sins of man, but Jesus tells us that God does love us. One of the apostles of Jesus said, "For God so loved the world that he gave his one and only Son, that whoever believes in him shall not perish but have eternal life." (John 3:16)

（イエスによれば、神は我々人間の創造主であり、人間を愛し、気にかけてくださる父である。イエスの使徒は、「神は人を愛するがゆえに、ひとり子を遣わせてくださった。そのひとり子を信じる者は、死ぬことはなく、永遠の命にあずかる」と述べている。）

The Parables of Jesus

（イエスの寓話）

Much of Jesus' teaching was in the form of stories with moral or spiritual meanings … parables. For example, Jesus told three parables to show God's love. One was about a good shepherd, who would leave the flock in the safety of the camp and go and search for one sheep that was lost. When he found the sheep he returned very happy and had a party to celebrate finding the lost sheep.

（イエスの教えは、〈寓話〉と呼ばれる道徳的、精神的物語の形式になっている。神の愛を示す寓話は3つあり、そのひとつは迷子になった一頭の羊を捜すために、群れをキャンプに残していった羊飼いの話である。迷子の羊を見つけた羊飼いは、喜んでキャンプに戻り、お祝いした。）

Another was about a widow who had 10 coins and lost one. She swept and cleaned her whole house and searched until she found the lost coin, then she was very happy and invited friends to celebrate with her.

（もう一つの話は、10枚のコインのうち1枚をなくしてしまった寡婦が、家中を掃除し、ついに見つけて喜び、友を招いて祝った話である。）

The third story was of a father who had two sons. The younger one was very selfish and asked for his inheritance even before his father died. He then took all he had and went to a foreign country and spent it all living it up. When all was gone, he became so poor and hungry that he had to work feeding pigs. He even thought about eating the food he was giving the pigs. He finally decided to return to his father's home and ask to be received, not as a son, but as a servant. Even a servant's life was better than the life he was living. When he was on the road back home, his father saw him and ran to him. He welcomed him with open arms and immediately threw a party to welcome his son home. The older son became very angry with his father, because he didn't think his younger brother deserved to be honored in that way. He would not even come into the house. He did not want to forgive his brother. The father also went outside and pleaded with his older son, asking him to forgive and accept his younger brother back into the family again. (Luke 15)

（三番目の話は二人の息子を持つ父親の話である。弟の方はわがままで、父親の生前に自分の分の遺産を求めた。遺産を手にした息子はそれを持って外国に行き、全て使い尽くしてしまう。（自分の身を落として）ブタに餌をやる仕事で何とか空腹をしのいでいたが、ブタの餌さえも食べようとする。ついに父親のもとに戻る決心をし、息子としてではなく、召使として受け入れてくれるように頼む。家に戻る途中に父親が息子を見つけ、駆け寄って招き入れ、祝宴を開く。兄はそれを見て、弟にはそれだけの扱いを受けるに値しないとして、不愉快に思う。祝宴の中に入ろうともしない。父親は外に出て、弟を赦して受け入れるよう、長男に頼む。）

These three stories show how much God cares for us. He will search for us even if we wander off. He will search for us because he considers us valuable. And he will forgive and receive us back no matter what kind of unloving things we have done.

> （この３つの寓話は、神がいかに私たちを愛してくださっているかを示している。私たちが神のもとを離れると捜し出し、私たちを価値ある者と考え、私たちがどんなことをしようとも、赦して受け入れてくださる。）

In another parable Jesus teaches us about the outrageous generosity of God. The story: A landowner went out early in the morning to hire workers for his vineyard. After agreeing with the laborers for the usual daily wage, he sent them into his vineyard. He went out again around 9AM and found some others who had no work, and told them to go into his vineyard, too, and he would pay them what was appropriate. Again at noon and at 3PM he found others who were waiting for a job, and he gave them opportunity to go to his vineyard and work. Once again at 5PM he found some men who hadn't been able to find work, and sent them into his vineyard, too. At the end of the day he paid them, beginning with the ones he hired last. Each of them received the usual daily wage. When the first ones came, they thought they would receive more, but each of them also received the usual daily wage. They complained, saying, "These last worked only one hour, and you have made them equal to us who have borne the burden of the day and the scorching heat." To that the landowner replied, "Friend, I am doing you no wrong; did you not agree with me for the usual daily wage? Take what belongs to you and go; I choose to give this last the same as I give to you. Am I not allowed to do what I choose with what belongs to me? Or are you envious because I am generous?" (Mat 20:1–16)

> （ほかの寓話の中で、イエスは神の途方もない寛容さを教えている。ブドウ畑の持ち主が、働き手を見つけるために早朝出かけ、通常の日当で雇い入れる。午前９時頃再び出かけ、仕事が見つかっていない人を雇う。正午と午後３時頃にも出かけ、仕事を捜している人を雇い入れる。夕方５時頃にも、仕事が見つからなかった人を雇い入れる。その日の仕事が終わり、最後に雇い入れた人から日当を払う。前の人たちがもらう日当を見て、最初に雇われた人はもっともらえるだろうと期待するが、同じ額だったので、不満の声を上げる。それに答えたブドウ畑の持ち主は、「あなたたちは、通常の日当で働くことを約束したではないか。私が自分の持っているもので何をしようが、私の自由ではないか。それとも、私が寛大であるため、あなた方はそれに嫉妬しているのか」と言って去らせる。）

God loves everyone … those he found early in the morning could work all day knowing that they would receive enough pay to buy things needed to survive. Those employed later in the day took the job hoping for even a little pay. Otherwise they would have nothing. They were overjoyed when they received a full day's wages. Jesus is teaching us that God is generous to all, and that without the gracious mercy of God we would all be lost.

> （早朝に仕事を得た者は一日中働き、生活に必要なものを買えるだけの賃金をもらえると考えて働いた。

遅くに仕事を得た者は、たとえわずかでも賃金がもらえることを期待し、丸一日分の賃金をもらうと、大いに喜んだ。イエスは、この話によって、神が全ての人に寛大であることを教えている。）

One more example of God's love and mercy can be seen in the parable Jesus told about a great banquet. The story: a man planned a large banquet and sent out invitations. When the banquet was ready, he sent his servant to contact each of the invited guests, telling them that all was ready and the meal was about to start. One after another, the guests made excuses for not coming. One had just bought some land and said he had to go see it. Another had purchased some oxen and said he had to try them out. Another said he was newly married and therefore could not come. When the master of the house hears these weak excuses, he becomes angry. He tells his servant to forget the guest list and go gather people up from the back streets and alleys of the town … inviting the poor, the crippled, the blind and the lame. When that didn't fill the house, he had his servant go out to the roads and country lanes and get people. He told his servant "Not one of those men who were invited will get a taste of my banquet." (Luke 14:15–24)

（神の愛と慈悲は、大宴会について語ったイエスの話に示される。宴会の準備が整った時招待客の所に召使を送るが、皆それぞれの理由をつけて来ようとしない。怒った主人は、招待客の代わりに貧しい人や、不具者、盲人などを集めて来るように召使に命ずる。それでも家が一杯にならないと、道に出て人を集めるように言う。主人は召使に「招待された者には、だれ一人として私の宴会の料理を食べさせない」と言う。）

Jesus here teaches that God accepts and gives grace to anyone who will come to him. Those who made silly excuses not to come will not be able to share in this love feast. However, those who come … regardless of their handicaps, problems, or hang-ups … will be able to enjoy the banquet in God's eternal house.

（イエスはこの話で、神のもとにやって来る者はその恩寵を受け、愚かな言い訳をして来ない者は、食卓を共にすることはないと言っている。ハンディや問題を抱えていても、神のもとにやって来る者は、誰でも神の永遠の家で宴会に席に付くことができる。）

Jesus told many other stories with very deep meanings, but those will have to be discussed in another book.

（イエスは他にも深い意味を持つ様々な話をするが、また別の機会に譲ることとする。）

The Story of the Believers (the Church): Acts & Letters

(使徒言行録、手紙)

THE book of Acts tells the story of the first century Christians and their activities for the first 30 years after the death, burial and resurrection of Jesus Christ. Peter and his teaching and life dominate the first ten chapters. He primarily taught Jews about Jesus and his resurrection. In the 10th chapter Peter is taught by a special vision that non-Jews were also welcome to become Christians. Saul, whose name was changed to Paul, dominates the rest of the book. He also taught Jews, but his primary work was teaching the Gospel of Christ to non-Jews, or gentiles. This is the biggest difference between the Old Testament (Jewish) religion and the New Testament religion. In the Jewish world one had to be a Jew in order to be acceptable to God. However, Jesus, Peter and Paul taught that race, citizenship or ethnic background are not important in order to please God. Anyone who through faith loves God with all his heart, soul, and strength and who loves his neighbor as himself is welcome to God's family.

(『使徒言行録』は、キリスト・イエスの死と復活の後の30年間にわたる使徒の行動を記している。最初の10章はイエスと復活について、ペトロがユダヤの民に伝えるものである。第10章で、ペトロはユダヤの民以外も信者になることができるということを示す。後半は、後にパウロと改名するサウルによるものである。パウロは主としてユダヤの民以外の人々に福音を伝えている。この点で、神に受け入れられるためにはユダヤの民でなければならないとする旧約聖書とは大きく異なる。イエスとペトロ、パウロは、神に喜ばれるようになるためには、人種などは重要ではなく、神を愛し、隣人を愛する者は神の家に招かれるということを教えている。)

The End of Time and Heaven: Revelation

(黙示録)

THE last book of the Bible, Revelation, is a highly figurative writing of the apostle John. It was written to seven churches in Asia for the purpose of encouraging them as they faced persecution from the Roman government. John encourages them to continue in their faith even in the face of death, because as Christians they not only have hope in this world, but also in life after death. He talks of the beauty of life eternal, with Jesus and God the Father in 'Heaven', a dwelling place for the good people who follow God.

(聖書の最後にある『黙示録』は、ローマの支配下にあって虐げられているアジアの7つの教会の人々を勇気づけるために、ヨハネによって書かれたものである。ヨハネは、「天の国」でイエスと父なる神と共にいる、永遠の命の素晴らしさについて語っている。)

Chapter II
★★
Idioms from the Bible
（聖書由来のイディオム）

1. The King James Version: A Monument in English
（英語における記念碑「欽定訳聖書」）

THERE are over 400 translations of the Bible in English alone. These translations cover various periods of the English language including:

（英語だけでも 400 以上の聖書の翻訳がある。こうした英訳は、以下のような英語の様々な時代にわたって見られる：）

Old English (pre-1066)	古英語期（1066 年以前）
Middle English (1066–1500)	中英語期 (1066–1500)
Early Modern English (1500–1800)	初期近代英語期 (1500–1800)
Modern Christian (1800)	現代キリスト教版 (1800)
Modern Jewish (1853)	現代ユダヤ教版 (1853)

Among the many English translations, The King James Version (KJV) of the Bible is regarded as a masterpiece of art. Scholars, poets, musicians and writers frequently acknowledge that the 1611 translation of the English Bible is a major inspiration for them. Even people who have no particular interest in religion recognize the beauty of the KJV. But as the English language evolves, it becomes necessary to constantly update the translations to make them understandable to current readers. For that reason, many students today prefer to read more modern versions of the Bible. It is important to understand that there is a long history of English versions of the Bible.

（聖書の英語訳が様々見られる中で、「欽定訳聖書 (KJV)」は最高傑作とみなされている。多くの学者、詩人、音楽家、そして作家が、1611 年に出版された英訳聖書によって刺激を与えられ、〈霊感〉を得てきたことを認めている。特に宗教には関心を持っていない人々でさえ、KJV の美を認識している。しかしながら、英語が言語として常に変化し続けているため、現在の読者が理解できるように、その翻訳も改訂され続けなければならない。そのため、今日多くの学生は、聖書の現代語訳の方を好むのである。聖書の英語訳には長い歴史があることを理解しておくことは重要である。）

Of course, there are many young people in the Western world who accept the challenge of studying the KJV. It was translated in the same time period of the English language as the writings of Shakespeare. In fact, both the KJV and *The Tempest* were published in the same year. So, for people who have an interest in the evolution of the English language, the KJV has particular appeal. For people less interested in the changes in the English language over the years, they can choose much more modern versions to read.

（西洋社会には、KJV を学ぼうとする若者も多くいることも確かである。KJV の書かれた時代の英語は、シェイクスピアの作品が書かれた時代の英語と同じ時代の英語である。事実、KJV と『大あらし (*The Tempest*)』は同じ年に出版されている。英語の歴史に関心を持つ人にとっては、KJV は特に訴えるものがある。英語の歴史にそれほど関心を持たない人は、もっと現代的な版で読むことができる。）

2. KJV Idioms in Modern Conversations
（現代の会話に見られる「欽定訳聖書」からのイディオム）

EVEN people who have no patience with studying the difficult grammar and vocabulary of the KJV still use many of its idioms in their ordinary conversations. They are probably unaware that so many expressions like "Salt of the earth," or "Go the second mile," have their origin in the KJV.

All of the various translations of the Bible since the KJV of 1611 acknowledge what a profound effect that version has had upon the world. The Preface to the Revised Standard Version (RSV, 1901) famously salutes its predecessor:

> The King James Version with good reason has been
> termed the noblest monument of English prose. Its
> revisers in 1881 expressed admiration for its "simplicity,
> it's dignity, its power, its happy turns of expression …
> the music of its cadences, and the felicities of its rhythm."

（KJV の難しい文法や語彙を学ぼうとする忍耐力を持たない人々も、日常の会話の中で KJV からのイディオムを多く使っている。「地の塩 (salt of the earth)」とか「さらに前に進む (go the second mile)」のような表現が、KJV に由来するものであるということに恐らく気づいてはいないだろう。
　1611 年の KJV 以降の（聖書の英語）訳は、KJV が世の中にどれほど大きな影響力を持っているのかを認めている。1901 年の「改訂標準版 (RSV)」の序文には、以下のように記されている。
欽定訳聖書が傑出した英語の散文であると言われているのはもっともなことである。1881 年にその改訂版を出した人々は、欽定訳聖書の「簡素さ、荘重さ、圧倒する力、表現の素晴らしさ、音楽のように流れる調子、そのリズムが与える至福」などを称賛している。）

1. An eye for an eye
目には目を

Matthew 5:38–42
マタイによる福音書　第 5 章　38-42 節

³⁸"You have heard that it was said, 'Eye for eye, and tooth for tooth.' ³⁹But I tell you, do not resist an evil person. If anyone slaps you on the right cheek, turn to them the other cheek also. ⁴⁰And if anyone wants to sue you and take your shirt, hand over your coat as well. ⁴¹If anyone forces you to go one mile, go with them two miles. ⁴²Give to the one who asks you, and do not turn away from the one who wants to borrow from you."

Revenge is a basic human instinct. When people hurt us, we want to hurt them back. The Old Testament had allowed some revenge. However, Jesus improved on the idea of human relations. He encouraged people not to take revenge. Under the old law, if someone took out your eye, you would be right in taking out that enemy's eye. But Jesus taught mercy and forgiveness.

³⁸「あなたがたも聞いているとおり、『目には目を、歯には歯を』と命じられている。³⁹しかし、私は言っておく。悪人に手向かってはならない。だれかがあなたの右の頬を打つなら、左の頬をも向けなさい。⁴⁰あなたを訴えて下着を取ろうとする者には、上着をも取らせなさい。⁴¹だれかが、一ミリオン行くように強いるなら、一緒に二ミリオン行きなさい。⁴²求める者には与えなさい。あなたから借りようとする者に、背を向けてはならない。」

復讐というものは基本的な人間の本能である。誰かが自分を傷つけたならば、その相手に仕返しをしたいと思うものである。旧約聖書では、そうした復讐が認められている場合がある。しかし、イエスは人間関係に関わる考え方を改善した。イエスは復讐などはしないようにと教えたのである。古い掟によれば、あなたの目を抉り出す人がいたら、その人の目を抉り出す権利を有するとなっていた。イエスはそれに対して慈悲と寛容を教えたのである。

　ミリオン＝マイル：1 マイル ≒ 1.609 km ／「目には目を」と「歯には歯を」は一緒に用いられる場合も多い。

Anne:　　When Ernest was the boss, he was unkind to Louis.
Jack:　　But now Louis is the boss. I'll bet[1] he will be unkind to Ernest.
Anne:　　I don't think so. Louis is a good man; he will not take "**an eye for an eye.**" [2]

1) **I'll bet**　きっと〜に違いない
2) **~ he will not take "an eye for an eye".**　Ernest は Louis にいじわるだったが、Louis はそんな態度を Ernest にはとらない。

2. As you sow, so shall you reap
自分の蒔いたものは自分で刈り取る

Galatians 6:7
ガラテアの信徒への手紙　第６章　７節

> ⁷*Be not deceived; God is not mocked; for <u>whatsoever a man soweth, that shall he also reap</u>*. (KJV)
>
> We must be careful to live good lives. If we get involved in illegal and criminal activities, we will end up in misery. A person who reads good books, listens to uplifting music, and engages in charitable works will have a happy peaceful life. In other words, the quality of our lives depends on our focus on good, wholesome things.

⁷思い違いをしてはいけません。神は、人から侮られることはありません。人は、**自分の蒔いたものを、また刈り取ることになるのです。**（8自分の肉に蒔く者は、肉から滅びを刈り取り、霊に蒔く者は、霊から永遠の命を刈り取ります。）

我々は良き人生を送るように注意しなければならない。不法行為や犯罪行為に関われば、みじめな最後を迎えることになってしまう。良い書を読み、精神を高揚させる音楽に耳を傾け、仁愛の精神に富む行いをすれば、幸福で平和な人生を過ごすことができる。言い換えるならば、人生の質は、良い、健全なことに集中することにかかっているのである。

soweth: sow の３人称単数現在形。／ **that shall he also reap** = he shall also reap it

---

Edna:　I can't believe it; I have just been awarded a complete scholarship for my senior year at the university!

Jack:　Congratulations. You really deserve[1] it.

Edna:　Of course you would say something nice like that. You are my good friend. You always say nice things to me.

Jack:　But it is true. You study hard. You're always helping[2] other students. You are the perfect example of "**As you sow, so shall you reap**".[3]

---

1) **deserve ~**（賞などをうけるに）ふさわしい
2) **be always ~ing**　always が現在進行形と一緒に使われると、~ing の動作がしばしば反復されることを表す。
3) **As you sow, so shall you reap.**　自分で行ったことは、よいことであれ、悪いことであれ、同じように自分に返ってくるということ。この会話は、Edna がいつもよく勉強し、他人を助けているので、大学から奨学金を授与されたのであると Jack が彼女を誉めている例である。

3. Broken heart
失意／失恋

Psalms 34:18 / Luke 4:18
詩編　34.18 ／ルカによる福音書　第4章　18節

Psalms 34:18
*¹⁸The Lord is nigh unto them that are of **broken heart**; and saveth such as be of contrite spirit. (KJV)*
*¹⁸The Lord is close to the **brokenhearted** and saves those who are crushed in spirit. (NIV)*

Luke 4:18
*¹⁸The spirit of the Lord is upon me, because he hath anointed me to preach the gospel to the poor; he hath sent me to heal the **broken-hearted**, to preach deliverance to the captives, and recovering of sight to the blind, to set at liberty them that are bruised. (KJV)*
¹⁸The Spirit of the Lord is on me, because he has anointed me to preach good news to the poor. He has sent me to proclaim freedom for the prisoners and recovery of sight for the blind, to release the oppressed. (NIV)

The expression, **broken heart**, or **broken-hearted**, appears in several different places in the Bible. The words are so common in conversations these days that most people don't realize that they are quoting the Bible when they use the term. Depending on the English version, the spellings vary:
Broken hearted, Brokenhearted, Broken-hearted.

　Today, when we refer to someone who has a **broken heart**, we usually mean someone who is disappointed in love. The expression is commonly heard on college campuses as boyfriends and girlfriends "break up" and move on with their lives. It can also refer to people who have disappointments other than romantic.

詩編 34.18
18 主は**助けを求める**人の叫びを聞き　苦難から常に彼らを助け出される。

ルカによる福音書 第4章 18節
18「主の霊がわたしの上におられる。貧しい人に福音を告げ知らせるために、主がわたしに油を注がれたからである。主がわたしを遣わされたのは、とらわれている人に解放を、目の見えない

人に視力の回復を告げ、圧迫されている人を自由にし、(19 主の恵の年を告げるためである。)」
「失意（の）／失恋（した）」という表現は、聖書のいくつかの箇所に見られる。語自体は最近の会話の中でよく使われるものであるため、この表現を使うとき、聖書から引用しているということに、気づいていない人が多い。英語聖書のどの版かによって、綴り方が異なる。すなわち、"broken hearted" なのか、"brokenhearted" なのか、あるいは "broken-hearted" なのか、というように。

　今日では、この表現を使うとき、通常は「失恋」している人に言及している。大学キャンパスにおいて、恋人同士が「破局」して、それぞれの人生を進むようなときによく耳にする。また、恋愛のような場面ではなく、何かに落胆している人に言及している場合もある。

　　nigh = near: 副詞・形容詞の古形。"neighbor" の下線部に見られる要素。／ **saveth** / **hath**: 3人称単数・直説法現在 "saves" / "has" の古形。／ **to set at liberty them** = to set them at liberty:「彼らを自由にする」／ **brush** = dismiss someone or something in an abrupt way (ODE)

(Broken heart in romance)

Derrick:　I feel so sorry for Mark. He is really very sad these days.

Anne:　　What happened?

Derrick:　After 3 years of dating, he and Edna have ended their relationship.

Anne:　　Well, I am sure that Edna is **broken hearted**[1] as well. Both of them are good people. Perhaps they will reconcile[2] soon.

(Broken hearted in personal failure)

Jack:　　I had high hopes for getting a new job. But I was rejected for the new position. This is the most **broken hearted**[3] I have ever been in my life.

Anne:　　Cheer up, Jack. You still have the current job.

Jack:　　Yes, that is true. I am glad that I did not quit this job.

Anne:　　I know you are not pleased with the salary on this job. Perhaps in a year or two you can apply again for another job.

Jack:　　Well, even though I am upset now, I think the best thing for me to do is to concentrate on doing my best here. Thank you for your concern.

---

1) **broken hearted**　（失恋して）悲しみに打ちひしがれている
2) **reconcile**　仲直りする
3) **broken hearted**　落ち込んでいる（状況）

4. Eat, drink and be merry
食らえ、飲め、(明日は死ぬのだから)

Isaiah 22:12–13 / Ecclesiastes 8:14–15:
イザヤ書　第22章　12-13節　飲み食いし、楽しむ (以上の幸福はない)：
コヘレトの言葉／伝道の書　第8章　14-15節

> ^{12}*The Lord, the LORD Almighty, called you on that day to weep and to wail, to tear out your hair and put on sackcloth. ^{13}But see, there is joy and revelry, slaughtering of cattle and killing of sheep, eating of meat and drinking of wine! "Let us **eat and drink**," you say, "for tomorrow we die!"* (Isaiah 22:12–13)
>
> ^{14}*There is something else meaningless that occurs on earth: righteous men who get what the wicked deserve, and wicked men who get what the righteous deserve. This too, I say, is meaningless. ^{15}So I commend the enjoyment of life, because nothing is better for a man under the sun than to **eat and drink and be glad**. Then joy will accompany him in his work all the days of the life God has given him under the sun.* (Ecclesiastes 8:14–15)
>
> This popular expression combines the ideas in two famous Bible passages. The idea is that we should not be sad or depressed. God is in control of our lives. We should enjoy the good things that God provides us.

<u>イザヤ書</u>
^{12} その日には、万軍の主なる神が布告された。嘆くこと、泣くこと　髪をそり、粗布をまとうことを。^{13} しかし、見よ、彼らは喜び祝い　牛を殺し、羊を屠り　肉を食らい、酒を飲んで言った。『**食らえ、飲め、明日は死ぬのだから**』と。

<u>コヘレトの言葉 (伝道の書)</u>
^{14} この地上には空しいことが起こる。善人でありながら　悪人の業の報いを受ける者があり　悪人でありながら　善人の業の報いを受ける者がある。これまた空しいと、わたしは言う。^{15} それゆえ、わたしは快楽をたたえる。太陽の下、人間にとって　**飲み食いし、楽しむ**以上の幸福はない。それは、太陽の下、神が彼に与える人生の日々の労苦に添えられたものなのだ。

良く知られているこの言葉は、聖書の2つの句に表されている考え方を合わせたものである。すなわち、人間は悲しんだり、落胆したりする必要はないということである。神は我々人間の人生・生命をコントロールしている。したがって人間は、神が与えて下さる良いものを楽しむべきなのである。

　　cf. カーニバル (Carnival: 謝肉祭) は、Ash Wednesday (灰の水曜日) に始まる、イエスの苦行・受難を思う期間である四旬節 (Lent) の直前の3日間の祝祭で、肉食を断つ四旬節の直前に大いに肉を食べ、酒を飲み、大いに楽しむ習慣がある。今日ではブラジルのリオデジャネイロで行われるカーニバルが世界的に知られており、裸に近い恰好で踊るサンバ (快楽の象徴) で有名になっている。

Anne: Jack, you worry too much.
Jack: I can't help it,[1] it's just my personality.
Anne: Well, you know what they say,[2] **"Eat, drink and be merry."**[3]

1) **I can't help it**　心配しないではいられない
2) **you know what they say**　よく言うじゃない（ことわざを引用する時に使う）
3) **Eat, drink and be merry**　飲み食いして、（大いに）楽しみなさい。

5. It is better to give than to receive
受けるよりは与える方が幸いである

Acts 20:35
使徒言行録　第20章　35節

[35]I have showed you all things, now that so laboring ye ought to support the weak, and to remember the words of the Lord Jesus, **It is more blessed to give than to receive.** (KJV)

Paul, one of the great Christian preachers during the first century, quoted Jesus Christ: **"It is more blessed to give than to receive."** Paul quoted Jesus as he was saying good-bye to some friends. Paul suspected that he would suffer persecution by people who did not like Christianity. He encouraged Christians to give priority to others. This is a complicated teaching in Christianity: each person should give priority to the other person. We probably see the opposite today. Most people have a degree of selfishness. Nevertheless, Paul teaches Jesus' idealized vision of human kindness. The problem is that scholars cannot find the exact place in the Bible where Jesus spoke these words. The reader must be satisfied that Paul's memory of Jesus' words is accurate.

（エフェソの長老たちに別れを告げる時のパウロの言葉）
[35] あなたがたもこのように働いて弱い者を助けるように、また、主イエス御自身が『受けるよりは与える方が幸いである』と言われた言葉を思い出すようにと、わたしはいつも身をもって示してきました。」

1世紀の偉大なキリスト教の布教者パウロは、イエス・キリストの言葉を引用して、「受けるよりは与える方が幸いである」と言っている。パウロは、友に別れを告げる際にイエスのこの言葉を引用している。彼は、キリスト教を良く思っていない人々によって迫害されるであろうと考えていた。彼は、キリストを信じる人々に、他者を優先させるように奨めている。この「各々が他者を優先させる」という教えは、キリスト教の教えの中でも込み入ったものである。今日では、そ

の反対のことを見ることが多い。ほとんどの人は、ある程度自分本位である。しかし、パウロは、人間のもつ親切な心をイエスが理想化した像を教えているのである。問題は、聖書のどこでイエスがこの言葉を言っているのか、その正確な箇所を学者が見つけ出すことができないことである。読者は、イエスの言葉をパウロが記憶しているということで満足しなければならない。

ye: 人称代名詞2人称複数主格。

Edna: If you have some free time next week, I hope that you will help with shopping.

Emiko: Sure. Nothing makes me happier than shopping.[1] Are you buying a new dress for the sorority[2] banquet next month?

Edna: No. I collected five thousand dollars from friends. We will buy children's clothes to send to a school in the countryside of Cambodia.

Emiko: Well, that is kind of you. But won't you also buy a new dress for the banquet?

Edna: I thought about a new dress, but I decided to use that money for the Cambodian Children's Project.

Emiko: Then, I will do the same. After all, **"It is more blessed to give than to receive."**

---

1) **Nothing makes me happier than shopping**（比較級を使って）「〜よりも…なものはない」
2) **sorority** 女子大生のための社交クラブ。主にアメリカで使われる。男子学生のための社交クラブは fraternity

6. Salt of the earth
地の塩

Matthew 5:13–16
マタイによる福音書 第5章 13-16節

*[13]You are **the salt of the earth**. But if the salt loses its saltiness, how can it be made salty again? It is no longer good for anything, except to be thrown out and trampled underfoot. [14]You are the light of the world. A town built on a hill cannot be hidden. [15]Neither do people light a lamp and put it under a bowl. Instead they put it on its stand, and it gives light to everyone in the house. [16]In the same way let your light shine before others, that they may see your good deeds and glorify your Father in heaven.*

Jesus uses this expression to compliment the hardworking people. Today, these words often describe good people who choose a simple, honest lifestyle.

「¹³ あなたがたは**地の塩**である。だが、塩に塩気がなくなれば、その塩は何によって塩味が付けられよう。もはや、何の役にも立たず、外に投げ捨てられ、人々に踏みつけられるだけである。¹⁴ あなたがたは**世の光**である。山の上にある町は、隠れることができない。¹⁵ また、ともし火をともして升の下に置く者はいない。燭台の上に置く。そうすれば、家の中のもの全てを照らすのである。¹⁶ そのように、あなたがたの光を人々の前に輝かしなさい。人々が、あなたがたの立派な行いを見て、あなたがたの天の父をあがめるようになるためである。」

勤勉である人を讃えるイエスの表現。今日では、質素で正直な人生を選ぶ「良き民」を表す表現として用いられる。

「地の塩」は、社会の腐敗を防ぐのに役立つ者のたとえ。「地の塩」と「世の光」は対になる表現として用いられることが多い。

Anne: Mark is such a good man, whenever he visits me, he finds something to repair around the house.

Jack: I know what you mean.[1] He helps a lot of people, and he never asks for any money.[2]

Anne: The world needs more people like him. He is **"the salt of the earth."**[3]

---

1) **I know what you mean** (君が言いたいことは) よくわかる
2) **ask for money** お金を要求する
3) **the salt of the earth** 謙虚で親切で人から信頼される、世のためになる人

7. Good Samaritan
善きサマリア人

Luke 10:33–35
ルカによる福音書 第10章 33–35節

³³But a certain Samaritan, as he journeyed, came where he was; and when he saw him, he had compassion on him. ³⁴And went to him, and bound up his wounds, pouring in oil and wine, and set him on his own beast, and brought him to an inn and took care of him. ³⁵And on the morrow when he departed, he took out two pence, and gave them to the host, and said unto him, Take care of him and whatsoever thou spendest more, when I come again, I will repay thee. (KJV)

Jesus told the story of a man who was beaten and robbed on the highway. Many of the man's fellow countrymen passed him by, not showing any concern for him. But finally, a foreigner stopped and took care of the man. He even put the injured man on his own donkey and took him to an inn. He left money at the inn for the further care of the injured man. We still speak of kind strangers as **Good Samaritans**.

(³⁰...「ある人がエルサレムからエリコへ下って行く途中、追いはぎに襲われた。追いはぎはその人の服をはぎ取り、殴りつけ、半殺しにしたまま立ち去った。...」³³ ところが、旅をしていたあるサマリア人は、そばに来ると、その人を見て憐れに思い、³⁴ 近寄って傷に油とぶどう酒を注ぎ、包帯をして、自分のろばに乗せ、宿屋に連れて行って介抱した。³⁵ そして翌日になると、デナリオン銀貨二枚を取り出し、宿屋の主人に渡して言った。『この人を介抱してください。費用がもっとかかったら、帰りがけに払います。』)

イエスは、街道で殴られ、持ち物を奪われてしまった男の話をした。同胞の人が大勢そばを通りかかったが、だれも関心を示さなかった。しかし、一人の異邦人が立ち止まり、その男を介抱し、自分のロバに乗せて宿屋まで連れていったのである。さらに介抱にお金がかかるならと、その人は宿屋にお金を置いていったのである。今日でも、親切な異邦人を「善きサマリア人」と言う。

morrow:「朝、翌日」。cf. tomorrow ／ **"Take care of ~ repay thee."**: 直接話法。／ **thou / thee**: 人称代名詞、2人称単数主格／目的格。／ **spendest**: spend の2人称単数現在形。

Stephan: In art class today, we studied the Rembrandt sketch of the **Good Samaritan**. Our instructor explained the Bible story which inspired the artist.

Yu: Yes, I know the sketch and the Bible story. I like the idea of such a kind stranger,¹⁾ but I don't believe such things really happen.

Stephan: Really? There are many examples of kind strangers. Yesterday, my car was stuck²⁾ in the ice on an incline.³⁾ A housewife came out of her house and laid expensive towels down so that my wheels could get traction. I was able to drive on within minutes.

Yu: Then, I stand corrected.⁴⁾ She is a truly a Good Samaritan. Did you give her money for the towels?

Stephan: She would not accept the money. She just said, "Help somebody else who has trouble."

---

1) **stranger** 異邦人、見知らぬ人
2) **be stuck** 動きがとれない（状態である）
3) **on an incline** 坂で
4) **stand corrected** 誤りを認める

8. Labor of love
愛の働き

Hebrews 6:10
ヘブライ人への手紙　第6章　10節

*¹⁰For God is not unrighteous to forget your work and **labor of love**, which ye have showed toward his name, in that ye have ministered to the saints, and do minister.* (KJV)
¹⁰God is not unjust; he will not forget your work and <u>the love</u> you have shown him as you have helped his people and continue to help them. (NIV)

The idea expressed here is that God sees all of the kind things we do. He is glad when we serve other people (feeding the hungry, doing volunteer work, etc.). God regards the kind things we do for other human beings as if we were personally doing the kind deeds to Him.

Often, today, we use this expression to refer to a task that a young man or a young woman might do to please or impress a lover. Of course love is not restricted to boyfriend-girlfriend romance. It can be a brotherly or neighborly love as well.

¹⁰神は不義な方ではないので、あなたがたの**働き**や、あなたがたが聖なる者たちに以前も今も仕えることによって、神の名のために示したあの**愛**をお忘れになるようなことはありません。

ここに示されている考え方は、神はわたしたちが行う全ての親切な行為を見ておられる、ということである。（飢える人々に食べ物を与えたり、ボランティアの仕事をしたり、というようなことをして、）他の人々を助けようとしているとき、神は喜ばれる。他の人のためにわたしたちが行う親切な行為は、わたしたちが神のためにしていることであるかのようにみなしてくださる。
今日では、この表現は、若い男子あるいは女子が愛する人を喜ばせたり、印象付けたりするために行う行為に言及して使われることが多い。もちろん愛は男女間のロマンチックな愛に限定されるものではなく、兄弟愛や隣人愛もありうるのである。

　　ye: 2人称複数主格の人称代名詞 (you) の古形。

(A conversation about neighborly love)
Edna:　　Mark spent all Saturday reading chapters of Ernest Hemingway's *The Old Man and the Sea* to his blind neighbor.
Derrick:　His neighbor? Maybe she is a beautiful lady, and he has fallen in love with her.
Edna:　　Well, certainly Mrs. Clark has a beautiful spirit. She is 73 years old,

and she is very kind. I think Mark loves her as if[1] she were his grandmother.

Derrick: Well, anyway, reading to Mrs. Clark is **a labor of love**[2] for Mark. He is a good guy.

(A conversation about romantic love)
Jack: Did you hear that Mark has a new girlfriend?
Anne: Everybody knows about that. For the last six Saturdays, Mark has been working overtime. He wants to buy her an engagement ring.
Jack: Wow, working so much overtime to buy a ring is really **a labor of love**.[3]

1) **as if** まるで〜であるかのように
2) **a labor of love** 奉仕活動
3) **a labor of love** 愛の働き

9. More than I can bear
わたしには負いきれない

Genesis 4:9–15
創世記 第4章 9-15節

*⁹Then the Lord said to Cain, "Where is your brother Abel?" "I don't know," he replied. "Am I my brother's keeper?" ¹⁰The Lord said, "What have you done? Listen! Your brother's blood cries out to me from the ground. ¹¹Now you are under a curse, and driven from the ground, which opened its mouth to receive your brother's blood from your hand. ¹²When you work the ground, it will no longer yield its crops to you. You will be a restless wanderer on the earth. ¹³Cain said to the Lord, **"My punishment is more than I can bear**. ¹⁴Today you are driving me from the land, and I will be hidden from your presence; I will be as a restless wanderer on the earth, and whoever finds me will kill me." ¹⁵But the Lord said to him, "Not so, if anyone kills Cain, he will suffer vengeance seven times over." Then the Lord put a mark on Cain so that no one who found him would kill him.*

The first murder recorded in the Bible is Cain's killing of his brother, Abel. This kind of murder is called fratricide. The motive was jealousy. It is not completely clear, but Cain assumed that God loved his brother more. God pronounced several punishments upon Cain. But, interestingly, God placed a mysterious mark upon Cain that would protect him from being harmed by others. Still Cain thought that the punishment was too severe.

⁹主はカインに言われた。「お前の弟アベルは、どこにいるのか。」カインは答えた。「しりません。わたしは弟の番人でしょうか。」¹⁰主は言われた。「何ということをしたのか。お前の弟の血が土の中からわたしに向かって叫んでいる。¹¹今、お前は呪われる者となった。お前が流した弟の血を、口を開けて飲み込んだ土よりもなお、呪われる。¹²土を耕しても、土はもはやお前のために作物を産み出すことはない。お前は地上をさまよい、さすらう者となる。」¹³カインは主に言った。「わたしの罪は重すぎて負いきれません。¹⁴今日、あなたがわたしをこの土地から追放なさり、わたしが御顔から隠されて、地上をさまよい、さすらう者となってしまえば、わたしに出会う者はだれであれ、わたしを殺すでしょう。」¹⁵主はカインに言われた。「いや、それゆえカインを殺す者は、だれであれ七倍の復習を受けるであろう。」主はカインに出会う者がだれも彼を撃つことのないように、カインにしるしを付けられた。

聖書における最初の殺人の記録は、カインが弟のアベルを殺したことである。こうした殺人は「兄弟殺し (fratricide)」と呼ばれる。その動機は嫉妬であった。明記されているわけではないが、カインは、神が弟の方をより愛していると考えていたのである。神はカインに対していくつかの罰を宣告した。しかし、興味深いことに、他の者がカインを傷つけないようにするために、神はカインに不思議なしるしを付けられた。それでもカインは罰が重すぎると考えた。

    cf. patricide（父親殺し）–matricide（母親殺し）–fratricide-sororicide（姉妹殺し）–homicide（人殺し）–genocide（集団大虐殺）–insecticide（殺虫剤）–germicide（殺菌剤）

Jack: I went to Las Vegas and gambled away three thousand dollars.
Anne: What did your wife say?
Jack: I haven't told her yet. Probably she will be angry with me for the rest of the year. **Her nagging**[1] **is more than I can bear**.[2]

---

1) **nagging**   常に小言を言ったり、厳しくけん責したりすること
2) **Her nagging is more than I can bear**   彼女の小言に耐えられない

10. Prodigal son
放蕩息子

Luke 15:11–32
ルカによる福音書　第 15 章　11–32 節

(For purpose of space saving, only verse 13 is cited here.)
¹³And not many days after, the younger son gathered all together, and took his journey into a far country, and there <u>wasted</u> his substance with riotous living. (KJV)

This is an especially interesting situation. Jesus told a story about a father who had two sons. One of the boys demanded his inheritance early. He took the money and lived wildly in a foreign country. The world over, this story is known as the Prodigal Son. However, those words are never used in the story. Even more interestingly, many people think the word prodigal means "bad" or "errant." Some people even think the word means a boy who has stayed away from his family a long time. In actuality the word means wasteful. The boy wasted the money in the foreign country.

(聖書に示されている物語は長いので、ここでは第13節のみを引用する。)
¹³ 何日もたたないうちに、下の息子は全部を金に換えて、遠い国に旅立ち、そこで*放蕩の限りを尽くして*、財産を無駄使いしてしまった。

この表現は興味深い状況を示している。イエスは2人の息子を持つある父親の話をしている。息子の一人が早めに財産を分けてほしいと要求し、そのお金を持って異国に行き、放埓三昧の生活をした。この物語は「放蕩息子」の話として世界中に知られているが、"prodigal son" という表現は物語の中では使われていない。さらに、"prodigal" という語が "bad（悪い）" とか "errant（さまよう）" という意味であると思っている人が多いのは、興味深いものである。この語は、実際には「浪費的な」という意味である。この息子は、異国でお金を「浪費した」ということである。

Jack: I haven't been home in over eight years. It will be good to see my brother and sister again.
Anne: Eight years, I am sure that your family will be happy to welcome the **Prodigal Son**[1] home.
Jack: Well, I have not been **prodigal**,[2] but I have been busy with my job here in the city.

1) **prodigal son** 放蕩息子
2) **prodigal** 【名】浪費家、放蕩者　【形】金遣いの荒い、浪費癖のある

11. Scapegoat
贖罪の山羊

Leviticus 16:6–10
レビ記　第16章　6–10節

*⁶Aaron is to offer the bull for his own sin offering to make atonement for himself and his household. ⁷Then he is to take the two goats and present them before the LORD at the entrance to the tent of meeting. ⁸He is to cast lots for the two goats— one lot for the LORD and the other for the **scapegoat**. ⁹Aaron shall bring the goat whose lot falls to the LORD and sacrifice it for a sin offering. ¹⁰But the goat chosen by lot as the scapegoat shall be presented alive before the LORD to be used for making atonement by sending it into the wilderness as a scapegoat.*

In the Old Testament, the scapegoat was an animal that was killed by the people. The people used that animal as a symbol. The people believed that they could transfer all of their bad actions and sins to the animal. The word is often used today. It means someone that everyone blames for their own bad behavior.

（モーセの兄アロンに対して神が与えた贖罪についての指示の一部。）
⁶ アロンは、自分の贖罪の献げ物のために雄牛を引いて来て、自分と一族のために購いの儀式を行う。⁷ 次いで、雄山羊二匹を受け取り、臨在の幕屋の入り口の主の御前に引いて来る。⁸ アロンは二匹の雄山羊についてくじを引き、一匹を主のもの、他の一匹をアザゼルのものと決める。⁹ アロンはくじで主のものに決まった雄山羊を**贖罪の献げ物**に用いる。¹⁰ くじでアザゼルのものに決まった雄山羊は、生きたまま主の御前に留めておき、購いの儀式を行い、荒れ野のアザゼルのもとへ追いやるためのものとする。

旧約聖書で贖罪の山羊というのは、象徴として使われ、人間によって殺される動物のことであった。人間の悪行や罪をこの動物に転嫁できると信じられていたのである。この語は今日でもよく使われ、自分の悪行の非難を向ける対象とされる人を意味している。

 cf. 「創世記 第22章」で、年老いてようやく生まれた一人息子のイサクを捧げ物とするよう、神に命じられたアブラハムが、苦しみながらも神の命令に従おうとしていたとき、アブラハムの信仰心を認めた神が、イサクの替わりに与えた雄羊。

Anne: Every time Henry gets in trouble,[1] he always blames his parents.
Jack: Yeah, he always says that his parents were too strict with him.
Anne: He should take responsibility[2] for his own actions. He should stop making his parents the **scapegoats**[3] for his problems.

1) **get in trouble**   トラブルに巻き込まれる、災難に見舞われる
2) **take responsibility**   責任を持つ
3) **scapegoat**   身代わり、罪をかぶせられる人

12. See eye to eye
見解が全く一致する

Isaiah 52:8
イザヤ書　第52章　8節

⁸*Thy watchmen shall lift up the voice; with the voice together shall they sing; for they shall **see eye to eye**, when the Lord shall bring again Zion.* (KJV)

The prophet Isaiah predicts a good time in the future. He has a vision of a time when people will not quarrel. He anticipates a time when Christians (and all people of goodwill) will praise God together. It is a vision of unity. Of course, this phrase appears frequently in modern conversation with no particular reference to the Bible or Isaiah's vision. We often hear this expression in the negative form these days, as in: "Well, **we just don't see eye to eye**," meaning we can't reach an agreement.

⁸その声に、あなたの見張りは声をあげ 皆共に、喜び歌う。彼らは目の当たりに見る 主がシオンに帰られるのを。

預言者イザヤは、未来の良き時を予言している。彼は、人々が争わなくなる時を見ている。彼は、キリスト教徒（およびすべての善意の人）が共に神を讃える時を予見しているのである。それは「一致」の姿である。この表現は、聖書やイザヤの描いた像に特に言及せずに、今日の会話においてしばしば見られるものでもある。最近では、否定文の形で使われることも多い。例えば、意見の一致に達することができない時、「意見が全く合わない」のように言う。

see eye to eye:「見解が全く一致する」／ **with the voice together shall they sing** = they shall sing with the voice together ／ **Zion**:「エルサレム旧市東南の、政治の中心であったシオン山」、「天における神の都」

Stephan: The city council is planning to tear down the old Majestic Theater in the center of town.
Anne: Well, it's about time.[1] That is an ugly old building. It is just an eyesore.[2] What are they planning to put in its place?
Stephan: I heard that they will sell the land and let a company build a new convenience store.
Anne: That sounds like a good idea to me.
Stephan: Anne, **we don't see eye to eye**.[3] The Majestic Theater was built in the early 1900s. I think we should preserve it. It could be restored to good condition. If it can't be a movie theater again, perhaps it could make a nice library.
Anne: You're right. **We don't see eye to eye**.

---

1) **about time** そろそろ〜してもよい頃
2) **eyesore** 目障りなもの
3) **not see eye to eye** 意見が一致しない

13. The blind leading the blind
盲人の道案内をする盲人

Matthew 15:10–14
マタイによる福音書　第 15 章　10–14 節

[10] And he called the multitude, and said unto them, Hear and understand; [11] Not that which goeth into the mouth defileth a man; but that which cometh out of the mouth, this defileth a man. [12] Then came his disciples, and said unto him, Knowest thou that the Pharisees were offended, after they heard this saying? [13] But he answered and said, Every plant, which my heavenly Father hath not planted, shall be rooted up. [14] Let them alone; they be blind leaders of the blind. And if the blind shall lead the blind, both shall fall into the ditch. (KJV)

Jesus was criticizing the Pharisees. They were supposed to be excellent students of religion, but, in fact, they missed many important ideas of the Bible. They had strict dietary laws about what foods to eat. Of course pork was forbidden to them. But Jesus expressed the idea that it is more important to be careful about decent behavior and decent speech, than to be concerned about which meats were appropriate for religious people. They were very proud of themselves, and they thought of themselves as superior to less educated people. Jesus said that they were only **blind people leading other blind people**. He meant that they lacked a full understanding of God's commands, and that they were not suited to educate others. They were **the blind leading the blind**.

[10] それから、イエスは群衆を呼び寄せて言われた。「聞いて悟りなさい。[11] 口に入るものは人を汚さず、口から出て来るものが人を汚すのである。」[12] そのとき、弟子たちが近寄って来て、「ファリサイ派の人々がお言葉を聞いて、つまずいたのをご存じですか」と言った。[13] イエスはお答えになった。「わたしの天の父がお植えにならなかった木は、すべて抜き取られてしまう。[14] そのままにしておきなさい。彼らは**盲人の道案内をする盲人**だ。盲人が盲人の道案内をすれば、二人とも穴に落ちてしまう。」

イエスはファリサイ派の人々を批判していた。ファリサイ派の人々は宗教に関して優れた人々尾であると考えられていたが、実際は聖書の重要な教えを見のがしていたのである。彼らは何を食べてよいのかということについて、厳しい規則をもっていた。もちろん豚肉は食べるのを禁じられていた。それに対してイエスは、宗教者にとってどんな食べ物が適切であるのかということに頭を悩ませるよりも、慎みのある行為、言葉に注意を払うことの方がもっと重要であるというこ

とを表した。ファリサイ派の人々は自尊心をもっていて、教養のない人々よりも優れていると思っていた。イエスは、ファリサイ派の人々は**盲人の道案内をする盲人**にすぎないと言っている。イエスの意図したところは、ファリサイ派の人々は神の命令を十分には理解しておらず、他の人々に教えることにはむいていないということである。彼らはまさに**盲人の道案内をする盲人**なのである。

『欽定訳聖書』では、直接話法においても引用符 (quotation marks) は使わないのが普通である。上記の例では、以下の2文が直接話法に当たる。

- *Hear and understand; Not that which goeth into the mouth defileth a man; but that which cometh out of the mouth, this defileth a man.*
- *Every plant, which my heavenly Father hath not planted, shall be rooted up. Let them alone; they be blind leaders of the blind. And if the blind shall lead the blind, both shall fall into the ditch.*

goeth / **defileth** / **cometh**: go / defile（汚す）/ come の3人称単数現在形。／ **hath**: have の3人称単数現在形 (has)。／ **Let them alone.** = Leave them alone.

Edna: Mark, I heard that you and Anne are studying together tonight.
Mark: Yeah, I am helping her with the homework for the Music Theory class.
Edna: Excuse me,[1] but didn't you make a "D" grade in that class last semester?
Mark: That is true.
Edna: Well, I am afraid that is **the blind leading the blind**.[2]
Mark: Not really, since doing poorly in that class, I studied much more carefully on my own. I think I am prepared to be a good tutor.
Edna: Well, good for you.

---

1) **Excuse me** 何ですって？（相手の言葉が意外であった時に使われる驚きの表現）
2) **the blind leading the blind** よくわからない人が他の人に教えること

14. The handwriting on the wall
壁に書かれた文字

Daniel 5:1–16
ダニエル書 第5章1–16節

¹*King Belshazzar gave a great banquet for a thousand of his nobles and drank wine with them.* ²*While Belshazzar was drinking his wine, he gave orders to bring in the gold and silver goblets that Nebuchadnezzar his father had taken from the temple in Jerusalem, so that the king and his nobles, his wives and his concubines might drink from them.* ³*So they brought in the gold goblets that had been taken from the temple of God in Jerusalem, and the king and his nobles, his wives and*

his concubines drank from them. ⁴As they drank the wine, they praised the gods of gold and silver, of bronze, iron, wood and stone. ⁵Suddenly <u>the fingers of a human hand appeared and wrote on the plaster of the wall</u>, near the lampstand in the royal palace. The king watched the hand as it wrote. ⁶His face turned pale and he was so frightened that his legs became weak and his knees were knocking.

… ¹³So Daniel was brought before the king, and the king said to him, "Are you Daniel, one of the exiles my father the king brought from Judah? ¹⁴I have heard that the spirit of the gods is in you and that you have insight, intelligence and outstanding wisdom. ¹⁵The wise men and enchanters were brought before me to read <u>this writing</u> and tell me what it means, but they could not explain it. ¹⁶Now I have heard that you are able to give interpretations and to solve difficult problems. If you can read <u>this writing</u> and tell me what it means, you will be clothed in purple and have a gold chain placed round your neck, and you will be made the third highest ruler in the kingdom."

A rich king gave a party. He wanted to impress all of the guests at his party. So, he used the most expensive gold and silver items on the table. It seems that the king thought of his gold and silver ornaments as "gods." But the Great God in Heaven produced a mysterious writing on the wall. The prophet Daniel interpreted the handwriting on the wall as a prediction of God's punishment for giving priority to money and riches over God. The idea is that something will end badly.

（壁に字を書く指の幻の話しが述べられているダニエル書第5章の一部。）
¹ベルシャツァル王は千人の貴族を招いて大宴会を開き、みんなで酒を飲んでいた。²宴も進んだころ、ベルシャツァルは、その父ネブカドネツァルがエルサレムの神殿から奪って来た金銀の祭具を持って来るように命じた。王や貴族、後宮の女たちがそれで酒を飲もうというのである。³そこで、エルサレムの神殿から奪って来た金銀の祭具が運び込まれ、王や貴族、後宮の女たちがそれで酒を飲み始めた。⁴こうして酒を飲みながら、彼らは金や銀、青銅、鉄、木や石などで造った神々をほめたたえた。⁵その時、人の手の指が現れて、ともし火に照らされている<u>王宮の白い壁に文字を書き始めた</u>。王は書き進むその手先を見た。⁶王は恐怖にかられて顔色が変わり、腰が抜け、膝が震えた。…¹³そこで、ダニエルが王のまえに召し出された。王は彼に言った。『…¹⁵賢者や祈祷師を連れて来させてこの文字を読ませ、解釈させようとしたのだが、彼らにはそれができなかった。¹⁶お前はいろいろと解釈をしたり難問を解いたりする力を持つと聞いた。もしこの文字を読み、その意味を説明してくれたなら、お前に紫の衣を着せ、金の鎖を首にかけて、王国を治める者のうち第三の位を与えよう。』

裕福な王が宴会を開いた。王は宴会の客を喜ばせようとして、最も高価な金銀の道具をテーブル

聖書由来のイディオム　35

に並べさせた。それは、王が金銀の祭具を「神」と考えているかのようであった。しかし、天の大いなる神は、壁に不思議な文字を現した。預言者ダニエルは、壁に書かれた文字を、神よりもお金や富を優先させたことに対する神からの罰と解釈した。この言葉が本当に意味することは、「あまりにも明白で、見のがすことはない」ということである。

be clothed in purple:「紫の衣を着せる」：昔ローマ皇帝や教皇庁の枢機卿が専用した、高貴な色とされる紫衣から、「王位、帝位；枢機卿の職；高位」を表すようになった。

Anne: It is getting more difficult to get a job if you don't have a college education.

Jack: That is so true. Companies are not paying attention to high school graduates.

Anne: **The handwriting is on the wall.**[1] We had better work hard and get university diplomas.

---

1) **The handwriting is on the wall.**　きわめて明白ね

15. The second mile
ニミリオン

Matthew 5:38–42
マタイによる福音書　第5章38-42節

(³⁸*You have heard that it was said, "Eye for eye, and tooth for tooth." ³⁹But I tell you, do not resist an evil person. If anyone slaps you on the right cheek, turn to him the other cheek also.*) ⁴⁰*And if someone wants to sue you and take your tunic, let him have your cloak as well. ⁴¹If someone forces you to go one mile, go with him two miles. ⁴²Give to the one who asks you, and do not turn away from the one who wants to borrow from you.*

In ancient times, soldiers would force a peasant to carry the heavy military equipment. Jesus always advises His followers to avoid confrontation. Don't get into an argument, do your best. Often this is interpreted to mean we should do more than we are required to do. If your teacher assigns ten pages of homework reading, then you should read twenty pages. Doing more than our job description requires is an indication of a dedicated and good worker. Don't wait to be told to do something. Think about what is good to do, and then do it.

(³⁸「あなたがたも聞いているとおり、『目には目を、歯には歯を』と命じられている。³⁹しかし、わたしは言っておく。悪人に手向かってはならない。だれかがあなたの右の頬をうつなら、左の

頬をも向けなさい。）⁴⁰ あなたを訴えて下着を取ろうとする者には、上着をも取らせなさい。⁴¹ だれかが、一ミリオン行くように強いるなら、一緒に二ミリオン行きなさい。⁴² 求める者には与えなさい。あなたから借りようとする者に、背を向けてはならない。」

昔、兵士は農夫を強いて、重い軍事用具を運ばせた。イエスは彼に従う者たちに、対立を避けるようにといつも言っている。言い争いをせず、最善を尽くしなさい、と。このイエスの言葉は、「我々は求められている以上のことをすべきである」という意味であると解釈されることがある。もし先生が宿題に 10 ページ読むように言ったなら、20 ページ読みなさい、というように。職務内容に求められている以上のことをするのは、献身的な良い労働者であることを示す。何かをするように言われるのを待つのではなく、何をするのが良いのかを考え、それを実行しなさい。

　ミリオン＝マイル／ **the second million**:「1 マイル進み、さらにそれに加えてもう 1 マイル進む」こと。

Anne: Well, my boss told me to work one hour overtime today.
Jack: Yeah, he told me to do the same thing. But I will work two hours overtime.
Anne: That is so much like you, Jack. You are a good man. You always **go the second mile.**[1]

---

1) **go the second mile**　求められている以上の仕事をする

16. There is nothing new under the sun
太陽の下、新しいものは何ひとつない）

Ecclesiastes 1:9
コヘレトの言葉 第 1 章　9 節

*⁹The thing that hath been, it is that which shall be; and that which is done is that which shall be done; and **there is no new thing under the sun**.* (KJV)

Many times we think that we are the originators of a great idea when actually that idea was expressed in ancient history. For example, Gary Jennings' novel *Aztec*, has a scene in which a man uses a special "reading stone"—he learned that by placing certain transparent stones on top of small objects and inscriptions, those things became enlarged and easier to see. Of course, modern eyeglasses are much more effective, but they have their origins in the primitive reading stones. There is truly **nothing new under the sun**.

⁹かつてあったことは、これからもあり　かつて起こったことは、これからも起こる。**太陽の下、新しいものは何ひとつない。**

我々は、大いなる考えを、自分が考えついたものであると思ってしまうことがよくある。しかし、実際には過去の歴史においてすでに述べられているものである。例えば、ゲーリー・ジェニングの小説『アステカ』には、「ものを読むための特別な石」を使う場面が出てくる。小さな物や碑文の上にある透明な石を置くと、大きくなり、見えやすくなるということを、その登場人物が知ったのである。もちろん現代の眼鏡の方がずっと優れているが、その源は原始的な読むための石にある。まさに、太陽の下、新しいものは何ひとつないのである。

　　hath: have の 3 人称単数現在形 (has)。

Makoto:　Well, Miriam, you have been studying here in Japan for 2 months already. Have you tried *yaki-imo*?

Miriam:　I am not sure. Is that some kind of food?

Makoto:　It sure is. In fact, I brought some to you. This is really a Japanese delicacy.[1]

Miriam:　Oh, this is a baked sweet potato. It may be a Japanese delicacy, but I have eaten plenty of these in my hometown, New Orleans.

Makoto:　Really, I thought it was exclusive to Japan.[2]

Miriam:　Not really, I am sure if you read 18th century American novels, you can find reference to sweet potatoes baked over hot coals. Don't you know? **There is nothing new under the sun**.[3]

---

1) **delicacy**　ごちそう、珍味
2) **exclusive to Japan**　日本にしかない
3) **nothing new under the sun**　この世に新しいものはない

17. Wit's end
途方に暮れて

Psalms 107:23–27
詩編 107.23–27.

---

²³*Some went out on the sea in ships; they were merchants on the mighty waters.* ²⁴*They saw the works of the LORD, his wonderful deeds in the deep.* ²⁵*For he spoke and stirred up a tempest that lifted high the waves.* ²⁶*They mounted up to the heavens and went down to the depths; in their peril their courage melted away.* ²⁷*They reeled and staggered like drunkards; they were* **at their wits' end**.

Often, people get very frustrated. When we have too many things to do at one time, or when we have big traumas, we feel like we will go "crazy." <u>Wit's end</u> expresses that situation.

²³彼らは、海に船を出し 大海を渡って商う者となった。²⁴彼らは深い淵で主の、御業を 驚くべき御業を見た。²⁵主は仰せによって嵐を起こし 波を高くされたので ²⁶彼らは天に上り、深淵に下り 苦難に魂は溶け ²⁷<u>酔った人のようによろめき、揺らぎ どのような知恵も呑み込まれてしまった</u>。…

人はしばしば苛立ち（挫折感）を感じることがある。一時に多くのことをしなければならないときや、大きなトラウマを感じるとき、「気が狂ってしまう」ように感じる。こうした場合を表す表現がこの wit's end で、「（健全な）精神が（限界まで達し）行き詰ってしまう」ことを表している。

　　at one's wit's [wits'] end の形で用いられることが多い。／**Psalms**: 旧約聖書中の「詩編」と呼ばれる書全体を表す。／**Psalm**: 「詩編」の中の個々の詩を指す。

> Anne: I have so much homework to do.
> Jack: You should have started¹⁾ doing it earlier.
> Anne: You are right, of course. I don't know how I can do all of this. I am **at my wit's end**.²⁾

1) **should have + 過去分詞** 〜すべきだったのに（過去の行為に対する非難や後悔の気持ちを表す）
2) **at one's wit's end** 途方に暮れて、困り果てて

18. Wolves in sheep's clothing
羊の皮を身にまとった狼

Matthew 7:15–20
マタイによる福音書 第7章 15–20節

¹⁵*Watch out for false prophets.* ***They come to you in sheep's clothing, but inwardly they are ferocious wolves.*** ¹⁶*By their fruit you will recognize them. Do people pick grapes from thornbushes, or figs from thistles?* ¹⁷*Likewise, every good tree bears good fruit, but a bad tree bears bad fruit.* ¹⁸*A good tree cannot bear bad fruit, and a bad tree cannot bear good fruit.* ¹⁹*Every tree that does not bear good fruit is cut down and thrown into the fire.* ²⁰*Thus, by their fruit you will recognize them.*

Paul warns Christians about people who claim to be Christian, but who are really not nice people. They want to control the Christians, and maybe they want to take the property which Christians own. Such people pretend to be kind, simple sheep, but really they are dangerous wolves.

（マタイによる福音書 第5~7章の山上の説教の一部）
[15]『偽預言者を警戒しなさい。彼らは羊の皮を身にまとってあなたがたのところに来るが、その内側は貪欲な狼である。[16] あなたがたは、その実で彼らを見分ける。茨からぶどうが、あざみからいちじくが採れるだろうか。[17] すべて良い木は良い実を結び、悪い木は悪い実を結ぶ。[18] 良い木が悪い実を結ぶことはなく、また、悪い木が良い実を結ぶこともできない。[19] 良い実を結ばない木はみな、切り倒されて火に投げ込まれる。20 このように、あなたがたはその実で彼らを見分ける。』

パウロは、キリスト者であると言いながら、実際には善人ではないような人に気をつけるよう警告している。そうした人々はキリスト者を支配しようとするか、キリスト者が持っている財産を欲しているかもしれないのである。そうした人々は親切で素直な羊であるかのように装うが、実際には危険な狼なのである。

聖書には、羊 (sheep, lamb) や狼 (wolf) が登場する表現がいくつか見られる。
cf. like a sheep [lamb] to the slaughter: 屠場にひかれる羊［子羊］のように、従順に

Anne: I like the new worker in our company. He always smiles and says nice things to me.
Jack: Be careful. I heard he works for another company. He is trying to steal the good ideas of our company.
Anne: Oh, I see. He is a **wolf in sheep's clothing**.[1] He seems nice, but actually he is a dishonest man.

1) **wolf in sheep's clothing** 偽善者

19. You can't take it with you
世を去るときは何も持って行くことができない

I Timothy 6:6–10
テモテへの手紙 一 第6章 6–10節

*[6]But godliness with contentment is great gain. [7]For we brought nothing into the world, and **we can take nothing out of it**. [8]But if we have food and clothing, we will be content with that. [9]Those who want to get rich fall into temptation and a trap and into many foolish and harmful desires that plunge people into ruin and*

destruction. ⁱ⁰For the love of money is a root of all kinds of evil. Some people, eager for money, have wandered from the faith and pierced themselves with many griefs.

This is a famous comment by Paul. He warns Christians not to be overly concerned about money and material possessions. We should be more concerned with living a kind, generous and good life. Paul uses the idea of newborn babies. They are naked when they come into this world. And, similarly, all of us will have to leave our riches behind on earth when we die.

⁶（もっとも、）信心は、満ち足りることを知る者には、大きな利得の道です。⁷なぜならば、わたしたちは、何も持たずに世に生まれ、世を去るときは何も持って行くことができないからです。⁸食べる物と着る物があれば、わたしたちはそれで満足すべきです。⁹金持ちになろうとする者は、誘惑、罠、無分別で有害なさまざまな欲望に陥ります。その欲望が、人を滅亡と破滅に陥れます。¹⁰金銭の欲は、すべての悪の根です。金銭を追い求めるうちに信仰から迷い出て、さまざまのひどい苦しみで突き刺された者もいます。

これはパウロによる利得に関する有名な言葉である。パウロは、お金や物質的な物にこだわり過ぎないように警告した。人間は親切で、寛容で、良い人生を送ることにもっと関心を向けるべきである。聖パウロは生まれたばかりの赤子を例にとっている。人は生まれる時には裸で生まれる。そして同様に、全ての人間は、死ぬ時には富をこの世に置いていかなければならないのである。

Anne: I want to buy a new car.
Jack: You are spending too much money.
Anne: We should enjoy the money we earn. **We can't take it with us** (when we die).¹⁾

1) **we can't take it with us.**（死んでしまったらそのお金は）使えないのだから。

20. A drop in the bucket
革袋からこぼれる一滴のしずく

Isaiah 40: 12–15
イザヤ書　第40章　12-15節

¹²Who has measured the waters in the hollow of his hand, or with the breadth of his hand marked off the heavens? Who has held the dust of the earth in a basket, or weighed the mountains on the scales and the hills in a balance? ¹³Who can fathom the Spirit of the L*ORD*, *or instruct the* L*ORD as his counselor?* ¹⁴*Whom did the* L*ORD consult to enlighten him, and who taught him the right way? Who was it that taught him knowledge, or showed him the path of understanding?* ¹⁵*Surely the nations are like* **a drop in a bucket**; *they are regarded as dust on the scales; he weighs the islands as though they were fine dust.*

The prophet Isaiah was impressed with the expansive power and knowledge of God. He compared the greatness of God to the futility of the politics of human beings. When we think about the importance of God, then all of the strivings and mean actions of men seem to be nothing at all. Today, we often use "**A drop in the bucket**" in reference to something too small—it is like comparing the water of the vast ocean to a mere drop in the bucket.

¹²手のひらにすくって海を量り　手の幅をもって天を測る者があろうか。地の塵を升で量り尽くし　山々を秤にかけ　丘を天秤にかける者があろうか。¹³主の霊を測りうる者があろうか。主の企てを知らされる者があろうか。¹⁴主に助言し、理解させ、裁きの道を教え　知識を与え、英知の道を知らせうる者があろうか。¹⁵見よ、国々は革袋からこぼれる一滴のしずく　天秤の上の塵と見なされる。島々は埃ほどの重さも持ちえない。

預言者イザヤは、神の大いなる力と知識に感銘を受けた。イザヤは神の偉大さを人間の政治の無益さと比較している。神の重要さを考えたとき、人間の奮闘やさもしい行為などは無に等しいように思われる。今日では、「革袋からこぼれる一滴のしずく」という表現は、ほんの小さなものに言及するときにしばしば使われる。すなわち、大海の水と比べられるときの、革袋からこぼれるわずか一滴のしずくのようなものである。

　イザヤ書の第40章12節から始まる創造と贖いの神の一部。

Anne: We did very well. We raised one hundred dollars to feed homeless people.
Jack: Yes, but we need to raise more money. There are so many homeless people in the world.
Anne: I suppose you are right. When I think about it, one hundred dollars is just **a drop in the bucket**.[1]

1) **a drop in the bucket**　焼け石に水、微々たるもの

21. Bite [Lick] the dust
塵をなめる

Psalms 72:9
詩編　72.9

> ⁹*They that dwell in the wilderness shall bow before him; and his enemies shall **lick the dust***. (KJV)
>
> Psalm 72 describes a good king who will lead the people of God. The king will be honest, and he will be protective of the people. (In the Bible, "the people of God" refers to several different groups: (1) All good and kind people, (2) The Israelites and Jews who believed in, and honored, The One God, (3) Obedient Christians, and (4) All honest and decent people of every nationality.) The Book of Psalms speaks of the suffering of the people who try to hurt the people of God. The good king will punish the enemies. The enemies will "**lick the dust**." Many people interpret this phrase to mean the enemies will fall down and die—in fact that is the most popular use of the phrase today. However, in the opinion of this writer, "Bite [Lick] the dust" could have meant that the enemies of God and the Good King would be forced to bow down very low before Him.
>
> Modern usage of the phrase almost always suggests that something has died, or has experienced a great failure.

(⁸ 王が海から海まで　大河から地の果てまで、遅配しますように。) ⁹ 砂漠に住む者が彼の前に身を屈め　敵が塵をなめますように。

詩編 72 は神の民を導く良き王のことについて述べている。王は正直で、民を護る者である。(聖書では「神の民」は様々な民について使われている：(1) 善人で親切な人々、(2) 唯一の神を信じ、崇めるイスラエルとユダヤの民、(3) 従順なキリスト教徒、そして (4) あらゆる国の全ての正直で思いやりのある人々。) 詩編の書は、神の民を傷つけようとする人々の苦しみを語っている。良き王は、敵を罰し、敵は「塵をなめる」ことになる。この表現が、〈敵が倒れ、死ぬ〉ということを意味していると解釈する人が多く、実際、今日最も一般的な意味として使われているものである。しかし、現著者は、「塵をなめる」というのは、〈神の敵と善王は（共に）神の前に身を低くし、ひれ伏さなければならない〉ということを意味していたのではないかと考えている。

　この表現の現代的使い方では、何かが死に、あるいは大きな失敗を経験したということを示している。

> Makoto: Stephan has returned to America. He could not learn Japanese well enough, so he dropped out of the exchange program.

Shirley: Oh well, **another one has bitten the dust.**[1]
Makoto: I heard that phrase in a movie last year. But it meant that a cowboy was killed by his enemy.
Shirley: Yeah, we do use the term that way sometimes. But it also means that someone has failed miserably, or that someone has been put out of a program.
Makoto: I think I can understand that idea. I wonder[2] where did that phrase originally come from?
Shirley: The King James Translation of the English Bible mentions it in Psalm 72:9.

1) **bite the dust** 失敗する。敗北する
2) **I wonder** 普通学校等で学ぶ形は "I wonder" の後に、接続詞 if あるいは whether が導く平叙文と同じ語順の節が現れるものであるが、この会話文では "where did that phrase originally come from?" という疑問文の語順が使われている。この場合、形式的には "I wonder" が主節であっても、意味上は「添え物」的に使われていることになる

22. Cast the first stone
最初の石を投げる

John 8:7
ヨハネによる福音書　第8章　7節

⁷So when they continued asking him, he lifted up himself and said unto them, He that is without sin among you, <u>let him first cast a stone</u> at her. (KJV)

The story about the woman involved in a sexual affair is very famous. Some people discovered her with the man. They brought the woman to Jesus for Him to decide her punishment. These days, feminists point out that only the woman was brought before Jesus. The man is not mentioned further in the story. The angry crowd wanted to kill the woman. But Jesus simply said, "Let the person who has never sinned <u>throw the first stone</u> at her." Of course everyone has sinned. The crowd dispersed, leaving Jesus alone with the woman. Jesus told her, "Don't sin anymore."

(² 朝早く、再び神殿の境内に入られると、民衆がみな、御自分のところにやって来たので、座って教え始められた。³ そこへ、律法学者たちやファリサイ派の人々が、姦通の現場で捕えられた女を連れて来て、真ん中に立たせ、⁴ イエスに言った。「先生、この女は姦通をしているときに捕ま

りました。⁵こういう女は石で打ち殺せと、モーセは律法の中で命じています。所で、あなたはどうお考えになりますか。」⁶イエスを試して、訴える口実を得るために、こう言ったのである。イエスはかがみ込み、指で地面に何か書き始められた。⁷しかし、彼らがしつこく問い続けるので、イエスは身を起こして言われた。)「あなたたちの中で罪を犯したことのない者が、**まず、この女に石を投げなさい。**」(⁸そしてまた、身をかがめて地面に書き続けられた。⁹これを聞いた者は、年長者から始まって、一人また一人と、立ち去ってしまい、イエスひとりと、真ん中にいた女が残った。¹⁰イエスは、身を起こして言われた。「婦人よ、あの人たちはどこにいるのか。だれもあなたを罪に定めなかったのか。」¹¹女が、「主よ、だれも」と言うと、イエスは言われた。「わたしもあなたを罪に定めない。行きなさい。これからは、もう罪を犯してはならない。」)

姦通の罪を犯した女の話は有名である。その女は男と一緒にいるところを捕えられ、その罰を決定するよう、イエスのもとに連れていかれた。今日、男女同権論者は、女だけがイエスのもとに連れていかれ、男の方はそれ以上話に出てこない点を指摘している。怒った群衆は女を殺そうとしたが、イエスは単に「罪を犯したことのない者に最初に石を投じさせよう」と言っただけであった。もちろん皆、罪を犯したことがあり、群衆は立ち去り、イエスと女だけが残された。イエスは女に「もう罪を犯してはならない」と言われた。

Emiko: I have just finished reading Victor Hugo's *Les Miserables*.

Makoto: Oh, I love that story. My favorite scene is when the criminal stole the silver candlesticks from the old priest. And the priest later forgave Jean Valjean, the criminal. In fact, the priest gave Jean Valjean the candlesticks as well as other valuables.

Emiko: Yes, I am amazed at that part of the story, too. The priest understood that everyone makes mistakes sometimes.

Makoto: He didn't want to **cast the first stone**[1] at Jean Valjean. And the criminal changed. He became a kind man.

---

1) **cast the first stone** （自分の過ちを省みず）他人を真っ先に避難する

23. Doubting Thomas
疑い深いトマス

John 20:24–25
ヨハネによる福音書 第20章 24-25節

---

²⁴*But Thomas, one of the twelve, called Didymus, was not with them when Jesus came.* ²⁵*The other disciples therefore said to him, "We have seen the Lord." But he said unto them, "Except I shall see in his hands the print of the nails, and put my finger into the print of the nails, and thrust my hand into his side, I will not believe."* (KJV)

Jesus originally had 12 disciples (or students) who were loyal to Him. After Jesus was put to death, he returned to life and appeared to various disciples at different times. Thomas, one of the followers, expressed disbelief when the others told him of the Resurrection. Jesus later appeared to Thomas and proved that he had, indeed, returned to life. The expression now refers to anyone who is very skeptical of something that many others accept.

²⁴ 十二人の一人でディディモと呼ばれるトマスは、イエスが来られたとき、彼らと一緒にいなかった。²⁵ ほかの弟子たちが、「わたしたちは主を見た」と言うと、トマスは言った。「あの方の手に釘の跡を見、この指を釘跡に入れてみなければ、また、この手をそのわき腹に入れてみなければ、わたしは決して信じない。」

イエスには彼に忠実な 12 人の弟子がいた。（十字架上での）死後、イエスは復活し、様々な時に弟子たちの前に現れた。弟子たちの一人であるトマスは、他の弟子たちがイエスの復活について語ったとき、「信じられない」と言った。イエスの後にトマスの前に現れ、実際に復活したことを証明した。この表現は、他の多くの者が信ずることに対して非常に懐疑的である人に言及するときに使われている。

Jack: Have you heard the news? The President of the United States will visit our campus today, and you and I have been chosen to have a private lunch with him.
Anne: Jack, you are such a joker. The President would never come to our small campus and have lunch with the two of us.
Jack: Anne, you are such a **Doubting Thomas**.[1] I knew you wouldn't believe me, so I asked the President if he would explain everything to you on the phone. Are you ready to speak with the President of the United States?!

1) **Doubting Thomas**　疑い深い人

24. Fall from grace
堕落する、神の恩寵を失う

Galatians 5:4
ガラテヤの信徒への手紙　第 5 章　4 節

⁴*Christ is become of no effect unto you, whosoever of you are justified by the law; ye are **fallen from grace**.* (KJV)

As you saw in the introduction, the Bible is divided into the Old Testament and the New Testament. Paul said that Jesus Christ freed people from the obligations of the complicated laws of the Old Testament. Jesus simplified religion. Some of the original Christians decided to return to the rituals and practices of the Old Testament (the Law). People in the times before Jesus Christ had to follow many rigid laws regarding diet and special sacrifices (they had to offer certain animals as sacrifices on certain occasions), and the male babies had to have a special operation, circumcision. The writer, Paul, says that the people who have ignored the freedoms that Jesus gave them have **fallen from grace**.

Today, we often hear this phrase used without any reference to the Bible. Often these words describe somebody who was once greatly admired, but that person is no longer in favor with his group. A movie actor who was once loved by the public, but who is now ignored by fans can be said to have **fallen from grace**.

[4] 律法によって義とされようとするなら、あなたがたはだれであろうと、キリストとは縁もゆかりもない者とされ、いただいた恵みも失います。

本書第1章にあるように、聖書は「旧約聖書」と「新約聖書」に分けられる。パウロによれば、イエス・キリストは旧約聖書の複雑な律法に記されている義務から、人間を解放したことになっている。イエスは宗教を単純明快なものにしたのである。キリスト教の原点に返ろうとする者は、旧約聖書の儀式や範（律法）に立ち返ろうとした。イエス・キリストの時代よりも前の時代の人々は、食事や生贄（ある場合には、ある特定の動物を生贄として捧げなければならなかった）に関する厳格な律法を守らなければならなかったし、男の子は特別な手術、すなわち割礼を受けなければならなかった。この手紙の筆者であるパウロは、イエスが与えてくださった自由を無視する者は、堕落し、神の恩寵を失ってしまう、と述べている。

今日では、聖書の意味に言及しない形で、この表現がよく聞かれる。かつて大いに尊敬されていた人が、もはや好まれてはいない、というような場面で使われる。かつて大衆に人気のあった映画俳優が、今やファンから見放されているとき、「落ちぶれてしまった」というように使われる。

ye: 人称代名詞2人称複数主格。

Jack: I saw the old movie, *Picnic*, last night. Do you remember it?
Anne: I think I saw it on television many years ago. The television station was showing classic films, but I have forgotten most of the story.
Jack: It was made in 1955. It starred Kim Novak and William Holden. They were so popular in those days. I think Kim Novak was so beautiful in that film.
Anne: Oh, now I remember. There was a famous dance scene in the movie.

> Jack: Yeah, I really liked that scene. I wonder whatever happened to those movie stars.
>
> Anne: Well, I guess **they have fallen from grace.**[1] Sometimes movie stars are popular for a few years, then forgotten.

1) **fall from grace**　ひいきされなくなる

25. Get your feet wet
足を水際に浸す

Joshua 3:15–16
ヨシュア記　第3章　15–16節

> ¹⁵*And as they that bare the ark were come unto Jordan, and <u>the feet of priests that bare the ark were dipped in the brim of the water</u>, (for Jordan overfloweth all his banks all the time of harvest,) ¹⁶that the waters which came down from above stood and rose up upon an heap very far from the city Adam, that is beside Zaretan: and those that came down toward the sea of the plain, even the salt sea, failed, and were cut off: the people passed over right against Jericho.* (KJV)

This is another example of an idiom from the Bible being very far removed from the original idea. In Joshua, God performed a special miracle. The Israelites were running away from their enemies. Their priests were carrying the Ark of the Covenant, a sacred box. They needed to cross Jordan River. As soon as the priests dipped their feet into the Jordan River, the water dried up and the priest could walk across. Finally a path was opened, and the priests could lead their people in an escape from their enemies.

Do not confuse this story with one that you may be more familiar with: Moses leading people through the Red Sea, Exodus 14. You may have seen the classic film, *The Ten Commandments* in which God parted the waters to allow the Israelites to pass through. When the last Israelite was on safe ground, the waters of the Red Sea closed over the Egyptian enemies chasing after them.

You might hear "**Getting your feet wet**" in a modern conversation: when a new worker joins a company, the senior employees help her and give many instructions. This time period of adjustment to the new situation is described as "**getting your feet wet.**"

(¹⁴ ヨルダン川を渡るため、民が天幕を後にしたとき、契約の箱を担いだ祭司たちは、民の先頭に立ち、) ¹⁵ ヨルダン川に達した。春の刈り入れの時期で、ヨルダン川の水は堤を越えんばかりに満ちていたが、箱を担ぐ祭司たちの足が水際に浸ると、¹⁶ 川上から流れてくる傷は、はるか遠くのツァレンタの隣町アダムで壁のように立った。そのため、アラバの海すなわち塩の海に流れ込む水は全く断たれ、民はエリコに向かって渡ることができた。(¹⁷ 主の契約の箱を担いだ祭司たちがヨルダン川の真ん中の干上がった川床に立ち止まっているうちに、全イスラエルは干上がった川床を渡り、民はすべてヨルダン川を渡り終わった。)

この表現も、元々の聖書における意味から大きくずれてしまった例の一つである。ヨシュア記の中で、神は一つの奇跡を行った。イスラエルの民が敵から逃げていたときである。祭司たちが聖なる「契約の箱」を担いで、ヨルダン川を渡ろうとしたとき、その足がヨルダン川の水に触れたとたんにその水が乾き、祭司たちは川を渡ることができた。道が開け、祭司たちは人々を敵の手から逃れさせることができたのである。

　この物語を、より馴染みのあるもう一つの物語、出エジプト記第14章に描かれている、モーセが人々を率いて紅海を渡る物語と混同してはいけない。古典的とも言える映画『十戒』を見たことのある人もいるであろう。そこに描かれているのは、神が海の水を二つに分け、イスラエルの民が渡れるようにしてくださり、最後のイスラエルの民が無事陸地に辿り着いたとき、紅海の水が再び閉じ、追って来たエジプト軍を飲み込んでしまったという物語である。

現在では、次のような場面でこの表現が使われるのを耳にすることがあるかもしれない。新入社員が入ってきたとき、先輩社員が手伝って色々な指示を出すことがある。新しい環境に慣れる期間を表すのに、この表現が使われる。

get [have] one's feet wet:「参加する」←「水（の中）に入る」←「足を（水に）浸ける」／ **overfloweth**: overflow の3人称単数現在形。

Brenda: Mark, I hope you will be patient with me. I am a new worker, and there is so much to learn.

Mark: Don't worry. All of us will help you. We remember our first days on the job.

Brenda: As you can tell, I am very nervous.

Mark: That is natural. You will be nervous until you **get your feet wet**.[1]

---

1) **get one's feet wet**　新しい環境に慣れる

26. Man after my own heart
御心に適う人

I Samuel 13:13–14
サムエル記上　第13章　13–14節

¹³"You acted foolishly," Samuel said. "You have not kept the command the Lord your God gave you; if you had, he would have established your kingdom over Israel

for all time. ¹⁴*But now your kingdom will not endure; the Lord has sought out* **a man after his own heart** *and appointed him leader of his people, because you have not kept the Lord's command."*

Saul had been king of Israel, but God did not approve his governing style. God appointed David [you can see the famous Michelangelo sculpture, *The David*, in the museum, Florence, Italy].

　When we approve of a woman or man and applaud their kindness, energy, and good behavior, we often say, "She (or he) is **a man (or woman) after my own heart.**"

¹³ サムエルはサウルに言った。「あなたは愚かなことをした。あなたの神、主がお与えになった戒めを守っていれば、主はあなたの王権をイスラエルの上にいつまでも確かなものとしてくださっただろうに。¹⁴ しかし、今となっては、あなたの王権は続かない。主は**御心に適う人**を求めて、その人を御自分の民の指導者として立てられる。主がお命じになったことをあなたが守らなかったからだ。」

サウルはイスラエルの王であったが、神はサウルの統治の仕方を認めなかった。神はダビデを王に指名した。（イタリアのフローレンスにある美術館所蔵の、ミケランジェロの有名なダビデ像を思い描くことができるでしょう。）
　ある男性または女性を認め、その親切さや活力や良い行いを称賛するとき、「彼女（彼）はわたしの心に適う人だ」と言うことがある。

Jack:	Anne, I know that you are the one who put the large bag of groceries in front of the poor family's house. That was so kind of you.
Anne:	Well, I went to their house in the dark of night. I didn't want them to see me as I left the food.
Jack:	Anne, you are **a woman after my own heart.**[1] You don't require people to thank you for your good deeds.

1) **a woman after my own heart**　思った通りの女性

27. To everything there is a season
何事にも時がある

Ecclesiastes 3: 1–8
コヘレトの言葉　第3章　1-8節

[1]To every thing there is a season, *and a time to every purpose under the heaven: [2]A time to be born, and a time to die; a time to plant and a time to pluck up that which is planted; [3]A time to kill, and a time to heal; a time to break down, and a time to build up; [4]A time to weep, and a time to laugh; a time to mourn, and a time to dance; [5]A time to cast away stones, and a time to gather stones together; a time to embrace, and a time to refrain from embracing; [6]A time to get, and a time to lose; a time to keep, and a time to cast away; [7]A time to rend, and a time to sew; a time to keep silence and a time to speak; [8]A time to love, and a time to hate; a time of war, and a time of peace.* (KJV)

This is perhaps one of the most famous Bible passages. It is really a poem. The phrase, **"To everything there is a season,"** is the first line of the poem, but the other lines of the poem are equally famous. The basic idea of the poem is that our lives are filled with good moments and bad moments. We must appreciate the cyclical nature of life. If you are in a bad time now, it will not last always. Japanese people, of a certain age, are fond of quoting the famous English poem, *Ode to the West Wind* by Percy Bysshe Shelley. He expresses the idea this way, "If winter comes, can spring be far behind?"

[1]何事にも時があり　天の舌の出来事にはすべて定められた時がある。[2]生まれる時、死ぬ時　植える時、植えたものを抜く時　[3]殺す時、癒す時　破壊する時、建てる時　[4]泣く時、笑う時　嘆く時、踊る時　[5]石を放つ時、石を集める時　抱擁の時、抱擁を遠ざける時　[6]求める時、失う時　保つ時、放つ時　[7]裂く時、縫う時　黙する時、語る時　[8]愛する時、憎む時　戦いの時、平和の時。

この句は聖書からの引用句の中で、恐らく最も有名なものの一つであろう。実際は詩であり、「**何事にも時がある**」というのは、その詩の1行目であるが、他の行もこの句と同じ位有名である。この詩の基本概念は、我々の人生には良い時もあれば、悪い時もあるということである。人は人生の循環する（移り変わる）性質を受け入れなければならない。もし今、悪い時期に当たっているとすれば、それは永遠に続くものではない。ある年代の日本人は、P. B. シェリーの有名な詩「西風に寄せる歌」を好んで引用する。そこに見られる表現は、「冬来りなば、春遠からじ」というものである。

Percy Bysshe Shelley: 英国のロマン派の詩人。"Ode to the West Wind" は 1819 年の作。

Emiko: Pardon me, Stephan, but I know that you are having some difficulties these days. Is there anything I can do for you?

Stephan: That's very kind of you, Emiko. Everybody knows about the many troubles I have had this year: my grandfather died, my master's thesis was rejected at the university, and I did not get the job I wanted.

Emiko: Well, just remember: **"To everything there is a season"**. These may be bad days, but I am sure good things are on the horizon[1)] for you.

Stephan: Thank you for your encouragement. I always feel good after talking with you.

1) **on the horizon**　近い将来

28. A baptism of fire
火のバプテスマ（聖霊による霊的洗礼）

Acts 2:1–4 / Matthew 3:11 / Proverbs 17:3, etc.
使徒言行録　第2章　1–4節；マタイによる福音書　第3章　11節；箴言　第17章　3節；他

(Acts 2:1–4)
¹And when the day of Pentecost was fully come, they were all with one accord in one place. ²And suddenly there came a sound from heaven as of a rushing mighty wind, and it filled all the house where they were sitting. ³And there appeared unto them cloven tongues like as of fire, and it sat upon each of them. ⁴And they were filled with the Holy Ghost, and began to speak with other tongues, as the Spirit gave them utterance. (KJV)

There are several places in the Bible in which fire is a symbol of purification. Proverbs 17:3 has the beautiful image of refining gold: "The fining pot is for silver and the furnace is for gold." The idea is that "raw" gold is subjected to extreme heat so that the lesser metals are separated from the pure gold. Acts 2:1–4 is the famous story of the frightened friends of Jesus. He had just been killed. They gathered in a room, not knowing what would happen to them. But then God gave them a special sign. He placed special, miraculous, flames of fire on top of their heads. These flames gave the frightened friends courage. They began to boldly speak about the Power of God.

As with so many of the Bible idioms in modern usage, the expressions are often more lighthearted than the original intent.

(使徒言行録第2章1–4節)
¹五旬祭の日が来て、一同が一つになって集まっていると、²突然、激しい風が吹いて来るような音が天から聞こえ、彼らが座っていた家中に響いた。³そして、炎のような舌が分かれ分かれに現れ、一人一人の上にとどまった。⁴すると、一同は聖霊に満たされ、"霊"が語らせるままに、ほかの国々の言葉で話しだした。

聖書の中には、火が清めの象徴とされている箇所がいくつかある。箴言第17章3節では金を精錬するすばらしい場面が描かれている。「銀にはるつぼ、金には炉（、心を試すのは主。）」という1節である。この意味するところは、精製されていない金が高温にさらされると、混じっている他の金属は純粋な金から分離されるということである。使徒言行録第2章1–4節は十字架上で処刑されたイエスの友が恐怖を抱いている場面である。彼らはこれからどのようなことが身に降りかかるのか分からず、ある部屋に集まっていた。すると神は特別な印を彼らに示したのである。彼らの頭上に、特別な、奇跡的な火を置いたのである。この火は彼らに勇気を与えた。かれらはその後、「神の御力」について勇気をもって語り始めたのである。
　聖書から引用された表現の多くは、現代の用法では、本来意図されたものよりも気楽な意味合いで使われていることが多い。

Pentecost（五旬祭）：過ぎ越しの祝い (Passover) の2日目から数えて50日目で、この日をモーセがシナイ山で十戒を授かった日として祝う。

Maya:　How was your year in America?
Asami:　Well, I did improve in English fluency. But I must say that the whole year was **a baptism of fire**.[1] It was tough adjusting to American culture, and I struggled hard to improve in English. But now that it is all over, I appreciate the experience so much.
Maya:　You have just convinced me to go to America for a year. If I come back to Japan with the same mastery of English as you have, I will be very pleased.

---

1) **a baptism of fire**　厳しい試練

29. A fig leaf
いちじくの葉

Genesis 3: 6–7
創世記　第3章　6–7節

⁶When the woman saw that the fruit of the tree was good for food and pleasing to the eye, and also desirable for gaining wisdom, she took some and ate it. She also gave some to her husband who was with her, and he ate it. ⁷Then the eyes of both of them were opened, and they realized that they were naked; so they sewed **fig leaves** together and made coverings for themselves.

Adam and Eve disobeyed God. They ate the fruit, which He had forbidden them. While they awaited the appearance of God (and the punishment that would be coming to them), they realized that they were naked. Hurriedly, Adam and Eve placed **fig leaves** over the private parts of their body. They were ashamed for God to see them naked. Today, the phrase refers to a simple "cover up" of a problem—not a serious remedy or repair of the situation.

⁶女が見ると、その木はいかにもおいしそうで、目を引き付け、賢くなるように唆していた。女は実を取って食べ、一緒にいた男にも渡したので、彼も食べた。⁷二人の目は開け、自分たちが裸であることを知り、二人はいちじくの葉をつづり合わせ、腰を覆うものとした。

アダムとイヴは神の教えに背いた。二人は神が禁じた木の実を食べてしまった。神が現れるのを待っているとき（また、彼らに与えられる罰を待っているとき）、二人は自分たちが裸であることに気付いた。二人は急いでいちじくの葉で陰部を隠した。神に裸でいるところを見られるのが恥ずかしかったからである。今日では、この表現は単に問題を「覆い　隠すもの」という意味で使われ、状況を治したり修正したりするものではない。

神を指す代名詞等は、He (His / Him)・God のように、文中でも大文字で示される場合が多いが、必ずしも全ての版に共通しているわけではない。

Anne: Mrs. Marsden painted her house yesterday. Now it is such a beautiful yellow color.

Jack: But that house is so old. It is falling apart. A simple paint job will not make the house sturdier.

Anne: Well, sometimes **a fig-leaf**[1] change can make us think that things are improved.

1) **a fig leaf**　不体裁を隠す物

30. A little bird told me
翼あるものがその言葉を告げる

Ecclesiastes 10:20
コヘレトの言葉（伝道の書）第 10 章　20 節

*²⁰Do not revile the king, even in your thoughts, or curse the rich in your bedroom, because **a bird in the air may carry your words**.*

We should be very careful about expressing negative opinions about others. If powerful people learn about our negative feelings, we suffer the consequences.

A bird in the air may overhear our true feelings and inform the powerful people what we truly think of them. Of course, "bird" is a metaphor. Birds cannot really speak, but other people can start rumors, or betray us.

²⁰ 親友に向かってすら王を呪うな。寝室ですら金持ちを呪うな。空の鳥がその声を伝え 翼あるものがその言葉を告げる。

他者について否定的なことを述べる際には注意深くなければならない。もし、権力を持つ者が我々の否定的な気持ちを知ったなら、我々はその結果に苦しまなければならない。空を飛ぶ鳥が我々の真の気持ちを聞きつけ、権力を持つ者について我々がどのように思っているのかを伝えるかもしれない。「鳥」というのはもちろん比喩である。鳥は本当の意味で語ることはできないが、人間は噂をし始めたり、我々を裏切ったりしてしまうかもしれない。

Anne: I heard that you will quit this job next year. I understand that you are not satisfied with your salary and work conditions.
Jack: I am surprised that you know that. Who told you about my plans?
Anne: Well, **a little bird told me.**[1)]

---

1) **a little bird told me**　ちょっと小耳にはさんだの。風の噂に聞いたの。

31. A two-edged sword
両刃の剣

Hebrews 4:12, etc.
ヘブライ人への手紙　第4章　12節、他

¹²*For the word of God is quick, and powerful, and sharper than any **two-edged sword**, piercing even to the dividing asunder of soul and spirit, and of the joints and marrow, and is a discerner of the thoughts and intents of the heart.* (KJV)

¹²*For the word of God is alive and active. Sharper than any **double-edged sword**, it penetrates even to dividing soul and spirit, joints and marrow; it judges the thoughts and attitudes of the heart.* (NIV)

This is another example of how a Bible term has acquired a meaning today that is different from the original intent. In the Bible, the expression specifically refers to the Bible itself: It is like a knife that separates good from bad. Perhaps the image is of a knife cutting away fat, or undesirable portions of meat, from the lean. Today, we use the words to refer to a situation that has good and bad consequences at the same time.

The Bible passage is a little confusing, but a very simplified rendering would be: "The Bible will be believed by some people and rejected by others."

¹² というのは、神の言葉は生きており、力を発揮し、どんな**両刃の剣**よりも鋭く、精神と霊、関節と骨髄とを切り離すほどに刺し通して、心の思いや考えを見分けることができるからです。

この表現も、聖書に見られる表現が、本来の意味とは違った意味を今日持つようになった例である。聖書においては、これは特に聖書そのものに言及する表現である。それは、善と悪を切り分けるナイフのようなものである。おそらくそのイメージは、赤みの肉から脂身を切り除くナイフのイメージであろう。今日では、同時に良い結果と悪い結果の両方をもたらす状況に言及する者として使われている。

聖書の一節は多少混乱を招くようなものであるが、単純化して表すとすれば、「聖書はある者には信じられ、他の者には拒絶される」ということになろう。

quick = alive cf. quicksilver = mercury

Jack: The new president of our company does not want us to work overtime anymore.
Anne: That's wonderful, now when I get off from work I can take the flamenco dance class in the evenings.
Jack: Yeah, but for me it is a **two-edged sword**.[1] I like having the time off, but I am disappointed that I will no longer get the extra money for overtime work.

1) two-edged sword　諸刃の剣

32. An upright man
まっすぐな人

Psalms 37:37
詩編 37.37

³⁷Mark the perfect man, and behold **the upright**; for the end of that man is peace.
(KJV)

Scientists use the expression "upright" to refer to the higher primates that can walk with the back straight, perpendicular to the ground. The upright position is one of the features that accompanies higher intelligence among animals. The Bible uses the same word, "upright," to refer to human beings who are honest and kind. Psalm 37:37 describes the kind of human beings who please God. The Psalm says that such people will have peace. The idea, of course, is that such people will eventually go to Heaven.

³⁷無垢であろうと努め、まっすぐに見ようとせよ。平和な人には未来がある。

科学者は、upright という語を、背中をまっすぐにし、地面に対して直角に保って歩行する高等霊長類を指す語として使っている。直立した姿勢は、動物の中でもより高い知性に伴う特徴である。聖書では、この語を、正直で親切な人間を表す語として使っている。詩編 37 の 37 節は、神を喜ばせるような人間を表している。そうした人には平和が訪れるとしている。その意味は、もちろん、そうした人は最終的には天国に行くものであるということを意味している。

Yu: Amy, do you remember old Professor Elias who taught us the class in Western Civilization?

Amy: Are you kidding me? Who can forget him?¹⁾ He was a real scholar. I still have my notebook from those classes four years ago.

Yu: So do I. He was really **an upright man**.²⁾ I was just thinking about him because I saw Louis a few minutes ago.

Amy: Louis? What is the connection? Was he a student of Professor Elias?

Yu: Yes, he was. Louis told me that one day Professor Elias asked him if he had enough money for lunch. Louis was embarrassed to say that he didn't have lunch money. Professor Elias bought him lunch in the cafeteria, and he sat down in the student section to eat with him.

Amy: **An upright man**—just as you said.

1) **Who can forget him?** = Nobody can forget him.　反語的疑問文
2) **an upright man**　清廉潔白な人

33. Apple of the [his] eye
ひとみ

Deuteronomy 32:10
申命記　第 32 章　10 節

¹⁰*He found him in a desert land, and in the waste howling wilderness; he led him about, he instructed him, he kept him as **the apple of his eye**.* (KJV)

聖書由来のイディオム **57**

The book of Deuteronomy represents God as the Father of many children. Some of the "children" rebelled against the Father's commands. Other children were obedient. God favored these children. Deuteronomy speaks of the Patriarch, Jacob. Deuteronomy 32:10 shows God's great love for this obedient son. The passage refers to God rescuing Jacob from a difficult experience. Jacob is described as the **"apple of his [God's] eye."** Sometimes, modern people speak of a particularly loved child as **the apple of their eye**.

¹⁰ 主は荒れ野で彼を見いだし　獣のほえる不毛の地でこれを見つけ　これを囲い、いたわり　**御自分のひとみのように守られた。**

申命記では、神を大勢の子供の父親として描いている。子供たちの中には父の命令の反抗する者もいた。また、他の子供たちは従順であった。神はこうした従順な子供たちを愛しんだ。申命記は、（イスラエルの民の）始祖ヤコブのことについて語っている。第32章10節の言葉は、従順な息子ヤコブに対する神の大いなる愛を示している。この一節は、苦難からヤコブを救い出そうとしている神のことに言及している。ヤコブが神の「ひとみ」とされているのである。今日では、（親に）非常に愛されている子供のことを「ひとみ」と言い表すことがある。

 apple:「ひとみ」そのものに加え、「非常に大切にしているもの、掌中の珠」の意味で用いられる。／ **Patriarch**: (1)Adam~Noah~Abraham までの人類の父祖とされる人々、(2) イスラエルの民の先祖である Abraham, Isaac, Jacob およびその父祖たち、(3) イスラエル 12 支族の祖先である Jacob の 12 人の子

Jack: I want to do something special for my parents' anniversary. Maybe I will take them to Crystal Lake Restaurant.
Anne: That is one of the most expensive restaurants in the city. Can you afford that?
Jack: I am planning on working extra hours so that I can save up the money.
Anne: That is very generous of you. Your parents deserve that gesture. They have always been devoted[1] to you. You are **the apple of their eye**.[2]

---

1) **devoted** 愛情深い
2) **the apple of one's eye** （目の中に入れても痛くないほど）かわいい子

34. By the skin of our teeth
命からがら、辛うじて

Job 19:13–20
ヨブ記　第19章　13-20節

¹³*He has alienated my family from me; my acquaintances are completely estranged from me.* ¹⁴*My relatives have gone away; my closest friends have forgotten me.* ¹⁵*My guests and my female servants count me a foreigner; they look upon me as a stranger.* ¹⁶*I summon my servant, but he does not answer, though I beg him with my own mouth.* ¹⁷*My breath is offensive to my wife; I am loathsome to my own family.* ¹⁸*Even the little boys scorn me; when I appear, they ridicule me.* ¹⁹*All my intimate friends detest me; those I love have turned against me.* ²⁰*I am nothing but skin and bones; I have escaped only* **by the skin of my teeth**.

Job was a good man who suffered very much. He lost his children and his money. He even endured a terrible skin condition. However, Job believed that God would eventually make his situation good again. In the middle of his sufferings, Job talks about how he almost died. He says that he escaped "with only *the skin of my teeth*." This unusual metaphor means that he just barely escaped death. Often people in modern times speak of barely escaping death or tragedy using these same words.

¹³ 神は兄弟をわたしから遠ざけ　知人を引き離した。¹⁴ 親族もわたしを見捨て　友だちもわたしを忘れた。¹⁵ わたしの家に身を寄せている男や女すら　わたしをよそ者と見なし、敵視する。¹⁶ 僕を読んでも答えず　わたしが彼に憐みを乞わなければならない。¹⁷ 息は妻に嫌われ　子供にも憎まれる。¹⁸ 幼子もわたしを拒み　わたしが立ち上がると背を向ける。¹⁹ 親友のすべてに忌み嫌われ　愛していた人々にも背かれてしまった。²⁰ 骨は皮膚と肉とにすがりつき　<u>皮膚と歯ばかりになって</u>　わたしは生き延びている。

ヨブは良き人であったが、大いなる苦しみを受けていた。子供たちを失い、財産も失っていたのである。彼はまた、皮膚も恐ろしい状態になって苦しんでいた。こうした状況の中にあっても、神が再び良い状態にしてくださるものとヨブは信じていた。苦しみの真っ最中、ヨブは自分が死にかかったことを述べている。かれは、「辛うじて」逃れたと言っている。この異例な隠喩は、かれが辛うじて死を免れたということを意味している。現代人もこの表現を使って、死とか悲劇を辛うじて逃れることができたということを表現している。

by [with] the skin of one's teeth: 歯の表層の薄さほどの差で　cf. **by a hair's breadth**: 髪の毛の幅ほどの差で → 間一髪のところで

聖書由来のイディオム　59

Anne: The earthquake was terrible, but we are alive.
Jack: Yes, we should be grateful that all of our family members are safe.
Anne: It was such a scary experience. We escaped **by the skin of our teeth**!¹⁾

1) **by the skin of one's teeth**　かろうじて

35. Fight the good fight
戦いを立派に戦い抜く

I Timothy 6:12
テモテへの手紙 ― 第6章　12節

*¹²**Fight the good fight** of faith. Lay hold on eternal life, whereunto thou art called and hast professed a good profession before many witnesses.* (KJV)

Although Christianity emphasizes peace and harmony among each other, it does endorse a "good fight." This seemingly paradoxical statement refers to two situations: (1) fighting the devil and evil forces in the world, (2) being persistent in doing good deeds, even if such behavior puts us in danger. The problem, of course, is that opponents in a war or disagreement will each think that their side is **fighting the good fight**.

> "'**We fought the good fight**.' We just didn't win, conceded House Speaker John Boehner as lawmakers lined up to vote on a bill that includes nothing for Republicans demanding to eradicate or scale back Obama's signature health care overhaul."
> (Published: Wed, October 16, 2013 @ 5:57 p.m. WASHINGTON (AP))

¹² 信仰の**戦いを立派に戦い抜き**、永遠の命を手に入れなさい。命を得るために、あなたは神から召され、多くの証人の前で立派に信仰を表明したのです。（信仰の戦いの一節）

キリスト教は相互の平和と調和を強調しているが、「良き戦い」を是認してもいる。この逆説にも思われる言葉は、2つの状況に言及している。すなわち、(1) 世の悪や邪悪な力と戦うこと、そして (2) たとえ危険にさらされようとも、良い行いを根気強く行うことである。もちろん、問題は、戦争の相手、不和の相手もまた、**良き戦い**をしていると考えていることである。

オバマ大統領が健康保険の調整にサインしようとするのを阻止し、制限しようとする共和党の要求に対して、何も配慮するところがない法案に、議員が票を投じようとしているときに、ジョン・

ボウナー下院議長が譲歩したときに言ったのが、「我々は良く戦った。（残念ながら）勝利を収めることができなかっただけである。」という言葉である。（ワシントン、AP 通信：2013 年 10 月 16 日水曜日、午後 5 時 57 分）

fight the good fight: 同族目的語の一例。本来自動詞であるもの (fight) が、(1) その派生語の名詞、あるいは (2) 意味上関係の深い名詞を目的語とするとき、その目的語を同族目的語 (cognate object) という。／ **lay hold on ~** :「〜をしっかりつかんでいる」／ **whereunto** = on [onto / upon] which ／ **thou**: 2 人称単数主格の人称代名詞の古形。／ **art**: BE 動詞の 2 人称単数・直説法現在形 (are) の古形。／ **hast**: 2 人称単数・直説法現在形 (have) の古形。／ **profess a good profession**: 同族目的語の一例。"profess" は「（公に）信仰を告白する」の意味。

Miriam: I gave my last lecture at the university today. I have concluded 35 years of teaching at the same school.

Dorothy: Congratulations. I hope you enjoy your retirement. You have certainly **fought the good fight**.[1)]

Miriam: Well, actually, I have enjoyed my work so much. I never thought of it as fighting.

Dorothy: Of course not, I was just using a figure of speech. I think it is wonderful that you have had such a good relationship with students and faculty all these years.

---

1) **fight the good fight** （大学の教育に）力を尽くす

36. Kiss of death
死の接吻

Matthew 26:47–50
マタイによる福音書　第 26 章　47–50 節

47While he was still speaking, Judas, one of the Twelve, arrived. With him was a large crowd armed with swords and clubs, sent from the chief priests and the elders of the people. 48Now the betrayer had arranged a signal with them: "The one I kiss is the man; arrest him." 49Going at once to Jesus, Judas said, "Greetings, Rabbi!" and kissed him. 50Jesus replied, "Do what you came for, friend." Then the men stepped forward, seized Jesus and arrested him.

Judas, the friend of Jesus, cooperated with the Roman soldiers to kill him. In a prearranged agreement, Judas walked up to Jesus and kissed him. This was a signal to the soldiers. Judas had identified Jesus, singling Him out from the other men standing in the garden. When people today talk of **"The kiss of death,"** they refer to some comments made to someone which probably make that person unpopular.

⁴⁷ イエスがまだ話ておられると、十二人の一人であるユダがやって来た。祭司長たちや民の長老たちの遣わした大勢の群衆も、剣や棒を持って一緒に来た。⁴⁸ イエスを裏切ろうとしていたユダは、『わたしが接吻するのが、その人だ。それを捕まえろ』と、前もって合図を決めていた。⁴⁹ ユダはすぐにイエスに近寄り、『先生、こんばんは』と言って接吻した。⁵⁰ イエスは、『友よ、しようとしていることをするがよい』と言われた。すると人々は進み寄り、イエスに手をかけて捕えた。

イエスの弟子であるユダは、ローマ兵に協力してイエスを殺そうとしていた。あらかじめ打ち合わせていたように、ユダはイエスに近づき、接吻した。それが兵士たちへの合図であった。ユダは（ゲツセマネの）園にいる他の者と区別してイエスを特定した。今日「死の接吻」という表現を使うとき、それは「ある人を不人気にする可能性のある、その人に関する言葉」を意味する。

Anne: I went to the party with Susan last night. She is so beautiful. All of the guys paid attention to her.
Jack: Well, I think you are the most intelligent woman in the world.
Anne: Thanks, but that is **the kiss of death**.¹⁾ Men want a beautiful woman that they can manipulate.

1) **the kiss of death**　命取りになる行為、わざわいのもと

37. Man does not live by bread alone
人はパンだけで生きるものではない

Matthew 4: 1–4
マタイによる福音書　第 4 章　1–4 節

¹*Then was Jesus led up of the Spirit into the wilderness to be tempted of the devil.* ²*And when he had fasted forty days and forty nights, he was afterward ahungered.* ³*And when the tempter came to him, he said, If thou be the Son of God, command that these stones be made bread.* ⁴*But he answered and said, It is written, Man shall not live by bread alone, but by every word that proceedeth out of the mouth of God.* (KJV)

The word "bread" is used as a symbol meaning different things in the Bible. Sometimes it means the body of Jesus Christ. Christians eat a small piece of bread on Sundays to remind them that Jesus died for them. Other times it means charity. "Cast your bread upon the waters" (Ecclesiastes 11:1) means we should give food, clothing and support to people in far away places. For example, when the Philippines suffered a great typhoon, Japan, America, and other countries sent money and medical supplies. In Matthew 4:4 the word bread simply means food. In that passage, Jesus teaches that all human beings need two kinds of food: (1) physical food such as meat, potatoes and bread, and (2) spiritual food such as beautiful words of inspiration and encouragement. Strangely, in Matthew 4:4, Jesus is speaking to the devil. The devil wanted to tempt Jesus by telling him to convert stones into bread. Even though Jesus was hungry, He refused the challenge that the devil gave Him.

[1] さて、イエスは悪魔から誘惑を受けるため、"霊"に導かれて荒れ野に行かれた。[2] そして四十日間、昼も夜も断食した後、空腹を覚えられた。[3] すると、誘惑する者が来て、イエスに言った。「神の子なら、これらの石がパンになるように命じたらどうだ。」[4] イエスはお答えになった。「『人はパンだけで生きるものではない。神の口から出る一つ一つの言葉で生きる。』と書いてある。」

bread（パン）という語は、聖書の中で様々な意味で使われている。イエス・キリストの体を意味することもある。キリスト教徒は、イエスが人のために死んだということを思い起こすため、日曜日にパンの一片を口にする。また、慈善を意味する場合もある。「あなたのパンを見ずに浮かべて流すがよい」（コヘレトの言葉第11章1節）というのは、遠くにいる人々に食べ物、衣服、支援を与えなければならないという意味である。例えば、フィリピンが台風で大きな被害を被ったとき、日本やアメリカなどの諸国がお金や医療品を送ったことがあげられる。マタイによる福音書第4章4節では、bread は単に食べ物を意味している。そこでイエスは、人間は2種類の食べ物を必要としていると教えている。(1) 肉、じゃがいも、パンなどの物質的な「食べ物」と、(2) 感動的な言葉や激励の言葉のような、精神的な「食べ物」とである。奇妙なことに、マタイによる福音書第4章4節では、イエスは悪魔に語りかけている。悪魔は、石をパンに変えてみろと言って、イエスを誘惑しているのである。イエスは（荒野での断食の後で、）空腹であったが、悪魔の挑戦を退けた。

ahungered = hungry: a- は形容詞を作る接頭辞。／ **thou**: 人称代名詞の2人称単数主格。／ **If thou be ~ made bread**: he (= the tempter) said に続く直接話法。／ **It is written ~ out of the mouth of God**: he (= Jesus) answered and said に続く直接話法。／ **proceedeth**: proceed の3人称単数現在形。

Derrick: Mark, I hear that you spend your free time reading to Mrs. Clark, the blind lady. That is so kind of you.

Mark: Actually, she is an inspiration in my life. We spend about half an hour reading. Then we have free conversation for another half hour.

Derrick: Well, does she pay you?

Mark:	Of course not. I think of our sessions as mutually beneficial.
Derrick:	Does she at least give you expensive boxes of cookies as gifts?
Mark:	You've got the wrong idea. She gives me good ideas. After all, **"Man does not live by bread alone."**[1]

1) **Man does not live by bread alone.** 「人はパンのみにて生きるにあらず」（人が生きていくためには、食べ物だけでなく、精神的な心の糧も必要であるということ）

38. A fly in the ointment
香料の中の蠅

Ecclesiastes 10:1
コヘレトの言葉（伝道の書）第10章 1節

¹As dead flies give perfume a bad smell, so a little folly outweighs wisdom and honor. (NIV)

¹Dead flies cause the ointment of the apothecary to send forth a stinking savor; so doth a little folly him that is in reputation for wisdom and honor. (KJV)

The image of this saying is an apothecary—an old time drugstore. The speaker is talking about how good, sweet-smelling fragrances (used as a medicine) were ruined by a fly falling into the substance. The dead fly would cause the ointment (or perfume) to become corrupt. The medicine would then be unusable. The speaker in Ecclesiastes is making the following comparison:

A) Flies that fall into a sweet-smelling ointment, and die, ruin the medicine.
B) Silliness or foolish behavior ruins the reputation of a person who is usually wise and thoughtful.

Often people speak of something, or somebody, who ruins a good moment or a good idea as **a fly in the ointment**.

¹ 死んだ蠅は香料作りの香油を腐らせ、臭くする。わずかな愚行は知恵や名誉より高くつく。

この言葉のイメージは、古代の薬屋である。話者は、（薬として使われていた）良い、甘い匂いのする香料が、その中に落ちた一匹の蠅によって台無しにされてしまうということを語っている。死んだ蠅は、香料（あるいは香水）を腐らせてしまうのである。そうすると、薬は使いものにならなくなってしまう。「コヘレトの言葉」に登場する話者は、以下のような対比を示している。

A) 甘い匂いの香料に落ちて死んだ蠅は、その薬を台無しにする。
B) いつもは賢明で思慮深いことで知られる人も、愚かな行いによってその名声を傷つけてしまう。

（この表現によって、）素晴らしい時や素晴らしいアイディアを台無しにしてしまうものや人について語ることが多い。

doth: "do" の3人称単数・直説法現在 "does" の古形／ **so doth a little folly him** = a little folly does him so = a little folly sends forth stinking savor: "so" は「〜もまたそうである」という意味を表す際に使われる代用形で、以下のような例に見られる。この "so" が文頭に現れる場合に、倒置法が使われる。"I am really exhausted." "So am I."

Edna: Anne, this was your first day as a university teacher. How did your class go?

Anne: Well, I was prepared. And, most of the students seemed to have appreciated the lesson.

Edna: It sounds as if your first day was a great success.

Anne: I can't say that it was one hundred percent successful.

Edna: Why? What happened?

Anne: One student laughed aloud in class. He joked about my Southern accent.

Edna: Oh, I am sorry to hear that. I guess he was just **a fly in the ointment**.[1]

---

1) **a fly in the ointment** 玉に瑕（きず）

39. Fall on his own sword
自分の剣の上に倒れ伏す

I Chronicles 10:4–6
歴代誌上　第10章　4–6節

*⁴Saul said to his armour-bearer, "Draw your sword and run me through, or these uncircumcised fellows will come and abuse me." But his armour-bearer was terrified and would not do it; so **Saul took his own sword and fell on it**. ⁵When the armour-bearer saw that Saul was dead, **he too fell on his sword and died**. ⁶So Saul and his three sons died, and all his house died together.*

Saul was a king who rebelled against the will of God. He refused to obey God. There was a battle between the armies that were loyal to Saul and the people who were loyal to God. Of course, Saul and his men were defeated. Saul had been wounded in battle, but he was not dead. He asked his own servant-soldier to finish killing him. The servant could not kill his master. Therefore, the weak King Saul set up his sword and fell on it in an act of suicide. The horrified servant did the same. Falling on our own sword is often used as an expression of a serious mistake or act that causes us great trouble—today it is not necessarily an act of suicide. In a recent court case in Los Angeles, the lawyer made a mistake in procedure. Because of that mistake, the criminal had to go free. The lawyer said, **"I have fallen on my sword."** He meant that he made a serious error.

⁴ サウルは彼の武器を持つ従卒に命じた。「お前の剣を抜き、わたしを刺し殺してくれ。あの無割礼の者どもに襲われてなぶりものにされたくない。」だが、従卒は非常に恐れ、そうすることができなかったので、サウルは剣を取り、**その上に倒れ伏した**。⁵ 従卒はサウルが死んだのを見ると、自分も**剣の上に倒れ伏して**死んだ。⁶ こうしてサウルとその三人の息子は死んで、その家もすべて絶えた。

サウルは神の意志に背いた王であった。彼は神に従うのを拒絶したのである。サウルに忠誠を誓う軍と、神に従う者たちの間に戦いが起こった。もちろん、サウルとその軍は戦いに敗れた。サウルは戦いで傷ついたが、まだ死んではいなかった。サウルは、自分にとどめをさすように従卒に命じたが、従卒はできなかった。そこで、弱ったサウルは、自分の剣を立て、自らその上に倒れ込んだ。それを見た従卒は、恐れ、自分も剣の上に倒れ伏して命を絶った。「自分の剣の上に倒れ伏す」という表現は、大きな問題を引き起こす重大な過ちとか行為を表すものとして使われている。今日では、必ずしも自殺行為に言及するものではない。最近、ロサンジェルスの法廷で、検事が訴訟手続きで間違いを起こし、そのため被告が自由の身になってしまった。その検事は「わたしは自らの剣の上に倒れてしまった」と言った。それは、重大な過ちを犯してしまったということを意味している。

Jack: I heard that George was caught cheating[1] on the examination.
Anne: Yes, and strangely, he is such a good student. He would have earned a good grade without cheating. I don't understand why he did that.
Jack: I don't understand, either, but certainly **he has fallen on his own sword.**[2]

1) **cheating**　不正行為
2) **fall on one's sword**　自刃する

40. How the mighty have fallen
勇士らは戦いのさなかに倒れた

II Samuel 1:17–27
サムエル記下　第１章　17-27節

[17]David took up this lament concerning Saul and his son Jonathan, [18]and he ordered that the people of Judah be taught this lament of the bow (it is written in the Book of Jashar): [19]A gazelle lies slain on your heights, Israel. **How the mighty have fallen!** *[20]Tell it not in Gath, proclaim it not in the streets of Ashkelon, lest the daughters of the uncircumcised rejoice. [21]Mountains of Gilboa, may you have neither dew nor rain, may no showers fall on your terraced fields. For there the shield of the mighty was despised, the shield of Saul—no longer rubbed with oil. [22]From the blood of the slain, from the flesh of the mighty, the bow of Jonathan did not turn back, the sword of Saul did not return unsatisfied. [23]Saul and Jonathan—in life they were loved and admired, and in death they were not parted. They were swifter than eagles, they were stronger than lions. [24]Daughters of Israel, weep for Saul, who clothed you in scarlet and finery, who adorned your garments with ornaments of gold. [25]***How the mighty have fallen*** *in battle! Jonathan lies slain on your heights. [26]I grieve for you, Jonathan my brother; you were very dear to me. Your love for me was wonderful, more wonderful than that of women. [27]***How the mighty have fallen!*** *The weapons of war have perished!*

King David was in a war with Jonathan and Saul. The former had been David's great friend. The latter was the manic-depressive father of Jonathan. The result of the conflict was the death of Saul and Jonathan. David makes his great comment upon the defeat of the two men who had at one time been very powerful. The remark shows the continued love that David had for his friend, Jonathan, and the respect he had for his friend's father.

[17] ダビデはサウルとその子ヨナタンを悼む歌を詠み、[18]「弓」と題して、ユダの人々に教えるように命じた。この詩は『ヤシャルの書』に収められている。[19] イスラエルよ、「麗しき者」は　お前の高い丘の上で刺し殺された。ああ、**勇士らは倒れた**。[20] ガトに告げるな。アシュケロンの街々にこれを知らせるな　ペリシテの娘らが喜び祝い　割礼なき者の娘らが喜び勇むことのないように。[21] ギルボアの山々よ、いけにえを求めた野よ　お前たちの上には露も結ぶな、雨も降るな。**勇士らのたてがそこに見捨てられ**　サウルの盾が油も塗られずに見捨てられている。[22] 刺し殺した者たちの血　勇士らの脂をなめずには　ヨナタンの弓は決して退かず　サウルの剣がむなしく納められることもなかった。[23] サウルとヨナタン、愛され喜ばれた二人　鷲よりも速く、獅子よりも雄々しかった。命ある時も死に臨んでも　二人が離れることはなかった。[24] 泣け、イスラエ

ルの娘らよ、サウルのために。紅の衣をお前たちに着せ　お前たちの衣の上に　金の飾りをおいたサウルのために。²⁵ ああ、**勇士らは戦いのさなかに倒れた**。ヨナタンはイスラエルの高い丘で刺し殺された。²⁶ あなたを思ってわたしは悲しむ　兄弟ヨナタンよ、まことの喜び　女の愛にまさる驚くべきあなたの愛を。²⁷ ああ、**勇士らは倒れた**。戦いの器は失われた。

ダビデ王はヨナタンとサウルと共に戦いに出ていた。ヨナタンはダビデの親友であった。サウルはヨナタンの躁鬱病の父親であった。サウルとヨナタンは戦死する。ダビデはかつて強力であった二人の男の敗北にあたって、哀悼の意を述べている。それは、友であるヨナタンに対するダビデの変わらぬ愛を表すものであり、友の父に対する敬意を表すものである。

Anne: A few years ago, everybody loved Herman.
Jack: Yeah, but now everybody is gossiping about his scandal.
Anne: It's amazing how a person can have a good reputation one day, and a bad reputation the next day.
Jack: **How the mighty have fallen!**[1]

---

1) **How the mighty have fallen**　地に落ちたものだ

41. Strait [Straight] and narrow
狭い門から入りなさい

Matthew 7:13–14
マタイによる福音書（狭い門）第7章　13–14節

---

¹³*Enter ye in at the strait gate; for wide is the gate and broad is the way that leadeth to destruction, and many there be that go in thereat.* ¹⁴*Because <u>strait is the gate and narrow is the way</u>, which leadeth unto life, and few there be that find it.* (KJV)

The choice given to all human beings is (1) to do what is popular, or (2) to do what is heroic and virtuous. Most people opt for the easy life. It is easy to make ourselves number one in our lives. It is easy to take advantage of the weak. The going through the "wide gate" means doing what most people do. But virtuous living requires us to be disciplined. We must do the right thing even if other people persecute us or laugh at us. Choosing the righteous but unpopular behavior means going through the **"narrow gate."** In William Saroyan's novel, *The Human Comedy*, a rich boy and a poor boy are enemies. They are rivals on the high school track team. During the race, the poor boy fell. The rich boy surprised everybody by stopping the race and reaching down to help the poor boy regain his footing. This is an example of doing the unpopular thing, helping our rival. It is an example of entering at the **narrow gate**.

¹³「**狭い門**から入りなさい。滅びに通じる門は広く、その道も広々として、そこから入る者が多い。¹⁴ しかし、命に通じる門はなんと狭く、その道も細いことか。それを見いだす者は少ない。」

全ての人間に与えられた選択肢は、(1) 大衆向きのことを行うことと、(2) 英雄的で高潔なことを行うことである。大半の人は、楽な人生を選ぶ。自分自身を人生におけるナンバーワンにすることはたやすく、弱者につけ込むのはたやすい。「広い門」を入るというのは、大半の人がすることを行うという意味である。それに対し、高潔な生き方をするには、規律正しくあることが求められる。他者によって迫害されようと、あざけられようと、正しいことを行わなければならない。正しいが大衆向きではないことを行うのは、「狭い門」を通るようなものである。ウィリアム・サロイアンの小説『人間喜劇』の中で、金持ちの少年と貧しい少年が対立関係にある。高校の陸上部で、二人はライバルになっている。レースの途中で貧しい少年が倒れたとき、金持ちの少年が走るのを止めて貧しい少年が立ち上がるのを助けて、皆を驚かせた。この話は、一般受けのしない、ライバルを助けるという一例であり、「狭き門」より入るということの例である。

strait / straight: There is some discussion whether the word should be spelled "strait" or "straight." The former spelling suggests a channel or canal for ships to enter. The latter spelling emphasizes an uncurved path. Either way, the idea is that good people follow righteous behavior and are not mere followers of the crowd. この語の綴り方に関し、異論がある。前者 (strait) は船が航行する「海峡、運河」を示し、後者 (straight) は曲がっていない「まっすぐな道」であることを強調している。いずれにしても、そこに示されている考え方は、善者は正しい行動をとり、単なる大衆の追随者ではないということである。/ *The Human Comedy*: アメリカの小説家・劇作家ウィリアム・サロイアン (1908–81) の代表作。/ **ye**: 人称代名詞 2 人称複数主格。/ **wide is the gate / broad is the way** = the gate is wide / the way is broad（倒置）/ **leadeth**: lead の 3 人称単数現在形。/ **therebe / thereat** = there + be / there + at / **strait is the gate / narrow is the way** = the gate is strait / the way is narrow（倒置）

Martin: You won't believe how lucky I am! I just bought coffee from the machine in the lounge. When I put my one hundred yen coin in the machine, so many coins were returned to me. I probably have enough money to buy a good book.

Sybil: Wait a minute! A cup of coffee from the machine only costs one hundred yen. You should not have gotten any money out of the machine.

Martin: That is what I am saying. The machine is broken. Instead of taking money, it is giving money.

Sybil: Well, I advise you to take the **strait and narrow** approach.[1] Return the excess money to the office.

Martin: You are always a kill-joy.[2] But you are right. I will return the money.

1) **the strait and narrow approach**　慣例に従ったやり方
2　**kill-joy**　座を白けさせるひと、興ざまし　cf. wet blanket

42. The spirit is willing, but the flesh is weak
心は燃えても、肉体は弱い

Matthew 26:41
マタイによる福音書　第26章　41節

> [41]*Watch and pray, that ye enter not into temptation:* **the spirit is** *indeed* **willing, but the flesh is weak**. (KJV)

Many times human beings disappoint themselves. Good people experience guilt. They feel ashamed when they have lost patience with a child or an older adult. Sometimes even very moral people cheat on examinations and on paying income taxes to their governments. They know the right thing to do. They want to do the right thing. But they are sometimes tempted to do things which violate their own high standards. For such situations some people repeat the words of Jesus Christ: **The spirit is willing, but the flesh is weak**.

　Even though the original context of the sentence is the serious situation of maintaining high moral integrity, the phrase can be used humorously these days.

（囚われの身となる直前に、ゲツセマネの園で一人祈っていたイエスが、弟子たちのところへ戻ったとき、彼らが皆眠っていたのを見て言った言葉。）
（[40]それから、弟子たちのところへ戻って御覧になると、彼らは眠っていたので、ペトロに言われた。「あなたがたはこのように、わずか一時もわたしと共に目を覚ましていられなかったのか。[41]誘惑に陥らぬよう、目を覚まして祈っていなさい。）**心は燃えても、肉体は弱い。**」

　人は（自らの）期待に背いてしまうことがある。善の人は罪を経験する。子供や年老いた人に対して忍耐を失ってしまったとき、恥ずかしい思いをする。非常に道徳的な人でさえ、試験でカンニングをしてしまったり、政府に税金を払う際にごまかしてしまったりすることがある。そうした人は、何が正しい行いであるのかを知っており、正しいことを行いたいと思っているのだが、自らの規範に背いた行為をする誘惑に駆られることがある。こうした場合に、「**心は燃えても、肉体は弱い**」というイエス・キリストの言葉を復唱することがある。
　本来のこの言葉の文脈は、道徳的に完全性を保たなければならない、重大な場面であるが、今日ではユーモアを交えた言葉として使われている。

　ye: 人称代名詞2人称複数主格。

> Emiko: Well, this is a very awkward situation, Edna. We both said that we were on strict diets,[1)] but here I find you at the ice cream parlor.
>
> Edna: I am so embarrassed. I had no idea that I would see anyone I know. I couldn't resist coming here today. **The spirit is willing, but the flesh is weak.**[2)]
>
> Emiko: That makes two of us. I said that I would not eat any ice cream for a year, but I received a coupon for a free scoop of ice cream. So, here I am.
>
> Edna: We should just enjoy this ice cream today. We can start our diets again tomorrow.

1) **on diet** ダイエット中
2) **The spirit is willing, but the flesh is weak** （ダイエット中だから）アイスクリームを食べてはいけないことはわかっているけれど、食べに来ちゃったの。

43. By the sweat of his brow
額に汗して

Genesis 3:16–19
創世記　第3章　16-19節

> [16]*To the woman he said, "I will make your pains in childbearing very severe; with painful labour you will give birth to children. Your desire will be for your husband, and he will rule over you."* [17]*To Adam he said, "Because you listened to your wife and ate fruit from the tree about which I commanded you, 'You must not eat from it,' Cursed is the ground because of you; through painful toil you will eat food from it all the days of your life.* [18]*It will produce thorns and thistles for you, and you will eat the plants of the field.* [19]***By the sweat of your brow*** *you will eat your food until you return to the ground, since from it you were taken; for dust you are and to dust you will return."*
>
> In the famous Bible story, God created Adam and Eve and placed them in a beautiful garden. Everything was perfect: there was no death. However, God forbade them to eat the fruit of one particular tree. Because they disobeyed God, the woman was forced to have pain in childbirth, and the man would have to work hard to earn his living.

（蛇の誘惑に負けて神の命にそむいた罰として、エデンの園からアダムとイヴを追放したときに言った神の言葉の一部。）

¹⁶神は女に向かって言われた。『お前のはらみの苦しみを大きなものにする。お前は、苦しんで子を産む。お前は男を求め　彼はお前を支配する。』¹⁷神はアダムに向かって言われた。『お前は女の声に従い　取って食べるなと命じた木から食べた。お前のゆえに、土は呪われるものとなった。お前は、生涯食べ物を得ようと苦しむ。¹⁸お前に対して　土は茨とあざみを生えいでさせる　野の草を食べようとするお前に。¹⁹お前は**顔に汗を流して**パンを得る　土に返るときまで。お前がそこから取られた土に。塵にすぎないお前は塵に返る。』

聖書に、「神はアダムとイヴを創られ、美しい園に置かれた」という有名な物語がある。（そこでは）全てが完璧であり、死というものはなかった。ただし、神はある特定の木の実を食べることを禁じていた。アダムとイヴが神の指示に背いたため、イヴは子を産む苦しみを味わうことになり、アダムは生きる糧を得るために厳しい労働をしなければならなくなったのである。

Anne:　David inherited a lot of money from his father.
Jack:　Yes, he is so lucky.
Anne:　But I prefer a man who earns his money **by the sweat of his own brow**.[1]

---

1) **by the sweat of one's brow**　額に汗して　in [with] the sweat of his brow の形で用いられることもある。

44. Feet of clay
　　陶土の足

Daniel 2:32–33
ダニエル書　第2章　32-33節

³²*This image's head was of fine gold, his breast and his arms of silver, his belly and his thighs of brass,* ³³*His legs of iron, his feet part of iron, and part of clay.* (KJV)

It happens sometimes that a person we assumed to be a hero turns out to have a serious fault. When such a person disappoints us, we say, "Well, he had **feet of clay** after all." The Bible reference is to a grand statue that appeared in the king's dream. Parts of the statue were made of gold; other parts were of iron, etc. But the feet were partly made of clay. The passage teaches us that all human beings have some weak points. The **clay feet** of the statue symbolized that the kingdom was vulnerable. One day, all the earthly kingdoms will be destroyed, but the kingdom of God will last forever.

　In modern usage, the idea is that no one is really perfect. Everybody has faults. The good person understands that he is not perfect. The good person strives to do his best. He does not let his faults dictate his lifestyle.

(³¹ 王様、あなたは一つの像を御覧になりました。それは巨大で、異常に輝き、あなたの前に立ち、見るも恐ろしいものでした。) ³² それは頭が純金、胸と腕が銀、腹と腿が青銅、³³ すねが鉄、足は一部が鉄、一部が陶土でできていました。(³⁴ 見ておられると、一つの石が人手によらずに切り出され、その像の鉄と陶土の足を打ち砕きました。³⁵ 鉄も陶土も、青銅も銀も金も共に砕け、夏の打穀場のもみ殻のようになり、風に吹き払われ、跡形もなくなりました。その像を打った石は大きな山となり、全地に広がったのです。³⁶ これが王様の御覧になった夢です。さて、その解釈をいたしましょう。)

英雄であると思っていた人が、重大な欠陥をもつ人であるということが分かるような場合がときにある。こうした人によって落胆させられたとき、「結局陶土の足だったんだ」のように言う。聖書で言及されているのは王の夢に現れる大きな像である。その像の一部は金でできており、他には鉄等でできている。しかし、足（の一部）は陶土でできているのである。この句が教えているのは、あらゆる人間は何らかの弱点をもっているということである。**像の陶土の足**は、王国が堅固ではないということを象徴している。いつの日か、全ての地上の王国は滅び行くが、神の王国は永遠に続くのである。

　現代の用法では、「本当に完全な人は一人もいない」ということを意味している。誰にも欠点があり、善き人は自分が完全な人間ではないということを知っている。善き人は最善を尽くそうと努力し、欠点によって人生を左右されるようにはしないのである。

Miriam: I am so disappointed in our city's chief of police. We elected him because he seemed so honest. His campaign slogan was "No more bribery." Now, we learn that he has accepted bribes.

Edna: He had **feet of clay**.¹⁾ He is a handsome man, and he is a good speaker, but as we have just learned, he has a weakness. He loves money more than he loves honesty.

Miriam: Well, I will never trust another politician again. They are all deceitful.

Edna: Don't be cynical. I happen to know that there are honest politicians.

Miriam: Name one.

Edna: My father—he is campaigning to be the new chief.

---

1) **feet of clay**　「粘土の足、不安定な土台」から、「人格上の弱点、思いもよらない弱点、重大な欠点」という意味を表す。

45. Laughingstock
物笑いの種

Job 12:4–5
ヨブ記　第12章　4–5節

⁴*"I have become a **laughingstock** to my friends, though I called upon God, and he answered a mere **laughingstock**, though righteous and blameless. ⁵Men at ease have contempt for misfortune as the fate of those whose feet are slipping.*

Job was an ideal man. He was very obedient to God. To prove that Job was righteous, God tested him. God allowed many misfortunes to happen to Job. Even though he suffered very much, Job remained faithful to God. Many people laughed at Job's suffering. He was a **laughingstock** even though he was innocent. It hurts when people laugh at us. Sometimes, cruel people intentionally embarrass other people in public. Recently, some people have been humiliated when someone else has posted embarrassing pictures. Maybe a "friend" will post a picture of someone drunk at party. The next day, many people see the picture on the internet. The victim has become a **laughingstock**.

⁴「神に呼びかけて　答えていただいたこともある者が　友人たちの物笑いの種になるのか。神に従う無垢な人間が　物笑いの種になるのか。⁵人の不幸を笑い、よろめく足を嘲ってよいと　安穏に暮らす者は思い込んでいるのだ。」

ヨブは理想的な人間であった。彼は神に従順であった。ヨブが正しい人であることを証明するため、神は彼を試した。神はヨブがあらゆる不運に見舞われるようにした。ヨブは大いなる苦しみを受けたが、神に対しては忠実であり続けた。周りの人々はヨブの苦しみを笑った。ヨブは無垢であったのだが、物笑いの種になってしまった。人に笑われるとき、我々は傷つく。ときに、残酷な者は、故意に人前で他者を困らせる。最近、誰かが恥ずかしいような写真を掲載して、屈辱を与えられた人が見られる。「友人」がパーティーで酔っぱらった人の写真を掲載するかもしれない。翌日には、大勢の人がインターネットでその写真を見、その犠牲となった人は物笑いの種になってしまう。

Anne: I always make sure that I am neatly dressed when I leave my house. Even when I just walk outside for a few minutes, my hair is perfectly groomed.

Jack: That seems extreme to me. You don't have to be perfectly dressed just to go outside for a few seconds.

Anne: Oh yes, I do. These days cameras are everywhere. I don't want to be a **laughingstock** on the internet.

46. My cup runneth over
わたしの杯を溢れさせてくださる

Psalms 23: 5
詩編 23.5

⁵*Thou preparest a table before me in the presence of mine enemies; thou annointest my head with oil; **my cup runneth over**.* (KJV)

This famous Bible passage is often read at funerals, weddings, and other special occasions. The speaker expresses his love for God, and his appreciation for the many good things that God provides him. In the very sentimental book and movie, *A Tree Grows in Brooklyn,* a poor little girl asks her father to arrange for her enrollment in a nice school in a nice neighborhood. He promises. Her words to him are: "Bend down, Papa. **My cup runneth over.**" Perhaps all human beings can remember a moment when they thought that God had been especially generous to them.

⁵わたしを苦しめる者を前にしても　あなたはわたしに食卓を整えてくださる。わたしの頭に香油を注ぎ　わたしの杯を溢れさせてくださる。

この有名な聖句は、葬儀、結婚式、などの特別な場面で読まれることが多い。この句を読む者は、神に対する愛を表し、神が与えてくださる良いものに対する感謝の気持ちを表している。非常にセンチメンタルで映画化もされている *A Tree Grows in Brooklyn* の中で、貧しい少女が、「良い環境で、良い学校に入れるようにして」と父親にお願いする場面がある。父親は約束する。少女は「パパ、かがんで。私幸せだわ。」と父親に言った。おそらく誰でも、神が自分に対して特別に寛容であったと思うような瞬間があったことを覚えているだろう。

A Tree Grows in Brooklyn: Betty Smith, 1943 ／ **thou**: 人称代名詞 2 人称単数主格。／ **runneth**: run の 3 人称単数現在形。／ **annointest**: annoint の 2 人称単数現在形。／ cf. His cup runs over [overflows].: 幸福が身に余る。

Mark:　　　　Mrs. Clark, I have come to read another chapter of Betty Smith's *A Tree Grows in Brooklyn* to you. Are you ready?

Mrs. Clark:　I certainly am. This story really touches my heart. I know, I am such a sentimental old woman.

Mark:　　　　Well, there is nothing wrong with being sentimental.

Mrs. Clark:　Before you start reading, I must share some wonderful news with you. My first grandchild, Maya, was born last week. "**My cup runneth over.**"[1]

Mark:　　　　That is wonderful news. I knew there was some reason for you being especially radiant[2] today.

---

1) **My cup runneth over**　幸せなの
2) **radiant**　幸せそうな、喜びに満ちた

47. Stumblingblock
障害物

Leviticus 19:14, etc.
レビ記 第19章 14節、他

¹⁴ *"Do not curse the deaf or put a **stumblingblock** in front of the blind, but fear your God. I am the LORD."*

(1) Some people have a strange sense of humor. They might want to play a joke on a blind person, putting something in his way and making him fall. That would be a literal way of using a **stumblingblock**. (2) But also, we should understand the expression in a figurative way. We should not do anything to encourage people to do bad things. A person who encourages another person to steal would be placing a **stumblingblock** in front of the innocent one. (3) Additionally, the word **stumblingblock** is sometimes used to refer to a problem that prevents someone from understanding something. A foreign student in Japan would have a stumblingblock before him if he cannot speak Japanese.

¹⁴「耳の聞こえぬ者を悪く言ったり、目の見えぬ者の前に障害物を置いてはならない。あなたの神を畏れなさい。わたしは主である。」

(1) 変わったユーモアのセンスをもった人がいる。そうした人は、盲人の行く手に物を置いてつまずかせ、からかおうとするかもしれない。これが文字通りの「障害物（つまずかせる物）」である。(2) この表現は、比喩的なものとしても理解しなければならない。他者に悪いことをするように勧めるべきではない。人に盗みを働くように勧める者は、純粋な人の前に「障害物（つまずかせる物）」を置くことになる。(3) さらには、「障害物（つまずかせる物）」という語は、何かを理解しようとするときに妨げとなる問題を意味するのに使われる場合がある。日本に滞在する外国人の学生は、日本語が理解できなければ、目の前に「障害物（つまずかせる物）」を持つことになる。

Anne: Margaret wants to get a Ph.D. in chemistry, but she does not have a good background in mathematics.
Jack: What a pity. It sounds to me as if she has a serious **stumblingblock**.[1] I doubt she will ever earn a Ph.D.
Anne: Well, she is very motivated. Sometimes motivation helps us to overcome all **stumblingblocks**.

1) **stumblingblock** 障害物、悩みの種

48. The bitter cup
苦いものを混ぜたぶどう酒

Matthew 27:34
マタイによる福音書　第27章　34節

³⁴They gave him <u>vinegar</u> to drink mingled with <u>gall</u>: and when he had tasted thereof, he would not drink. (KJV)

Just before Jesus died on the cross, he endured humiliation. People laughed at him. He was mocked. He was offered a bitter drink. Some scholars say that there was a tradition of giving this bitter drink to people who were about to be crucified. Supposedly, the drink was a narcotic that would have made the death less painful. The exact reason for the drink is debatable. What is certain is that Jesus refused the drink. Perhaps he wanted to show his determination to endure the suffering, demonstrating his commitment to be a Sacrifice on the part of sinful human beings.

In modern times, people who endure a very difficult experience speak of it as drinking **the bitter cup**. It can even be used in not-so-serious situations.

(³² 兵士たちは出て行くと、シモンという名前のキレネ人に出会ったので、イエスの十字架を無理に担がせた。³³ そしてゴルゴタという所、すなわち「されこうべの場所」に着くと、) ³⁴ 苦いものを混ぜたぶどう酒を飲ませようとしたが、イエスはなめただけで、飲もうとされなかった。(³⁵ 彼らはイエスを十字架につけると、くじを引いてその服を分け合い、³⁶ そこに座って見張りをしていた。)

十字架上での死の直前、イエスは辱めを耐え忍んだ。人々はイエスを笑い物にし、あざけり、イエスに苦い飲み物を与えた。十字架上での刑に処せられる人にこうした苦い飲み物を与える慣習があったとする学者もいる。おそらくその飲み物は麻薬のようなもので、死に対する恐怖を和らげるものと考えられていたのだろう。正確な理由については議論の余地があるが、確かなのはイエスがその飲み物を拒否したということである。イエスは、罪深い人々のために自分が「犠牲」となる責任を負っていることを示すために、苦しみに耐える心構えができていることを示したかったのであろう。

今日、非常に困難な体験を耐え忍ぶ人が「苦い飲み物を飲む」と言われる。この表現はそれほど深刻ではないような場面でも使われうる。

vinegar: 原義は「酸っぱいぶどう酒」／ **gall**:（牛の胆嚢から得られ、薬用にしていた）「胆汁」から意味が拡大され、「ひどく苦いもの」を表す。

Susan: Edna, please pray for me. Tomorrow I will have examinations all day.
Edna: I am sure you will do well. You have studied hard. Now, the important thing is to relax.
Susan: I will relax after tomorrow. By then I will have finished drinking from **the bitter cup.**[1)]

1) **drink the bitter cup**　苦杯を飲む

49. Written in stone / Nothing is written in stone
（神の指で）記された石の板／何も記されていない石の板

Exodus 31:18
出エジプト記　第31章18節

[18]And He gave unto Moses, when He had made an end of communing with him upon Mt. Sinai, two tables of testimony, tablets of stone, <u>written with the finger of God</u>. (KJV)

This is the famous story of Moses going up to Mount Sinai to speak with God. At that time, God gave Moses two stone tablets on which He had "written with His finger"—the Ten Commandments. These are the basis of moral behavior that are still the foundation of Western Civilization: honoring parents, no stealing, no sexual immorality, etc. Many people in their 60's and 70's have fond memories of watching the Charlton Heston movie, *The Ten Commandments*. The tableau etched in the memory of these senior citizens is the scene of the powerfully built actor, in the role of Moses, lifting the heavy stone tablets high above his head as he addressed the misbehaving Israelites.

Today, **"written in stone,"** is an idiom which means a law or policy that is irreversible. Sometimes when we want to describe a situation that can change at any minute, we say, "Well, it is not **written in stone**."

[18]主はシナイ山でモーセと語り終えられたとき、二枚の掟の板、すなわち、**神の指で記された石の板**をモーセにお授けになった。

これはシナイ山に登り、神と語るモーセの有名な話である。その時、神はモーセに「自らの手で記した」2枚の石板、すなわち十戒を与えられた。この十戒は、今日でも西洋文明の基盤となっている道徳律の基礎である。その中には、親を敬い、盗みを働かず、性的不道徳な行いをせず、というようなことが含まれている。1960年代から70年代の人であれば、チャールトン・ヘスト

ンの有名な映画「十戒」を見た記憶があるだろう。年長者たちの記憶に刻み込まれた石板は、モーセの役を演じた屈強な俳優が、重い石板を頭上高く掲げ、間違った行いをしているイスラエルの民に向かって語る姿を思い出させる。

今日、「石板に記された」という表現は、取り消すことのできない法律や政策を意味するものとして使われている。いつでも変更できる状況を説明したいときには、「それは石板には記されていない」と言うことがある。

he gave unto Moses two tables of testimony, tablets of stone = He gave two tables of testimony to Moses = He gave Moses two tables of testimony

---

Derrick: Here are my plans for the next five years: (1) I will get married, (2) I will have two children, and (3) I will be employed at the American Embassy in Nairobi.

Susan: That sounds so ambitious. Are you sure that you will accomplish all of those things in five years?

Derrick: Well, of course nothing is **written in stone**,[1] but those are the things I hope to do.

Anne: I have faith in Derrick. I think he will do all those things.

Susan: It is good that you are so supportive of Derrick.

Anne: Well, it is sure that he will be married within the next five years. We are engaged. That part is definitely **written in stone**.[2]

---

1) **written in stone**　決定事項
2) **written in stone**　変えられないこと

50. A prophet is without honor in his own country
預言者が敬われないのは、その故郷、家族の間だけである

Matthew 13:53–58
マタイによる福音書　第13　53–58節

---

*⁵³When Jesus had finished these parables, he moved on from there. ⁵⁴Coming to his home town, he began teaching the people in their synagogue, and they were amazed. "Where did this man get this wisdom and these miraculous powers?" they asked. ⁵⁵"Isn't this the carpenter's son? Isn't his mother's name Mary, and aren't his brothers James, Joseph, Simon and Judas? ⁵⁶Aren't all his sisters with us? Where then did this man get all these things?" ⁵⁷And they took offence at him. But Jesus said to them, "**A prophet is not without honour except in his own town and in his own home.**" ⁵⁸And he did not do many miracles there because of their lack of faith.*

Jesus Christ was a Jew. Yet, many Jews rejected Him, but foreigners accepted Him as Lord. Jesus used these words to describe human behavior: often we believe that people from far away places know more than the local people. Even today, universities invite guest speakers from far away places when there are teachers just as qualified on the local faculty.

（故郷のナザレで受け入れられないイエスが述べた言葉。）
⁵³イエスはこれらのたとえを語り終えると、そこを去り、⁵⁴故郷にお帰りになった。会堂で教えておられると、人々は驚いて言った。『この人は、このような知恵と奇跡を行う力をどこから得たのだろう。⁵⁵この人は大工の息子ではないか。母親はマリアといい、兄弟はヤコブ、ヨセフ、シモン、ユダではないか。⁵⁶姉妹たちは皆、我々と一緒に住んでいるではないか。この人はこんなことをすべて、いったいどこから得たのだろう。』⁵⁷このように、人々はイエスにつまずいた。イエスは、『預言者が敬われないのは、その故郷、家族の間だけである』と言い、⁵⁸人々が不信仰だったので、そこではあまり奇跡をなさらなかった。

イエスはユダヤ人であった。多くのユダヤ人はイエスを拒否したが、異邦人はイエスを主として受け入れた。イエスは人間の行動を説明するためにこの言葉を使った。すなわち、人間は、遠くの地からやって来た人はその土地の人よりも物事をよく知っている、と考えがちになる。今日、大学においても、そこに有能な教師がいても遠くから講師を招くことがよくある。

Anne: Our university invited a famous professor from England to speak to our class.
Jack: But our university has many great teachers. Why do we need someone to come from England?
Anne: Well, **a prophet is without honor in his own country.**[1]

1) a prophet is without honor in one's own country　預言者故郷に容れられず

51. Old as Methuselah
メトシェラのように長生きをした

Genesis 5:27
創世記　第5章　27節

²⁷*And all the days of Methuselah were nine hundred sixty and nine years: and he died.*

Methuselah's name appears in the family lineage of Adam and Eve. He is primarily known as the oldest person mentioned in the ancient scriptures. He is a descendant of Adam and an ancestor of Noah (who is famous for building the Ark to survive the Great Flood). The name Methuselah is simply used, today, to refer to anything that is extremely old.

²⁷ メトシェラは九百六十九年生き、そして死んだ。

メトシェラという名前は、アダムとイヴの系図に現れる名前である。古代の聖書で述べられている人物の中で最も長生きした人物として知られている。彼はアダムの子孫であり、ノアの先祖である。(ノアは、大洪水を生き残るための方舟を造った人物として有名である。) メトシェラという名前は、今日では、「非常に古い」ものに言及する言葉として使われている。

Derrick: Wow! I can't believe you still have your cat, how old is she?!
Susan: She is **as old as Methuselah**.¹⁾
Derrick: I can believe that. I saw that cat for the first time when I was 8 years old.
Susan: Actually, Lily is only 16 years old.
Derrick: Well, I guess you really take very good care of her.
Susan: Of course, she is like a member of my family.

1) **as old as Methuselah**　メトシェラと同じ位長生きしている

52. Two are better than one
ひとりよりもふたりが良い

Ecclesiastes 4: 9–12
コヘレトの言葉　第4章　9–12節

⁹Two are better than one, because they have a good reward for their labor. ¹⁰For if they fall, the one will lift up his fellow; but woe to him that is alone when he falleth; for he hath not another to help him up. ¹¹Again if two lie together, they have heat; but how can one be warm alone? ¹²And if one prevail against him, two shall withstand him. And a threefold cord is not quickly broken. (KJV)

This is a good reading to use in wedding ceremonies. The passage is saying that it is good for human beings to have a devoted husband or wife. When they face difficulties, they can help each other. The passage goes on to speak of a threesome: "For a threefold cord is not easily broken." The idea is that the people in a happy marriage are the wife, the husband and God. That combination is like a strong rope, twisting three strong pieces into one powerful cord.

⁹ひとりよりもふたりが良い。共に苦労すれば、その報いは良い。¹⁰倒れれば、ひとりがその友を助け起こす。倒れても起こしてくれる友のない人は不幸だ。¹¹更に、ふたりで寝れば暖かいがひとりでどうして暖まれようか。¹²ひとりが攻められれば、ふたりでこれに対する。三つよりの糸は切れにくい。

この句は、結婚式で読むのにふさわしい。人間にとって献身的な夫あるいは妻をもつことは良いことであると言っている。困難に出くわしたとき、互いに助け合うことができるからである。この表現はさらに「3」にまで話が進み、「三つよりの糸は切れにくい」と結ばれている。その背景には、幸せな結婚生活を送る者とは、妻と夫、そして神であるという考え方がある。この組合せは、強い3本の糸をより合わせて作られた（1本の）頑丈なロープに例えられている。

falleth / **hath**: fall / have の3人称単数現在形。

Mahmud: Are you planning to attend Mike and Julia's wedding?
Emiko: Of course, I went shopping for a good gift for them. Do you think they would like a crystal punch bowl?
Mahmud: I suppose so. I am planning to give them money in a nice wedding card.
Emiko: Well, that is a practical gift.
Mahmud: I am so happy for them. They will be the ideal husband and wife. They were happy as single people. Now they will be happy as married people. You know what people say, **"Two are better than one."** [1]

---

1) **Two are better than one** （ひとりより）ふたりの方がよい　cf: Two heads are better than one　三人よれば文殊の知恵

53. A flood of biblical proportions
聖書の規模の洪水

Genesis 7:20–22
創世記　第7章　20-22節

²⁰*Fifteen cubits upward did the water prevail; and the mountains were covered.* ²¹*And all flesh died that moved upon the earth, both of fowl and of cattle, and of beast and of every creeping thing that creepeth upon the earth, and every man:* ²²*All in whose nostrils was the breath of life, of all that was in the dry land, died.* (KJV)

One of the most consistent stories within all ancient cultures is that a great flood occurred, destroying much of life on earth. One version is recorded in the ancient manuscript of *The Epic of Gilgamesh* (fragments from the 18th century BC survive). Of course, in the Western world, the Biblical account in the Book of Genesis is the most famous. Jews and Christians believe that God, angry with the sinful ways of mankind, destroyed everything on earth except for Noah, his family, and the animals that Noah let aboard the Ark. When dramatic flooding occurs in modern times, newspaper headlines often refer to **Floods of Biblical Proportions**. Such were the announcements of the 2013 catastrophes in Tacloban, Philippines (November) and in Colorado, USA (September).

[20] 水は勢いを増して更にその上十五アンマに達し、山々を覆った。[21] 地上で動いていた肉なるものはすべて、鳥も家畜も獣も地に群がり這うものも人も、ことごとく息絶えた。[22] 乾いた地のすべてのもののうち、その鼻に命の息と霊のあるものはことごとく死んだ。

古代文化のうちに一貫して見られる話は、大洪水が起きて地上の生命のほとんどを破壊してしまうというものである。その一つが、(紀元前18世紀の断片が残っている)『ギルガメシュ叙事詩』の写本に記されている。西洋社会では、創世記にある記述が最も有名である。ユダヤ教徒やキリスト教徒は、人間の罪深い行いに怒った神が、ノアとその家族、ノアが方舟に乗せた動物を除く地上の全ての命あるものを滅ぼしたということを信じている。今日でも、大洪水が起こると、新聞には「聖書の規模の洪水」というような見出しが見られることがある。2013年11月のフィリピン、タクロバンでの災害や、同年9月のアメリカ、コロラド州における災害の際に、そうした見出しが見られた。

> ***The Epic of Gilgamesh***: バビロニアの伝説の王ギルガメシュを主人公とした、紀元前2千年頃の叙事／ **his family**: Noah とその妻、3人の息子 Shem（長男；セム族の祖）、Ham（次男；エジプト人・ヌビア人。カナン人などの祖）、Japheth（三男）およびその妻たちの8人。／ **Tacloban, Philippines**: 2013年11月の台風により、甚大な被害を受けた。／ **cubit**: 腕尺。昔の長さの単位で、ひじから中指の先端までの長さ。約17-21インチ。／ **fowl**: 現代英語では「家禽類」を指すが、原義は「鳥」一般。／ **beast**: 植物に対する「動物」／ **creepeth**: creep の3人称単数現在形。／ **in whose nostrils was the breath of life**: the breath of life が主語の倒置文。創世記第2章7節に記されている、「主なる神は土（アダマ）の塵で人（アダム）を形づくり、その鼻に命の息を吹き入れられた。人はこうして生きる者になった。」参照。

Mark: The weatherman forecasts a big storm for next week.

Miriam: Well, maybe we will get lucky and the classes at the university will be cancelled. I have two research projects to present, and I am not really prepared.

Mark: My advice to you is to prepare to attend classes and do your presentations. This school has a reputation for holding classes even in inclement weather.[1] Nothing less than **a flood of biblical proportions**[2] stops the activities of this university.

> Miriam: You are right, of course. I should not be wishing for dangerous weather just so I can escape my responsibilities.

1) **in inclement weather**　悪天候の中で
2) **a flood of biblical proportions**　聖書に書かれているような大規模な洪水（大規模なハリケーンが襲ってくるような時に天気予報等でこのような表現を使うことがある）

54. Fire and brimstone
火と硫黄

Psalms 11: 5–7
詩編 11.5–7

> *⁵The Lord trieth the righteous; but the wicked and him that loveth violence his soul hateth. ⁶Upon the wicked he shall rain snares, **fire and brimstone**, and an horrible tempest; this shall be the portion of their cup. ⁷For the righteous Lord loveth righteousness; his countenance doth behold the upright.* (KJV)
>
> In several places in the Bible, God shows His anger with criminals and evil-doers. God is patient, giving bad people ample time to change their wicked ways. But sometimes such people exhaust God's patience, and He gives them severe punishment. On one famous occasion, God sent fire and brimstone (sulfur) from the skies to burn up two very sinful towns, Sodom and Gomorrah (Genesis 19: 1–38) But Psalm 11:6 promises that God will protect the good people, and He will punish the bad people with **fire and brimstone**.
>   Often this expression is used in a humorous way in modern conversation. It can refer to the words of an overly emotional or excited speaker. Originally of course, it referred to God's anger. These days, the expression is often used with no reference to the Bible or to God.

⁵主は、主に従う人と逆らう者を調べ　不法を愛する者を憎み　⁶逆らう者に災いの火を降らせ、熱風を送り　燃える硫黄をその杯に注がれる。⁷主は正しくいまし、恵の業を愛し　御顔を心のまっすぐな人に向けてくださる。

聖書のあちこちで、神は犯罪者、悪を行う者にたいしてその怒りを顕わにしている。神は（いつもは）忍耐強く、悪を行う者がその邪悪な道を変えるための時間を十分に与えている。しかし、悪を行う者たちの中には神を辟易させてしまう者もいて、その場合、神はそうした人々に厳しい罰をお与えになる。ある有名な場面で、神は邪悪な町ソドムとゴモラに天から火と硫黄を送り、焼き尽くしてしまった（創世記第19章1–38節）。しかし、詩編11の6節では、神は善の人々を守り、**火と硫黄**でもって悪を行う人々を罰するとされている。

現代の会話では、この表現はユーモラスな使われ方をする場合が多い。感情過多の語句や、興奮した話者に言及する場合もある。もちろん元来は、神の怒りを表すものである。今日の用法では、聖書や神に言及しない使われ方が多い。

trieth / loveth / doth: try / love / do の３人称単数現在形。

Jack: Carl, I noticed that your library book is overdue. You had better return it immediately. There is a one dollar fine for every day that you are late.

Carl: I know that, but I just didn't have time to return it.

Jack: Not only will you have to pay a lot of money, but you will have to endure the **fire and brimstone**[1] of Dr. Erickson, the head librarian. He gets so angry when students are late returning the books.

1) **the fire and brimstone**　地獄の責め

55. Manna from Heaven
天の恵み／天からのマナ

Exodus 16:4
出エジプト記　第16章

*⁴Then the Lord said unto Moses, Behold, I will rain **bread from heaven** for you; and the people shall go out and gather a certain rate every day, that I may prove them, whether they will walk in my Law, or no.* (KJV)

*⁴Then the Lord said to Moses, "I will rain down **bread from heaven** for you. The people are to go out each day and gather enough for that day. In this way I will test them and see whether they will follow my instructions. (⁶On the sixth day they are to prepare what they bring in, and that is to be twice as much as they gather on the other days.)* (NIV)

This is an extended story. Basically, the idea is that the Israelite people were wandering a long time in their escape from slavery in Egypt. God had made special arrangements for the Israelites to escape the slavery in Egypt. But at some point in their long sojourn, the people began to complain. They remembered that they had food to eat in Egypt. Some began to think it was better to be a slave who had food than to be a free man who was starving. God, irritated with the small-mindedness of the people, sent special meat and "bread" from heaven. The people had so much to eat that they got sick.

Today, the expression refers to any unexpected supply of something you really need.

⁴ 主はモーセに言われた。「見よ、わたしはあなたたちのために、天からパンを降らせる。民は出て行って、毎日必要は分だけ集める。わたしは、彼らがわたしの指示どおりにするかどうかを試す。(⁵ ただし、六日目に家に持ち帰ったものを整えれば、毎日集める分の二倍になっている。)」

この表現にまつわる話も長いものである。その概略は、以下のとおりである。イスラエルの民がエジプトにおける奴隷生活から逃れ、長い間さまよっていた。神はエジプトでの奴隷生活から逃れることができるように、イスラエルの民のために特別な計らいをしてくださった。長い間さまよっているうちに、民は不平を口にするようになった。エジプトでは食べ物があったことを思い出したのである。飢えに苦しむ自由の身であるよりも、食べ物が与えられる奴隷の身であった方がましだと考え始めた者が出始めた。イスラエルの民の小心さに怒った神は、天から特別な食べ物、パンを与えたのである。食べ物があまりにも多すぎたので、人々はうんざりしてしまった。今日では、この表現は、本当に必要としているものが予期せぬ時に与えられるということを表すものとして使われている。

meat: 本来の意味は "food"

Jack: Anne, you seem especially happy today, what's up?
Anne: You know¹⁾ that I volunteer in Cambodia every summer. My friends and I are building a new library for the village. Well, the New York City Library is donating 300 new books for our project!
Jack: Wow, that is good news. It is like **manna from heaven**²⁾ for the village library.

1) **You know~**　ご存知の通り、あのね（文頭で）
2) **manna from heaven**　天からの贈り物

56. Old wives' tale
愚にもつかない作り話

I Timothy 4:7
テモテへの手紙 一　第4章　7節

⁷*But refuse profane and <u>old wives' fables</u>, and exercise thyself rather unto godliness.*
(KJV)

The word "wife" in Old English really just meant "woman." Originally it did not indicate marital status.

Paul was a prolific writer. He wrote a major portion of the New Testament by himself. He wrote two letters to a young Christian, Timothy. In the first letter, he reminds Timothy to teach the original Christian message and not to change any of the teachings of Jesus Christ. Paul predicted that, in the future, there would be false Christian teachers who would teach different ideas. In cautioning Timothy against such false teachers, Paul reminds Timothy that all Christians must study the Bible and reject "**old wives' tales**." Women in ancient times did not receive high levels of education, and often they passed around non-scientific myths about daily life. He wanted to make a distinction between the good teachings of Jesus and the myths passed on by uneducated women—and by dishonest "preachers." Today, the expression refers to any idea which is not scientifically proven. A man or a woman could be the source of an **old wives' tale**.

⁷俗悪で愚にもつかない作り話は退けなさい。信心のために自分を鍛えなさい。

古英語では "wife" は "woman" の意味で使われ、結婚歴は含んでいなかった。
　パウロは多作の人で、新約聖書の大部分を自分で書いた。彼は若い信者のテモテに宛てて2通の手紙を書いている。その第一の手紙で、聖パウロは、キリスト教の本来の教えを伝え、イエス・キリストの教えを少しも変えてはならないということを思い出させている。パウロは、将来、異なる教えを説く間違ったキリスト教の師が現れるであろうと予言している。こうした間違ったキリスト教の師に対して注意を促すため、パウロはテモテに、キリスト教徒たる者は全て、聖書を学び、「愚にもつかない作り話」を退けなければならないということを思い出させているのである。古代の女性は高等教育を受けておらず、日常生活について、非科学的な作り話を広めてしまうことがしばしばあった。パウロは、イエスの良い教えと、教養のない女性たちによって広められる作り話、また不正直な「説教者」によって広められる作り話とを区別したかったのである。今日では、この表現は科学的に証明されていない考え方を示すものとして使われている。男性も女性も、「愚にもつかない作り話」の作り手になりうるのである。

　　"old wives' tale": 文字通りの意味は、「(教養のない) 老女の (たわいない) 話 [繰り言]」／
　　woman: 古英語では単に「女の人」という意味で、結婚の有無は表していなかった。

Mark:　　When I visited Japan last October, I enjoyed eating persimmons—they are not very popular in America.

Makoto:　Oh, you are making me homesick. I really miss persimmons in Japan! We call them *Kaki*.

Mark:　　They are so sweet. I think I could eat three or four of them at one time. But an elderly Japanese man told me that I should not eat persimmons late at night.

Makoto:　Oh, that is not scientific. Some old Japanese people say that eating persimmons late at night lowers body temperature.

Mark: Really? Well it could be true. Sometimes **old wives' tales**[1)] have a basis in truth.

Makoto: I thought you said an elderly man told you that about persimmons. In that case it's an old man's tale.

Mark: In English, **old wives' tale** just refers to an old myth—it really has nothing to do with gender.

1) **old wives' tale**　くだらない迷信

57. Out of the mouth of babes and sucklings
幼子、乳飲み子の口から

Psalms 8:1–2
詩編 8.1–2

*¹Oh Lord, our Lord, how excellent is thy name in all the earth! who hast set they their glory above the heavens. ²**Out of the mouth of babes and sucklings** hast thou ordained strength because of thine enemies, that thou mightest still the enemy and the avenger.* (KJV)

*¹Lord, our Lord, how majestic is your name in all the earth! You have set your glory in the heavens. ²**Through the praise of children and infants** you have established a stronghold against your enemies, to silence the foe and the avenger.* (NIV)

In modern times, the expression is often rendered: "**Out of the mouths of babes and sucklings** comes wisdom." It refers to the occasional, remarkably enlightened things that young people or untutored people say. For example, if a new worker comes into a company and offers some brilliant advice, an older worker might say, "**Out of the mouth of babes ….**"

Simplified rendering: Even babes and uneducated people recognize your greatness!

²主よ、わたしたちの主よ　あなたの御名は、いかに力強く　全地に満ちていることでしょう。天に輝くあなたの威光をたたえます。³幼子、乳飲み子の口によって。あなたは刃向かう者に向かって砦を築き　報復する敵を断ち滅ぼされます。

現代では、この表現は "Out of the mouths of babes and sucklings comes wisdom"（赤子、乳飲み子の口から智恵の言葉が出てくる）という形で使われる。その意味するところは、若者や学のな

い人が時折言う、非常に賢明な事柄を指して使われる。たとえば、入社したての人が素晴らしいことを言ったとき、年長の社員が "Out of the mouth of babes ..." と言うようなことがあげられる。簡単な表現として、「赤ん坊や教養のない人でもあなたの偉大さには気が付くだろう！」があげられる。

thou / thy / thine: 2人称単数代名詞の主格・所有格。thine は母音の前、thy は子音の前。／ **hast**: have の2人称単数現在形。／ **mightest**: might (may) の2人称単数。／ **still**: 動詞

Jack: There is an amazing student in the freshman class. She says that the university should have a satellite campus in Ethiopia. Students could do volunteer teaching there, and they could get credit for graduation.

Anne: I am surprised that a new student has such wonderful ideas. It seems like she is not shy.

Jack: Yes, she spoke very eloquently at the student meeting today—**Out of the mouth of babes and sucklings** comes wisdom!

---

58. Thorn in the flesh
わたしの身に一つのとげ（が与えられた）

II Corinthians 12:7
コリントの信徒への手紙二　第12章7節

*⁷And lest I should be exalted above measure through the abundance of the revelations, there was given to me **a thorn in the flesh**, the messenger of Satan to buffet me, lest I should be exalted above measure.* (KJV)

Paul was privileged to have special communication with God. He was a mystic who had visions and experiences that most people did not have. He said that God did not want him to be  proud or to think himself superior to others, so God gave him a mysterious problem or sickness that kept him humble. Many scholars have tried to guess what the problem could have been. Some have conjectured that the **thorn in the flesh** was partial blindness. The people who suggest that blindness was the problem note that on at least one occasion Paul said that he was writing in large letters (apparently so that he could better see what he was writing). They also note that physical blindness would be a balance to the very beautiful visions of Heaven that Paul was granted. In other words he was gifted with precious

> spiritual sight, so physically impaired sight might be the best thing to keep him humble.
>
> Very often today, **Thorn in the flesh** refers to one of two situations: (1) a problem or sickness that a person must endure, or (2) another person who is a severe irritation or annoyance.

⁷また、あの啓示された事があまりにもすばらしいからです。それで、そのために思い上がることのないようにと、**わたしの身に一つのとげが与えられました**。それは、思い上がらないように、わたしを痛めつけるために、サタンから送られた使いです。

パウロは神とコミュニケーションを取る特権を与えられていた。彼は秘法伝授者で、ほとんどの人が有しない予見力と経験を持っていた。彼の言うことによれば、神は彼に尊大にならないよう、他者よりも自分が優れていると考えないように望み、彼が謙虚でいられるように、不可思議な課題、病を与えた。その課題とはどのようなものであるのか、学者たちが推測しようとしてきた。**肉体のとげ**とは、部分的な盲目状態であると推測する学者もいる。盲目が課題であるとする人々は、少なくとも一度、パウロが大きな文字で書いていると言ったことに注目している。(そうすれば、明らかに自分が何を書いているのかよく見えるからである。)また、肉体上の盲目は、パウロが与えられた天国の美しい光景とバランスが取れると見なしている。言い換えるならば、彼は豊かな精神的視野を与えられ、従って肉体上欠陥としての盲目は、彼を謙虚な人間にしておく最善の方法なのである。

今日では、**肉体のとげ**は、(1) 人間が耐えなければならない課題問題や病、(2) 他者を苛立たせ、悩ませる人に言及する表現となっている。

a thorn in the [one's] **flesh** [side] ／ **buffet** [bʌfit]: 続けざまに痛めつける

(An Annoying Person)
Mark: Professor Wilson really gave us too much homework last week. I am only half way through the readings. How about you?
Emiko: I have not done any of the readings. I am having a hard time in the dormitory. One girl plays loud music all night, and I can't concentrate.
Mark: I have heard about that girl before. Sounds like she is your **thorn in the flesh**.[1)]
Emiko: I am wondering what I can do about this problem.
Mark: Students with a high grade point average are allowed to live off campus. I suggest you ask the student office to help you find an apartment.
Emiko: I think that is the best solution.

(A Personal Problem)
Emiko: Oh Mark, you seem to be having asthma problems again.

Mark: Yes, I have been struggling with asthma most of my life. It is my **thorn in the flesh**, but I refuse to let it ruin my life. I just carry on the best I can.
Emiko: You have a good attitude.

1) **thorn in the flesh** 悩みの種

59. Your number is up!
あなたの治世は終わった

Daniel 5:24–28
ダニエル書　第 5 章　24-28 節

²⁴Then was the part of the hand sent from him; ²⁵and this was written, Mene, Mene, Tekel, Upharsin. ²⁶This is the interpretation of the thing. Mene; God hath numbered thy kingdom, and finished it. ²⁷Tekel; Thou art found wanting. ²⁸Peres; Thy kingdom is divided and given to the Medes and the Persians. (KJV)

In the original Bible passage, King Belshazzar was a foreign king who occupied Jerusalem. He was not obedient to the God of Israelites (who lived in Jerusalem). Part of the message was "**Your number is up!**" The actual meaning of those words is that you will die soon, but modern day English speakers often use the phrase to mean, "It is time for you to go on stage," or "It is time for you to do something important."

（ダニエル書の「壁に字を書く指の幻」の話しの続き。）
²⁴ そのために神は、あの手を遣わして文字を書かせたのです。²⁵ さて、書かれた文字はこうです。メネ、メネ、テケル、そして、パルシン。²⁶ 意味はこうです。メネは数えるということで、すなわち、神はあなたの治世を数えて、それを終わらせたのです。²⁷ テケルは量を計ることで、すなわち、あなたは秤にかけられ、不足と見られました。²⁸ パルシンは分けるということで、すなわち、あなたの王国は二分されて、メディアとペルシアに与えられるのです。」

聖書の原文では、ベルシャザール王はエルサレムを支配する異国の王であった。王は、エルサレムに住むイスラエルの民の神に対して従順ではなかった。そこに記されていることの一部は「あなたの（この世での）日数は終わった」ということである。その意味するところは、「間もなく死ぬことになる」ということであるが、現代では、「舞台に上がるときが来た」あるいは、「何か重要なことをする時期である」という意味で使われている。

Then was the part of the hand sent from him: 副詞 then が文頭に使われていることによる、主語と動詞の倒置。(cf. The part of the hand was sent from him then.) ／ **hath**: 3 人称単数の直説法現在 "has" の古形。／ **thy / thou**: 2 人称単数目的格／主格の人称代名詞の古形。／ **art**: BE 動詞の 2 人称単数・直説法現在形 (are) の古形。／ **want**:「欠けている、不足している」の意味。

(In reference to death)

Edna: I heard that Mrs. Clark died last night. She was such a sweet old lady. I really liked her.

Mark: Yes, I really respected her. She was blind, but she managed to help other people.

Edna: You were kind to read to her on some Saturdays. I am sure you are grieving.

Mark: Yes, I feel so sad. But she had a good life. It was just her time to die. **Her number was up**.

(In reference to a performance)

Susan: I hear that you will make an important speech to the company in a few hours.

Jack: Yes, unfortunately, I must announce that we have to cut salaries. People will get smaller paychecks.

Susan: No one will be happy to hear that.

Jack: I am nervous about making the announcement.

Susan: Well, you must do it. You cannot force someone else to make the speech. **Your number is up**.[1]

1) **one's number is up** 年貢の納め時

60. Jot and tittle
一点一画

Matthew 5:17–18
マタイによる福音書　第5章　17–18節

Jesus explains His respect for the ancient Scriptures:
¹⁷*Think not that I am come to destroy the law, or the prophets; I am not come to destroy them, but to fulfill.* ¹⁸*For verily I say unto you, Till heaven and earth pass,* **one jot or one tittle** *shall in no wise pass from the law, till all be fulfilled.* (KJV)

¹⁷"*Do not think that I have come to abolish the Law or the Prophets; I have not come to abolish them but to fulfill them.* ¹⁸*For truly I tell you, until heaven and earth disappear,* **not the smallest letter, not the least stroke of a pen**, *will by any means disappear from the Law until everything is accomplished.* (NIV)

These words originally referred to diacritical markings in the Greek alphabet. In modern day English, it would translate as the horizontal bar on the letter "t" and the dot above the letter "i". However, this phrase has come to refer to the attention paid to the smallest details of a manuscript or an arrangement, as in "I checked and re-checked the letter many times, analyzing every **jot and tittle**."

Occasionally, the famous phrases of the Bible are used in one version or translation and not others. That is the case with *jot and tittle*. These words are found in the classic King James Version, and not in some other translations.

律法について
[17]「わたしが来たのは律法や預言者を廃止するためだ、と思ってはならない。廃止するためではなく、完成するためである。[18] はっきり言っておく。すべてのことが実現し、天地が消えうせるまで、律法の文字から一点一画も消え去ることはない。[19] だから、これらの最も小さな掟を一つでも破り、そうするようにと人に教える者は、天の国で最も小さい者と呼ばれる。しかし、それを守り、そうするように教える者は、天の国で大いなる者と呼ばれる。[20] 言っておくが、あなたがたの義が律法学者やファリサイ派の人々の義にまさっていなければ、あなたがたは決して天の国に入ることができない。」

jot と tittle は、元々ギリシャ語アルファベットの文字に付けられた符号・補助記号のことを意味している。現代英語における "t" の横棒とか、"i" の点などと理解されている。しかし、このフレーズは、原稿や取決めなどの細部の詳細に向けられた注意に言及するものとなってきた。「その手紙を、あらゆる細かなところも分析して、何度も、何度もチェックした」のような表現に見られる。
聖書の有名な表現が、ある版では使われているが、他の版では使われていない、というようなことがしばしば起こる。**jot and tittle** という表現についても当てはまる。欽定訳聖書では使われているが、他の版には見られないのである。

通例否定語と共に用いられ (not a jot or tittle)、「ほんの少しも…（し）ない」という意味。

Jack: Anne, I must make a special presentation before the board meeting next week. Would you please proofread my manuscript?

Anne: I don't mind at all. You are a good writer, and you have excellent command of grammar, but I will be sure to check **every jot and tittle**.[1)]

Jack: Thanks a lot, I appreciate your willingness to help.

1) **jot and tittle**　詳細な点

Chapter III
★★★
The Bible and Popular Culture
(聖書と大衆文化)

Scripture in Political Speeches

(政治演説で使われる聖書の言葉)

It is almost impossible to escape references to the Bible in popular culture. There are Bible verses included in newspaper stories, in famous novels, and in the speeches of modern politicians. David Cameron, the Prime Minister of Britain, has quoted the Bible several times in his speeches. On the 400th anniversary of the publication of the King James Version of the Bible (1611–2011), he spoke about the continuing influence of that great English translation. He talked about the many Bible idioms which are used in everyday conversations—often by people who are not aware of the source of those words:

> "We live and breathe the language of the King James Bible, sometimes without realizing it."[†]

[†]Interestingly, even this quotation by Cameron about the Bible uses the Bible idiom. "live and breathe." Some scholars see this as a variation of Acts 17:28—"For in Him we live and move."

(大衆文化においては、聖書に言及しないですませるわけにはいかない。新聞記事、小説、政治家のスピーチのいずれにも、聖書の引用句が含まれている。英国首相のジェイムズ・キャメロンは、その演説の中で幾度となく聖書の言葉を引用している。欽定訳聖書の出版400年記念日に、キャメロン首相は演説の中で、この英語訳が今日でも大きな影響力を持っていることを述べている。表現の由来について何も知らない人々の日常会話の中で、聖書の言葉が多く使われているのである。
「我々は、それと気づかずに、欽定訳聖書と共にあり、その言語を呼吸しているのである。」)

Although he has said that his faith "comes and goes" (it means sometimes he is religious, sometimes he is not religious), he delivered a Christmas speech in 2013 which indicated his knowledge of the Bible. He quoted the well-known words of Jesus from Acts 20:35, "It is more blessed to give than to receive." In the western world, those words of Jesus are familiar even to non-Christians. The idea is that giving things to other people makes us feel good. Frequently, people speak of the happiness that they get from helping other people. At Christmastime, and at other seasons, audiences hear those Bible words over and over.

（キャメロン首相は、「自分の宗教心は時に厚く、時に薄くなりはする」と述べているが、2013 年のクリスマスの演説では、聖書に関する知識を表し、『使徒言行録』第 20 章 35 節の「受けるよりは与える方が幸いである」という有名なイエスの言葉を引用している。西洋社会では、この言葉はキリスト教徒ではない人にもよく知られている。そこにある思想は、〈他者に与えることによって人は良い気分になれる〉ということである。クリスマスの時も、また他の季節でも、そうした聖書の言葉がよく聞かれる。）

Almost every American President has included some Bible expressions in formal speeches. President George Bush often referred to his Christian conversion. In one interview, he spoke about the effects of a particular Bible verse on his life. He said:

The more I got into the Bible, the more (I understood) the admonition, '*Don't try to take a speck out of your neighbor's eye when you got a log in your own.*' [†]

([†]A Library of Quotations on Religion and Politics by George W. Bush, http://www.beliefnet.com/News/Politics/2000/07/A-Library-Of-Quotations-On-Religion-And-Politics-By-George-W-Bush.aspx.)

Of course that verse teaches people to be careful about criticizing others. Everybody makes mistakes, everybody should be quick to forgive and to understand.

（ほとんどのアメリカ大統領は、その演説の中で、聖書の表現を使っている。ジョージ・ブッシュ大統領は、自身の信仰的目覚めによく言及して、あるインタビューにおいて、聖書の句が自身の人生に大いに影響を与えていると述べている。
「聖書に入りこめば入りこむほど、『自分の目に丸太があるのに、他人の目の汚点を取り除こうとするな』という戒めがよく理解できる。」
もちろんこの言葉の意味は、〈他者を非難する際には気をつけよ〉ということである。誰も過ちを犯すことがあり、人は進んで赦し、理解すべきである。）

Some people have noted that Mr. Obama is especially keen at using the Bible to comfort Americans who have suffered in mass tragedies. When mentally disturbed men have used guns to kill innocent people in public schools and in shopping malls, the President has flown to those sites to embrace the mourners. At the funeral service for Americans killed in a Tucson, Arizona gun attack on January 12, 2011, Obama recited:

There is a river whose streams make glad the city of God, the holy
place where the Most High dwells.
God is within her, she will not fall;
God will help her at break of day. (Psalms 46:5–6)

Psalms 46:5–6 is a beautiful poem about God's protection. It says that God is always in our midst. When tragedies come, God uses good people to bring us comfort.

（オバマ大統領も、大きな悲劇を被ったアメリカ国民を慰めるために、とりわけ熱心に聖書を利用している。精神障害のある人が、公立学校やショッピング・モールで無実の人々を殺害したとき、大統領は現地に赴き、嘆き悲しむ人を抱擁した。2011年1月12日にアリゾナ州ツーソンで銃殺された人々の葬儀で、オバマ大統領は以下のように引用している。
「大河とその流れは、神の都に喜びを与える　いと高き神のいます聖所に。 神はその中にいまし、都は揺らぐことがない。夜明けとともに、神は助けをお与えになる。」詩編 46:5–6
詩編 46 第 5–6 節は、神のご加護を示す美しい詩である。この部分は、神は常に我々の内にあり、悲劇の際には善なる人をもって我々を慰めてくださるのである。）

Scripture in Cities

（市民が使う聖書の言葉）

Not only is the Bible used to comfort people who have experienced tragedies. Sometimes ordinary people, on ordinary days, speak in the words of the Bible. The following paragraphs are stories from the internet. They are about homeless people in America who have been discovered to have amazing talents.

（聖書は、悲劇に遭遇した人々を慰めるために利用されるばかりではない。普通の人々が、日々の生活の中で聖書の言葉を使っている。以下に記すのは、インターネットに掲載されているもので、素晴らしい才能を持っていることがわかった、ホームレスの人たちの話である。）

The Homeless and the Gifted
（ホームレスと恵まれた者）

Recently, countries around the world are experiencing an influx of homeless people sleeping under bridges, in all-night fast food stores, in little villages of blue tarpaulin tents. Amazingly, some of the people living in these conditions are intelligent and articulate. Several of them have become internet sensations as they demonstrate remarkable talents such as singing, public speaking, and playing the piano. Some of these homeless people are well-versed in the Bible. They often cite God as the one who gave them talent. People who happen to witness the miracle of these talents are often prompted to quote the Bible or to praise God.

（最近、世界中でホームレスが大勢見られるようになった。彼らは、橋の下で眠ったり、深夜営業のファースト・フード店で過ごしたり、青い防水シートのテント村で寝たりしている。こうしたホームレスの中には、非常に知的で、理路整然とした考えを持っている人がいる。歌や、スピーチや、ピアノでその才能を示し、インターネット上でセンセーションを巻き起こしている人々もいる。聖書に非常に詳し

いホームレスもいる。そうした人々は、自分に才能を与えてくれた者として、神を引き合いに出す。こうした人々の才能を目撃したとき、聖書を引用したり、神を讃えたくなるものである。)

Nathaniel Ayers, Street Violinist
(路上バイオリニスト、ナサニエル・エイアーズ)

ONE such case appears to be Nathaniel Ayers, the schizophrenic violin virtuoso. He lives in a homeless shelter. At night, Nathaniel prays the famous Lord's Prayer (Our Father, which† art†† in Heaven …), Matthew 6:9–13. The walls of the shelter are covered with a neon sign which cites Romans 6:23, "For the wages of sin is death, but the gift of God is eternal life through Jesus Christ our Lord." Ayers' true story has inspired a book, *The Soloist: A Lost Dream, an Unlikely Friendship, and the Redemptive Power of Music*, by Steve Lopez. Many people know of Ayers through the award winning film, *The Soloist*, which starred Robert Downey Jr. and Jaime Foxx.

　　†初期近代英語期の関係代名詞で、先行詞はFather。／††初期近代英語期の、BE動詞の3人称単数現在形。

(こうした人の例として、総合失調症のバイオリンの名手、ナサニエル・エイアーズをあげることができる。彼はホームレスのシェルターに住み、夜になると『マタイによる福音書』第6章の9–13節の主の祈り（天にまします我らの父よ、…）を唱える。シェルターの壁は『ローマの信徒への手紙』第6章23節の「罪が支払う報酬は死です。しかし、神の賜物は、私たちの主キリスト・イエスによる永遠の命なのです。」という引用文のネオン・サインで覆われている。エイアーズの実話は、スティーブ・ロペスの著書 *The Soloist: A Lost Dream, an Unlikely Friendship, and the Redemptive Power of Music*（『ソリスト：失われた夢、予期せぬ友情、そして音楽の救いの力』）の基となっている。ロバート・ダウニーⅡ世とジェイミー・フォックスが出演した「ソリスト」という受賞映画を通して、エイアーズを知っている人も多い。)

David Allen Welsh
(デイビッド・アレン・ウェルシュ)

AMID the news of frightening international conflict, networks and newspapers all over the world reported the inspiring story of David Allen Welsh. CNN posted a video of the homeless man who is not formally trained and who cannot read music, but who has the amazing power to create classical-style music and play instantly. David visits a second-hand shop in Vancouver, Canada. People come to the store to hear him play—and to weep. One man, James Maynard, quoted the Bible and said that there is no clear explanation of Welsh's great talent. Maynard quoted, "It is the joy that passeth† understanding" (a near perfect reference to Philippians 4:7).

　　†passの3人称単数現在形。

(国際紛争のニュースを報じる中、世界中の報道機関はデイビッド・アレン・ウェルシュの素晴らしい話を報じた。CNN (Cable News Network) は、それまでに訓練を受けたこともなく、譜面も読めないが、クラシック調の曲を作り、即興で演奏する才能を持ったホームレスの映像を流した。デイビッドがカナダのバンクーバーにある中古品店を訪れると、多くの人が押し寄せ、彼の演奏を聞いて、涙を流した。その中の一人、ジェームズ・メイナードが、「それは人知を超える喜びである」という聖書の言葉を引用し、ウェルシュの才能を明確に表す言葉は他にないと言っている。この表現は、『フィリピの信徒への手紙』第4章7節の、「そうすれば、あらゆる人知を超える神の平和が、あなた方の心と考えとをキリスト・イエスによって守るでしょう」に相当するものである。)

Ted Williams—"The Man With the Golden Voice"
(テッド・ウィリアムズ―「黄金の声を持つ男」)

TED Williams, a former radio announcer who had a wife and nine children succumbed to drug addiction and lost everything. His family disowned him, and he lost his radio job. One day while holding a sign on the street, he attracted the attention of a driver. The sign said, "I have a God-Given voice …" The driver offered him a dollar to prove his ability. As the driver filmed him, Ted Williams spoke in the most beautifully refined tones. The video received worldwide attention, and Williams became an overnight star. One of the popular American Television shows broadcast Ted's reunion with his mother, a devout Christian woman. Her words were predictable for those who are familiar with the Bible:

Ted Williams: I love you mother.
Julia Williams: The Prodigal son has come home.

The mother, Julia Williams, reminded her son that she had tried very hard to raise him a faithful Christian, but that he had disappointed her with his lifestyle of addiction.

(元ラジオ・アナウンサーで、妻と九人の子供を持つテッド・ウィリアムズは、麻薬中毒に負け、家族も仕事も全てを失ってしまった。ある日、通りで「私には神に与えられた声があります」と書かれたサインを掲げていると、一人のドライバーが彼に注目した。ドライバーはその能力を証明してくれるならばと、1ドルを差し出した。ドライバーが撮影し、テッド・ウィリアムズはこの上もなく素晴らしい声で話し始めた。そのビデオは全国の注目を集め、テッド・ウィリアムズは一夜にしてスターになった。あるテレビ局が、テッドが敬虔なクリスチャンである母親と再会する場面を放送した。彼の母親の言葉は、聖書に親しんでいる人には、予測できるものであった。
　テッド：愛しているよ、お母さん。
　母　親：放蕩息子がようやく帰って来たわね。
彼を忠実なクリスチャンに育てようと一生懸命努力した母親のジュリア・ウィリアムズは、彼が麻薬中毒になって母親をがっかりさせてしまったと思いださせようとしたのであった。)

Books and Films
(本と映画)

THE Bible is freely quoted in important books (fiction and non-fiction). The list provided is not exhaustive, of course. There is not enough space in this publication to name all of the movies and all of the novels which are influenced by the Holy Bible. Perhaps you have seen some of these movies and you were not aware of the quotations from the Bible.

> (聖書はフィクションであれ、ノンフィクションであれ、重要な本の中で頻繁に引用されている。本書で扱われているものは当然その全体を示すものではない。聖書に影響されている小説や映画を網羅するスペースは本書にはない。御覧になった映画もあるだろうが、恐らく聖書からの引用には気づいておられないだろう。)

The Influence of the Bible on Western Culture
(西洋文化に見られる聖書の影響)

THE English Bible, particularly the King James Version of 1611, continues to be a powerful influence on Western culture. Dialogues in English language movies, conversations of ordinary citizens, and passages of famous novels are saturated with Biblical quotations. In this chapter, we would like to consider how the Bible permeates the societies of English speaking countries. Presidents, movie stars, and homeless people have exhibited a love of Scripture.

> (英語訳聖書、とりわけKJVは、西洋文化に大きな影響を与え続けている。映画での対話、一般市民の会話、そして有名な小説の一節は、聖書からの引用文で溢れている。本章では、英語圏の社会に聖書がいかに浸透しているか、考えてみたい。大統領、映画スター、そしてホームレスも、聖書を好む姿を示してきている。)

Scripture in Hollywood

（ハリウッド映画と聖書）

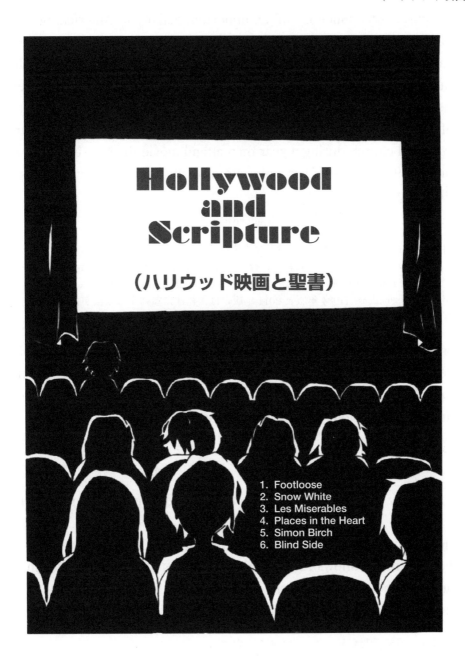

FREQUENT movie goers are subjected to a steady recitation of Bible verses. Not only are specific verses alluded to, but the films also have references to famous Bible stories and characters.

（映画を良く観る人は、特定の聖書の一節だけでなく、聖書の中の物語や登場人物が示されていることに気がつくことがある。）

Footloose, 2011
『フットルース 2011』

NOTE: Church attendance is still an important activity in America. Surveys vary, but according to two famous polling organizations, Pew and Gallop, 40 per cent of Americans report going to church every Sunday.* Of course that is a much smaller figure than in earlier decades. However, think about it: although 40 percent of Americans report weekly church attendance, another poll suggests that only 11 percent of Americans report going to a movie theater once a month. Clearly more Americans attend church during a year than attend movie theaters in a year. *Footloose* (two versions, 1984, and 2011) is only one of many movies which have scenes of families attending a worship service.

* http://en.wikipedia.org/wiki/Church_attendance

(教会に行くことは、アメリカ社会では今日でも大切なこととされている。有名な統計調査機関によると、アメリカ人の40%が毎週日曜日に教会に行くと答えている。*昔に比べるとその数はかなり減っているが、1ヶ月に1度映画を観に行く人が11%であるという調査結果と比較するといかに大きな数字であるかが分かる。*Footloose*（1984年版と2011年版）は、礼拝に参列する家族が描かれている映画の一つである。)

The original 1984 film starring Kevin Bacon is a cult classic; that simply means that people still enjoy watching the movie many years after it was made. Often, movies like *Footloose* have fan clubs, and people gather together to see the film repeatedly. The dancing in both versions of the film is phenomenal.

(ケヴィン・ベーコン主演の1984年版は、礼拝のクラシックとも言える映画である。こうした映画にはファン・クラブがあり、人々は繰り返し観ている。この映画のダンスシーンは圧巻である。)

There are a few changes to the story in the 2011 version. But the major differences are:
1. The 1984 movie depicts an all-white community.
2. The 2011 movie shows African Americans interacting with whites in the community, school and the church.
3. The dancing in the 2011 is updated, featuring hip hop dancing.

(2011年版には若干の変更が見られ、その主なものは
1. 1984年版は白人社会を描いている。
2. 2011年版では、アフリカ系アメリカ人（黒人）が、社会、学校、教会で白人と混じり合っている。
3. 2011年版のダンスは、ヒップ・ホップになっている。)

The movie shows a father who is a preacher. He seems to focus more on God's punishment of sinners than he does on God's love of all of us. His sermons are scary. He makes the people very uncomfortable in church. Perhaps he should have more balance in his teaching. He should spend sometimes talking about the goodness of God.

（映画には伝道師である父親が登場する。その父親は、全ての人に対する神の愛よりも罪人に対する神の罰の方に重きを置いている。その説教は脅しのようなもので、信者は不安な気持ちになる。）

Reverend Shaw Moore spends more time in sermon preparation than he does in paying attention to his daughter. Ariel desperately wants her father to pay attention to her.

（ショー牧師は、娘に注意を向けるよりも説教の準備に時間を費やしている。娘のアリエルは自分にもっと目を向けてほしいと願っている。）

Bible Quotations（聖書からの引用）

The Bible is quoted exactly the same in both films. The key scriptures are:
1. Psalm 149
2. II Samuel 6: 14
3. Revelation 9: 1 - 2

（どちらの映画も同じ聖書の一節を引用している。その主なものは、
1. 詩編　第149
2. サムエル記下　第6章　14節
3. ヨハネの黙示録　第9章　1–2節
である。）

Characters（登場人物）

Ren McCormack
Ariel Moore
Reverend Shaw Moore

Plot（あら筋）

THE story is about a small town which has banned public dancing. It may come as surprise, but there are conservative communities and churches in America which consider dancing a sin. In this story, Bomont, Georgia has made a law against teenagers dancing and staying out late at night. Ren McCormack, a teenager, has moved to this town from Boston to live with his relatives. He is shocked by the cultural differences. When he goes to Church on Sunday, he is irritated by Reverend Moore's emotional sermon about the wickedness of the music of young people. Ren is immediately attracted to the preacher's daughter. But he discovers that she is unfriendly and has a mean boyfriend. Additionally, Ariel is very rebellious, doing all the things that her father dislikes. In America, there is a stereotype, PK's—Preachers' Kids. The unfair stereotype represents the children of the minister or preacher as being very misbehaved. As with all stereotypes, the image is unjust—not all children of preachers are bad. Ariel Moore is a presentation of the stereotype. She lies to her father, telling him that she is going to her friend's house to study. But she goes to the local teenager gathering spot and joins in the dancing.

（物語の舞台は公共の場でのダンスを禁じている小さな町である。アメリカには、ダンスを禁じている社会や教会がある。ジョージア州ボーモントでは、10代の若者がダンスをし、夜遅くまで外出することを法律で禁止している。10代のレン・マコーミックは、親戚の家に住むため、ボストンからやって来たが、文化の違いにショックを受ける。日曜日に教会に行くと、ムーア牧師の音楽の邪悪さを説く説教にイライラしてしまう。レンは牧師の娘にすぐさま魅了されるが、彼女には悪いボーイフレンドがいて、レンは親しくなれない。アリエルは父親に対して反抗的で、アメリカでは典型的とされる「伝道者の子ども」である。もちろん全ての伝道者の子どもがそうだというわけではないが、アリエルはその典型である。父親には「友達の家で勉強する」と言いながら、実際には他の十代の若者たちとダンスに行く。）

Ren has a difficult time adjusting to the conservative lifestyle of his new home. And, he has a difficult time impressing Ariel.

（レンはこうした保守的な生活に慣れ、アリエルの目を引くのに苦労する。）

Psalm 149:1–3 （詩編 149.1–3）

AT a town hall meeting, the teenagers and the adults gather to discuss what to do about the disobedience of the teenagers. Some of them (including Ariel, the preacher's daughter) have been seen dancing. Ren McCormack stands up to defend dancing. He is interested in having a high school prom where the students can dance. When he is given permission to speak, he surprises everyone by quoting Psalm 149: 1–3.

（市庁舎での会合で、若者と大人たちが集まって、反抗的な十代の若者をどのようにすべきか議論する。アリエルも含め、若者たちがダンスをしているのを目撃されている。高校でプロムをしたがっているレンは、ダンスを弁護するために立ち上がる。そこで詩編を引用したレンに皆が驚く。）

This is a well-known passage which indicates that in the old days, some form of dancing was actually a spiritual exercise:

Praise ye[†] *the Lord. Sing unto the Lord*
A new song, and his praise in the congregation of the saints.
Let Israel rejoice in him that made him:
Let the children of Zion, be joyful in their King.
Let them praise his name in the dance:

Let them sing praises unto him with the timbrel††
And the harp . . .

† 人称代名詞 2 人称複数主格。You の古形。／†† 鈴の付いた手打ち小太鼓。

(詩編のこの一節は、昔ある種のダンスは精神の鍛錬になると考えられていたことを示すものである。
¹ ハレルヤ。新しい歌を主に向かって歌え。主の慈しみに生きる人の集いで賛美の歌をうたえ。
² イスラエルはその造り主によって喜び祝い　シオンの子らはその王によって喜び踊れ。
³ 踊りをささげて御名を賛美し　太鼓や竪琴を奏でてほめ歌をうたえ。)

Reverend Moore looks at Ren with new appreciation. He didn't suspect that such a lively teenager would have any knowledge or appreciation of Scripture. Ren continued reading. This time he quotes another Old Testament passage, II Samuel 6:14

And David danced before the Lord with all
His might; and David was girded with a linen ephod†
　So David and all the house of Israel brought up
　The ark of the Lord with shouting and with the
　Sound of the trumpet.

† 古代イスラエルの祭儀用の法衣。

(ムーア牧師はレンを高く評価する。彼のような若者が聖書の知識を持っていることを疑わなかった。レンは続いて旧約聖書の『サムエル記下』の一節を朗読する。
¹⁴ 主の御前でダビデは力のかぎり踊った。彼は麻のエフォドを着けていた。¹⁵ ダビデとイスラエルの家はこぞって喜びの叫びをあげ、角笛を吹き鳴らして、主の箱を運び上げた。)

The above passage concerns King David of Israel moving the holy religious objects to another city. The ark was simply a big box which held some things that were precious to the Hebrew people. God required that David and the Israelites treat the ark with great respect. At the start of the trip, the ark was not treated with proper respect. But later, David and the group became more careful. King David was so happy as the ark neared the new destination, that he danced.

(この話は、イスラエルのダビデ王が神聖なる物を他の町に移そうとしている場面である。櫃とはヘブライ人にとって大切なものを入れる箱のことである。神はダビデとイスラエルの民に、櫃を崇めるように要求した。旅の当初はそれほど大切にされなかったが、櫃が目的地に近づくと、ダビデ王は至福に満ち、踊り始めた。)

Of course Ren was pleased to find a passage of Scripture which showed a great man of the Bible doing a dance. Everyone is surprised that Ren read the Bible to the adults on the city council.

(レンは、聖書の偉大なる人物が踊る場面を見つけて喜んだ。)

Revelation 9:1–2 （黙示録　第 9 章　1–2 節）

Later, Ren walks into the church on Saturday. Reverend Moore is practicing his sermon for the next day. Ren listens to a small part of the practice before the Reverend becomes aware that somebody is in the building. Ren steps forward. The passage that Reverend Moore had been practicing comes from The New Testament, Revelation 9:1 –2.

> *[1] And the fifth angel sounded, and I saw a star fall from heaven unto the earth: and to him was given the key of the bottomless pit[†]. [2] And he opened the bottomless pit; and there arose a smoke out of the pit, as the smoke of a great furnace; and the sun and the air were darkened by reason of the smoke of the pit.* (KJV)

　　[†] the key of the bottomless pit was given to him の倒置。

（土曜日にレンが教会に行くと、ムーア牧師が翌日の説教の練習をしていた。レンはその一部を耳にした。牧師が練習していたのは、新約聖書の『黙示録』の一節であった。
[1] 第五の天使がラッパを吹いた。すると、一つの星が天から地上へ落ちて来るのが見えた。この星に、底なしの淵に通じる穴を開く鍵が与えられ、[2] それが底なしの淵の穴を開くと、大きなかまどから出るような煙が穴から立ち上り、太陽も空も穴からの煙のために暗くなった。）

Although Ren uses the Bible to defend the dancing that he and friends want to do, there is some fault in his reasoning. The dancing that is done in the 2011 version, especially, is quite sexual in some parts. The dancing that David did in the Bible was probably not as sexually explicit as the dance which the teenagers did in the movie. Nevertheless, it is rather charming that the teenager impressed the adults with his Bible knowledge.

（レンはダンスを正当化しようとして聖書を使ったのだが、その理屈には欠点があった。2011 年版に見られるダンスには、かなり性的な部分が見られる。ダビデの踊りはそれほど性的なものではなかったと考えられる。それでも、若者が聖書の知識を使って大人を引きつけたのはかわいいものである。）

　In English, we call this situation "Beating somebody at his own game." That means an amateur shows more skill than the professional.

（英語ではこうした状況を示すのに、「プロ本人の試合でそのプロを打ち負かす」という表現を使う。）

Dialogue

Junko:　The dancing in *Footloose 2011* is really spectacular.
David:　Yes, and I really liked it when Ren quoted my namesake,[1)] King David of Israel.
Junko:　I remember the scene when he read Psalm 149. The first words are **"Praise ye the Lord."**

David: People often say those words when they are relieved that a problem has been solved.

Junko: Just this morning, my grandmother used those words. When she finally found her house keys, she said, **Praise the Lord!**[2]

1) **namesake** 同名の人
2) **Praise the Lord** 主をほめたたえよ

Snow White and the Seven Dwarfs
(『白雪姫と七人のこびと』)

Film: *Snow White and the Seven Dwarfs**
Company: Walt Disney Studios
Date of the Original Animation: 1937

* *The American Heritage Dictionary* and *The Oxford English Dictionary* offer two plural forms of the word: Dwarves or Dwarfs.

Characters: (主な登場人物)
The Wicked Stepmother Queen
Snow White
Prince Charming
The Seven Dwarfs
Numerous animals of the forests

Plot (あら筋)

THE wicked stepmother is extremely vain. She owns a magic mirror. Frequently she speaks with the mirror and asks the question: "Who is the fairest woman in the land?" For a long the time the mirror answered in her favor. But one day, the mirror suggests that Snow White is the most beautiful woman. The Queen determines that Snow White must die. She orders her servant to take Snow White deep into the forest and to murder her. The servant is too tenderhearted to carry out the plan.** Instead of placing Snow White's heart in a special box for delivery to the Queen, he encourages her to run far away. Meanwhile, he puts a pig's heart in the box to give to the Queen. Snow White spends time with the Seven Dwarfs whom she domesticates by instructing them to wash before dinner, etc.

** Art scholars might be interested in the scene of servant raising his knife to kill Snow White (and then deciding against it). That scene of the raised knife has some resemblance to the famous Rembrandt painting in which the Angel tells Abraham not to kill Isaac.

（召使が白雪姫を殺そうとして一旦はナイフを振りかざしながら最後には断念した場面が、レンブラントが描いた聖書の場面、アブラハムが生贄としてささげるためにイサクを殺そうとナイフを振りかざした時に天使がそれを止めさせたシーンと重なり、美術学者は興味を抱くかもしれない。）

（意地悪な継母は虚栄心のかたまりで、魔法の鏡に向かって「この世で一番美しいのは誰？」と尋ねている。鏡はずっと彼女が気に入るような答えを言っていたが、ある日、白雪姫が一番美しいと言う。継母は白雪姫を殺そうと思い、召使に白雪姫を森の奥に連れていって殺すように命令する。心優しい召使は殺すことをためらい、白雪姫の心臓を箱に入れて女王のところに持っていく代わりに、遠くに逃げるよう勧める。召使はブタの心臓を代わりに箱に入れ、女王に差し出す。白雪姫は７人のこびとと暮らす。）

Eventually the Queen learns that her servant has spared the life of Snow White. Curiously, the beautiful queen elects to transform herself into an ugly old witch. Her plan is to disguise herself so that she might tempt Snow White to eat the "Apple of Death."

（召使が白雪姫の命を助けたことを知った女王は、醜い年老いた魔女に姿を変え、白雪姫に「死のリンゴ」を食べさせようと企てる。）

It is curious that the Queen takes on an ugly disguise. The premise of the story is that her vanity is her major problem. She is fixated on her own beauty. She decides to have Snow White killed because she doesn't want a rival. Of course she doesn't want Snow White to recognize her. But she could have changed herself into another person—not necessarily an ugly person.

（女王が醜い姿に返送するというのは興味深いが、この物語の前提は虚栄心であり、自分の美しさに執着していることである。ライバルの存在を望まない女王は、白雪姫が自分に気づくことも望まなかった。）

But of course we ruin fairytales by being too logical.

（論理的でありすぎると、おとぎ話も面白くなくなってしまう。）

Tempted by the witch's promise that one bite of the apple will secure the love of Prince Charming, Snow White eats and dies. The Seven Dwarfs cannot bear to bury their beautiful princess. They place her in a glass coffin where her body remains uncorrupted.*** Finally, the Prince arrives. The Dwarfs open the glass cover, allowing the Prince to kiss Snow White. She is instantly revived, and the two go off to live happily ever after.

*** There is an old idea among Roman Catholic Christians that certain very good people do not deteriorate after they die. St. Bernadette Soubiroux is one of many saints which the Roman Catholic church displays in a glass coffin, claiming that her body remains uncorrupt.

（ローマカトリック教会では、特に徳の高い人は死後も遺体が腐敗しないという考えが古くからある。聖ベルナデット・スービルーもその一人で、教会は遺体をガラスの棺に入れ、遺体が腐敗して

いないと言っている。)

(リンゴを一口食べると、チャーミング王子の愛が得られるという魔女の誘いに、白雪姫はリンゴを食べて死んでしまう。美しい白雪姫を墓に埋葬するに忍びず、こびとたちはガラスの棺にいれる。王子がやってきて、ガラスの棺の中の白雪姫にキスをすると、白雪姫はたちまち生き返り、二人はその後幸せな生活を送る。)

Although there are no direct Biblical quotations (except the "Amen" at the end of Snow White's prayer), there are several instances that a Bible reader might construe as references to Scripture. Here are only three:

1. Snow White's Name
2. Snow White's Prayer
3. The Apple of Death

(白雪姫の祈りの最後の「アーメン」を除き、聖書からの直接的な引用は見られないが、聖書を読んだことのある人ならば、聖書に関係していると解釈するような場面がいくつかある。
1.「白雪姫」という名前
2. 白雪姫の祈り
3. 死のリンゴ)

Snow White's Name（白雪姫という名前）

HEARING this name, a Bible reader would readily recall Psalm 51. This is a poem written by King David. He had sexual relations with a married woman, and he had her husband killed. Finally, King David is very ashamed of himself. He confesses his sins to God. He begs God for forgiveness:

Purge me with hyssop, and I shall be clean;
wash me, and I shall be whiter than snow. Psalm 51:7

(白雪姫という名前を聞いて、詩編第51番を思い出す。ダビデ王によって書かれた詩で、王はある女性と不倫し、その夫を殺させた。王はその罪を恥じ、神に告白して許しを請う。
⁷ わたしは咎のうちに産み落とされ
母がわたしを身ごもったときも
わたしは罪のうちにあったのです。)（詩編 51.7）

Many Christian songs use the symbolism of whiteness with reference to innocence and purity. In recent years, some sensitive people have objected to the persistent idea that whiteness equates goodness.

(キリスト教の讃美歌では、白を純潔の象徴としている。最近では白を善とする考え方に反対する人もいる。)

Snow White's Prayer（白雪姫の祈り）

Just before the visit of the Queen (disguised as an old woman), Snow White happily kneels down beside her bed and says a short prayer: "Bless the seven little dwarfs. Amen." Standing up after her prayer, she immediately decides to add a PS to her prayer. She prays for Grumpy, the Dwarf who opposed her "domestication" of the other dwarfs. Although Grumpy's irritability does not exactly fit the extreme image of "enemies," Snow White's prayer on his behalf is definitely in the spirit of *The Sermon on the Mount*:

> . . . and pray for them which despitefully use
> you and persecute you. (Matthew 5:44.)

（老女に変装した女王がやって来る直前、白雪姫はベッドのわきにひざまづき、「七人のこびとたちに幸いあれ。アーメン」という短い祈りを捧げる。立ち上がった直後に追伸として、白雪姫がこびとたちを「飼いならしている」ことに反発しているグランピーのために祈る。グランピーのイライラは「敵」のイメージとは多少ずれるが、グランピーのために祈るということは、明らかに「山上の垂訓」に示される精神である。

44 しかし、わたしは言っておく。敵を愛し、自分を迫害する者のために祈りなさい。（マタイによる福音書　第5章44節））

The Apple of Death（死のリンゴ）

Most people are aware that Satan tempted Eve with a forbidden fruit. God provided generously for Adam and Eve in the Garden. He only required that they not eat the fruit of one particular tree. Satan appealed to the vanity of Adam and Eve. He promised them that they would be like gods (Genesis 3:5). That of course resulted in God's anger and the expulsion of Adam and Eve from the Garden. The witch appealed to the vanity of Snow White, telling her that the love of the Prince would be assured if she ate the Apple of Death. There is no statement in the Bible that the forbidden fruit in Genesis was an apple. But culturally, the fruit has been interpreted as an apple.

（サタンがイヴをそそのかし、禁断の木の実を食べさせた話はよく知られている。神はアダムとイヴに「ある一本の木の実だけは食べてはならない」と命じていたが、サタンはアダムとイヴの虚栄心に働きかけ、食べても死ぬことはないと誘惑する（創世記　第3章5節）。当然神の怒りを招き、二人はエデンの園を追放される。魔女に変装した女王は、白雪姫の虚栄心をくすぐり、リンゴを食べると王子の愛を得ることができると誘惑する。創世記では、禁断の木の実がリンゴであるとは言っていないが、長年リンゴであると考えられてきた。）

Dialogue

Makoto: I was surprised that my professor showed the Disney classic *Snow White* in our world literature class yesterday.

Stephan: I think it is a cute children's movie, but I wouldn't think it is worthy of academic study.

Makoto: Professor Elias was showing us the subtle Christian imagery and ideas in the film.

Stephan: Can you cite an example?

Makoto: Yes, Snow White kneels down and prays to God before getting into bed. She ends the prayer with "Amen." That little word has such important Christian meaning. Among the Hebrew people, it meant, either "So be it[1]," or "I agree."

Stephan: Everyday I learn something new.

Makoto: Amen!

1) **So be it** そうあらしめよ （祈りの最後に唱える言葉）= Amen

Les Miserables (The Musical)
(『レ・ミゼラブル』)

Film: *Les Miserables*
Company: Universal Studios
Date of DVD: 2012

Characters: （主な登場人物）
- Jean Valjean
- Javert
- Fantine
- Marius
- Cosette
- Bishop

Plot （あら筋）

This film is a grand musical production of Victor Hugo's extremely lengthy and beloved novel, of 1862. It tells the story of Jean Valjean who steals a loaf of bread* for his little hungry nephews. For that, he is imprisoned for nearly 20 years. While incarcerated in the cruel French prison system, he becomes a hardened brute of great strength. He loses his faith and depends only on himself and his remarkably powerful body. He is released from prison, apparently early. The problem is that he is an ex-convict who must always carry papers identifying him as a criminal. Of course no one will hire him. He happens to meet the kindly Bishop who welcomes him to his home. The Bishop gives Jean Valjean food and a place to sleep. But Jean is unaccustomed to such human kindness, and in the night he escapes with the silverware he has stolen from the good-hearted Bishop. When the police quickly capture Jean Valjean and return him to the Bishop, everyone is surprised when the Bishop says the items were not stolen but were gifts from him to Jean Valjean. In fact, the Bishop says that Jean Valjean forgot to take everything that was given to him. He presents Jean Valjean with two silver candlesticks to add to the things he has taken. Of course, Jean Valjean is stunned by such extreme kindness, and he is determined to live a worthy life as a tribute to the generosity of the Bishop.

> * It is sad that Jean Valjean had to steal bread to feed the hungry children. Many times in the Bible, bread is used as symbol of kindness. Good people should have been eager to share their bread. Note the cover design of this book, "Cast your bread upon the waters" (Ecclesiastes 11: 1–6) in Chapter II.
>
> (ジャン・バルジャンはお腹を空かせた子どもたちのためにパンを盗んだとされている。聖書でも、パンは親切さの象徴として頻繁に登場する。善なる人はすすんでパンを分かち合わなければならない。本書の表紙の挿絵、「あなたのパンを水に浮かべて流すがよい。」(コヘレトの言葉　第11章1–6節) 参照。)

(この映画は、1862年出版のヴィクトール・ユーゴーの長編作をミュージカルにしたものである。お腹を空かせた幼い甥のためにパンを盗んでしまったジャン・バルジャンは、20年の懲役刑に処せられてしまう。過酷なフランスの投獄生活の中で、彼は屈強な男になる。出獄した彼は、元受刑者であることを記す書類を携帯していなければならなくなる。仕事も見つけられないジャン・バルジャンは、親切な司教に出会い、食べ物と寝る場所を提供してもらう。人の親切さに慣れていないジャン・バルジャンは、夜のうちに銀の食器を盗み、立ち去る。警察に捕まったジャン・バルジャンが司教のもとに連れていかれると、司教は銀の食器は盗まれたのではなく、彼にあげたものだと言う。また、あげたものなのに全部は持っていかなかったとも言う。さらに、2本の銀の燭台まで差し出す。司教の親切さに呆然となったジャン・バルジャンは、その恩に報いるため、まっとうな人生を送ることを決心する。)

Eventually Jean becomes a rich merchant. He has changed his name and follows a life of virtue. Upon meeting a sick prostitute, Fantine, who has been mistreated throughout her life, he offers her a place to stay. She informs him that she has a child in another place. She implores him to find and look after her child, Cossette. Fantine dies, and Jean finds Cosette, eventually caring for her as his own daughter. He provides wonderfully for Cosette, and becomes extremely protective of her. Meanwhile, she falls in love with Marius, a handsome young man who participates in the French Revolution.

(裕福な商人になったジャン・バルジャンは、名前を変えて徳に満ちた生活を送っている。ずっとひどい扱いを受けていた病気の売春婦ファンティーヌに会ったジャン・バルジャンは、彼女に泊まる場所を

提供する。子どもがいることを打ち明けた彼女は、子どものコセットの面倒を見てほしいとジャン・バルジャンに懇願する。ファンティーヌの死後コセットを見つけ出したジャン・バルジャンは、自分自身の娘として育てる。成長したコセットは、フランス革命に参加しているハンサムな若者マリウスを愛するようになる。)

Jean Valjean is heartbroken that his "daughter" has found a gentleman who wants to marry her. He fears that Cossette will erase him from her life (although her love for her "father" is so great that she envisions a future with all three of them living together).

（自分の「娘」が結婚を望む男を見つけたことを知り、ジャン・バルジャンは、コセットが自分を見捨ててしまうのではないかと悩む。コセットの方は、「父親」に対する愛情が非常に深く、将来は3人で暮らすことを考えている。）

The tension in the novel and the film is that Jean Valjean is pursued by Detective Javert. The detective is a man completely without love. His life is based on exacting the law. Javert is unmoved by any acts of kindness that Jean Valjean may show him. He wants to put Jean Valjean back in prison. Much of the story involves Jean Valjean's escapes from the relentless Javert—and the near apprehensions.

（小説および映画の中で緊張するのは、ジャベール警視がいつもジャン・バルジャンを追っていることである。警視には愛のかけらもない。ジャン・バルジャンがいかに親切な行為を示そうとも、警視の心は動かされず、再び監獄に送り込みたいと考えている。）

The Bible in *Les Miserables* (『レ・ミゼラブル』における聖書)

THE movie has many scenes in which the cross is either overtly shown in the foreground or subtly shown in the background. The film opens with many men, prisoners, at hard labor in a shipyard. They sing a song of desperation saying, "Sweet Jesus doesn't care." The camera focuses on the masthead of the great ship (mastheads are often used as symbols of the Cross of Jesus Christ). A short while later in the film, Jean Valjean wanders in the countryside looking for work and for food. He passes a simple cross erected on a rocky mound. Later, after he is treated so kindly by the Bishop, Jean Valjean kneels in a beautiful church which has a marble carving of Jesus Christ on the Cross. Jean sings about the Sacrifice of Jesus Christ as he promises to live a better life:

> What have I done?
> Sweet Jesus, what have I done?

Become a thief in the night,
Become a dog on the run,
Have I fallen so far

(映画の中では、十字架が時にはっきりと、時にそれとなく映し出されている。映画は造船所で働かされている囚人たちが歌を歌う場面で始まる。カメラは十字架の象徴とされる大きな船のマストを映し出す。それから、仕事と食べ物を求めて田舎を彷徨っているジャン・バルジャンが登場する。道の途中に粗末な十字架が見える。司教の親切さに触れたジャン・バルジャンは、立派な教会の中で、大理石像のイエスの前でひざまづく。そこでジャン・バルジャンは、次のような歌を歌う。
私が何をしたというのでしょうか。
優しきイエス様、私が何をしたというのでしょうか。
夜には盗人となり
逃げ回る犬となり
私はここまで落ちてしまった。)

Later in that same song he regrets his past life of brutishness. He is sorry that he spent so much of his life, taking "an eye for an eye" (see that phrase in the list of Bible idioms). Jean Valjean uses the expression, "Eye for an eye," to say that he used to want to revenge on all of the people who had hurt him. Now, in his intent to live a Christian life, he wants to live in a gentler way. Certainly, he is turned into a loving father of Cosette.

(同じ歌の中で、ジャン・バルジャンは自分の過去の残虐さを後悔する。「目には目を」という復讐の気持ちを持って過ごしてきた時間を悔い、優しい気持ちを持ったキリスト者として暮らそうとしている。娘コセットを愛する父親になっている。)

"A Thief in the Night" (夜の盗人)

In his moment of great shame, Jean Valjean says that he has become "A thief in the night." He has stolen the silverware of the one man who had been so kind to him. He did, indeed, escape into the night with the stolen goods. His use of the phrase is very interesting. Jesus used that same phrase in Matthew 24: 42–44.

(恥いったジャン・バルジャンは、自分が「夜の盗人」となったと言っている。実際、親切な司教から銀食器を盗んで、夜中に逃げ出したのである。イエスも同じ表現をマタイによる福音書第24章42–44節で使っている。)

Oddly, Jesus used the image of a thief who comes unexpectedly in the night in reference to Himself. Jesus was teaching that He will return to the earth at the end of the world. He will come back to earth when people least expect it. Many people do bad things. Maybe these bad people think that they will change to good behavior in the future. They plan on sinning now, and converting to good behavior just in time for

Jesus' return. Of course that is foolish thinking. We don't know when the end of the world will come. We don't know when Jesus will appear again. So, the best thing is to plan on being good always. That way, whenever Jesus returns, He will be pleased with us.

(イエスは、ご自身を夜に不意にやって来る盗人に例えている。悪事を行う者は、そのうち改心すれば間に合うだろうと考えているが、イエスの再臨、すなわち「世の終わり」は不意にやって来る。常にその準備をしておくことが大事である。)

Jean Valjean used "Thief in the night" to confess his past bad behavior. Jesus used "Thief in the night" to describe the suddenness and unexpectedness of His return to rescue the good people.

(ジャン・バルジャンは「夜の盗人」という表現で自分の過去の悪行を告白している。)

Dialogue:

Derrick: I enjoyed going to the theater with you tonight, Susan.
Susan: Yes, *Les Miserables* is a wonderful musical, although it is a bit long. I could see many Bible references in the film.
Derrick: I did hear Jean Valjean refer to himself as **"A thief in the night."** He was feeling guilty because he stole silverware from the kind priest, and he escaped into the night.
Susan. Yes, in the Matthew 24: 42 -44, Jesus used those words to describe His eventual return to the earth. No one knows the date of the end of the world. The return of Jesus will be sudden and surprising as the breaking-in of a thief in the house.
Derrick: Jesus used **"Thief in the night"** to refer to his sudden return one day. Jean Valjean used the expression to refer to his shameful theft.

Places in the Heart
(『プレイス・イン・ザ・ハート』)

Film: *Places in the Heart*
Company: TriStar Pictures
Date of DVD: 1984
Honors: 1984, Best Picture; Best Actress, Sally Field; Best Supporting Actor, John Malkovich; Best Director; Best Writing, and others.

(1984年最優秀映画賞、最優秀女優賞・サリー・フィールド、最優秀助演男優賞・ジョン・マルコヴィッチ、最優秀監督賞、最優秀脚本賞、他)

Characters: (主な登場人物)
　Edna Spalding
　Sheriff Royce Spalding
　Mr. Will
　Moze

Setting: Waxahachie, Texas
Time: 1935

Plot（あら筋）

THE film depicts a time when women, children, disabled people and African Americans were not accorded full rights. All of these disenfranchised groups are represented in the film.

　　(女性、子ども、障害者、アフリカ系アメリカ人がその権利をまだ十分に認められていなかった時代。)

The story opens as the sheriff and family are about to have dinner. He is summoned to a scene of domestic disturbance. A young black man gets drunk and starts firing his gun. When the sheriff arrives on the scene, the black man accidentally shoots him. Immediately, angry whites kill the youth.

　　(物語は保安官が家族と夕食を食べようとする場面で始まる。酔っぱらった黒人男性が銃を撃ち始めた、という知らせで保安官が現場に駆けつけると、運悪く撃たれ、怒った白人がその青年を殺してしまう。)

The death of the sheriff plunges his family into hard times. In the 1930s, many widows, divorced women, and unmarried women had a difficult time; often they could not get loans from banks. And, of course, employment opportunities for women were limited, especially in the rural South. Edna has a sister, but she cannot help financially. In fact, the sister has her own problems; her husband is having an affair with another woman.

　　(保安官の死によって、家族は途方に暮れてしまう。1930年代には、未亡人、離婚した女性、そして未婚の女性にとっては厳しい時代であった。銀行からの借り入れもできず、女性が仕事に就くことも、特に南部では難しかった。エドナには姉妹がいたが、夫の不倫問題もあり、経済的援助を頼りにすることはできなかった。)

Edna is determined to survive. She and her children plant cotton. When a hungry homeless man (another African American) comes to the door begging for food, Edna reluctantly agrees to give him something to eat. He sits on the doorstep, and says his prayer before eating. Edna's intelligence does not allow her to transfer feelings of hatred to this second black man. Moze hires on as a helper at the house. He helps orchestrate the cotton planting routines.

(エドナは生き抜く決意をし、子どもたちと共に綿花を栽培した。お腹を空かせた黒人のホームレスが食べ物を請うたとき、エドナは渋々食べ物を与えた。彼は玄関先に座り、食べる前に祈りを捧げた。この黒人に対して、エドナは嫌悪の情を向けることができなかった。モーゼは綿花の栽培を手伝う。)

Edna accepts yet another man into her home, as a renter, Mr. Will. He is blind, and bitter about his disability. All of these people become a newly composed "family" living in the house: Edna, Mr. Will, Moze, and the children. As they struggle together against prejudice and poverty, they become very protective of each other. Learning of a $100 award for the first load of cotton to be taken for processing, "the family," works hard to do the seemingly impossible task. Because of their respect for each other, and because of their decision to work together, they win the award.

(エドナはもう一人、ウィル氏を間借り人として家に入れる。彼は盲人である。新しい「家族」として共同生活を始める。偏見と貧困と闘いながら、互いに守り合うようになる。最初の出荷に対する100ドルの賞金のことを知り、新しい「家族」は不可能とも思える仕事に取り掛かる。互いを敬う気持ちと共に働くという決意のおかげで、「家族」は賞金を手にする。)

Most people are surprised at the very end of the film. Suddenly there is a scene in a Christian church. The film director places everybody together in the church service. The young black man who was killed sits peacefully next to the sheriff he had killed. The cheating husband sits beside his wife. Perhaps the scene is not realistic. It is idealistic. It is a beautiful depiction of forgiveness.

(映画の最後の場面に驚かされる。教会の中で、殺された黒人の若者が、彼が殺した保安官のそばに座り、不倫の夫がその妻のそばに座っているシーンで終わっている。現実ではなく、理想の光景ではあるが、赦しの美しさを描いている場面である。)

It is probably one of the most authentic church scenes ever shown in a movie. There is a communion service in the manner of Protestant Christian churches. As the minister reads the Bible, the choir sings a well-known hymn, *In the Garden*. Then the people pass a plate with small pieces of bread which represent the Body of Christ.

(映画で映しだされる教会のシーンとしては、最も信頼できるシーンの一つであろう。牧師が聖書を朗読し、聖歌隊が「園において」を歌い、イエスの御身体を象徴するパンが入った皿を回している。)

Bible Themes in *Places in the Heart* （『プレイス・イン・ザ・ハート』に見られる聖書のテーマ）

1. Adoption of non-DNA family members（血縁関係のない「家族」）
2. Reconciliation（和解）

Bible Quotations （聖書からの引用）

The minister reads a very famous Bible passage:

> *¹Though I speak with the tongues of men and of angels, and have*
> *Not charity, I am become as sounding brass, or a tinkling cymbal.*
> *²And though I have the gift of prophecy, and understand all mysteries,*
> *All knowledge; and though I have all faith, so that I could remove*
> *Mountains, and not charity, I am nothing.*
> *³And though I bestow all my goods to feed the poor, and though I*
> *Give my body to be burned, and have not charity, it profiteth* me nothing.*
> *⁴Charity suffereth† long, and is kind; charity envieth† not; charity vaunteth† not itself, is not puffed up,*
> *⁵Doth† not behave itself unseemly, seeketh† not her own, is not easily provoked, Thinketh† no evil;*
> *⁶Rejoiceth† not in iniquity, but rejoiceth† in the truth;*
> *⁷Beareth† all things, believeth† all things.*
> *⁸Charity never faileth†; but whether there be prophecies, they shall fail; Whether there be tongues, they shall cease; whether there be knowledge, It shall vanish away* (KJV: I Corinthians 13: 1–8)

　　† 動詞 (profit, suffer, envy, vaunt, seek, think, rejoice, bear, fail) の 3 人称単数現在形。

（牧師は聖書の有名な一節を朗読する。
『コリントの信徒への手紙一』第 13 章　1–8 節
¹ たとえ、人々の異言、天使たちの異言を語ろうとも、愛がなければ、わたしは騒がしいどら、やかましいシンバル。
² たとえ、預言する賜物を持ち、あらゆる神秘とあらゆる知識に通じていようとも、たとえ、山を動かすほどの完全な信仰を持っていようとも、愛がなければ、無に等しい。
³ 全財産を貧しい人々のために使い尽くそうとも、誇ろうとしてわが身を死に引き渡そうとも、愛がなければ、わたしに何の益もない。
⁴ 愛は忍耐強い。愛は情け深い。ねたまない。愛は自慢せず、高ぶらない。
⁵ 礼を失せず、自分の利益を求めず、いらだたず、恨みを抱かない。
⁶ 不義を喜ばず、真実を喜ぶ。
⁷ すべてを忍び、すべてを信じ、すべてを望み、すべてに耐える。
⁸ 愛は決して滅びない。預言は廃れ、異言はやみ、知識は廃れよう、

Dialogue:

Karen: I really like the final scene of *Places in the Heart*. The minister in the movie read a Bible passage, I Corinthians 13.

Michael: I haven't seen the movie, but I know those words very well. I especially like verse 8: **"Charity never faileth."** [1] The sentence simply means that Love is a powerful force.

Karen: No, he didn't say anything about charity. He was talking about love.

Michael: Oh, I see the problem. The minister in the movie was using a modern translation. In the King James Version of the Bible, <u>Charity</u> means <u>Love</u>.

Karen: Well, the idea of the power of love is beautiful, no matter which translation of the Bible is used.

1) **Charity never faileth.** 愛は不滅である。

Simon Birch
(『サイモン・バーチ』)

Film: *Simon Birch*
Company: Hollywood Pictures
Date of DVD: 1998

Characters: (主な登場人物)
- Simon Birch
- Joe Wenteworth
- Rebecca Wenteworth
- Reverend Russell
- Marjorie

Plot (あら筋)

This movie is based on the novel *A Prayer for Owen Meany* by John Irving (please see the commentary on that book elsewhere in this publication). Of course the film maintains the general theme of the book, while making many changes in the storyline.

(これはジョン・アーヴィング著『オーウェン・ミーニーのための祈り』を映画化したものである。小説の基本的テーマを保ちながら、脚色もしている。)

Simon Birch has an underdeveloped body. He was born too small, and he remains too small throughout his life. His parents do not love him. They only provide food and shelter. Although the parents appear to lack intelligence, their son, Simon, exhibits an amazing intellect. Simon is about 12 years old, and despite his physical deformity, he has the normal reactions of a boy just entering puberty. Simon is attracted to girls, especially Marjorie (a girl whose body is developing fast). Marjorie seems to think that Simon is cute. However, Simon does not really believe that Marjorie could actually love someone who is as handicapped as he is.

（サイモン・バーチは体の発達が遅れている。生まれつき体が小さく、一生小さいままである。両親には愛されず、食べ物と住む場所を与えられているだけである。両親には知性が感じられないが、サイモンは素晴らしい才能を示す。12歳のサイモンは、体は小さくても思春期の普通の少年と同じ反応を示す。体つきが大きくなったマージョリーに魅せられ、マージョリーはサイモンをかわいらしいと思っているらしいが、ハンディを背負ったサイモンを愛してくれるとは信じられない。）

The bright spot in Simon's life is his friendship with Joe Wenteworth. Joe's mother, Rebecca, seems to love her son and Simon almost equally. However, while batting in the little league game, Simon accidentally bats a foul ball that hits Rebecca in the head. In that instance, Simon killed his surrogate mother, and he made his best friend, Joe, an orphan. Joe, though deep in grief, forgives Simon for the accident.

（サイモンの人生にとって明るい点は、ジョー・ウェントワースとの友情である。ジョーの母親レベッカは息子と同じ位サイモンを愛してくれる。しかし、リトル・リーグでサイモンが打ったファウル・ボールがレベッカの頭に当たり、レベッカは死に、ジョーは孤児になってしまう。ジョーは深く悲しむが、サイモンを赦す。）

Both boys have a problem: (1) Simon is handicapped and unloved by his parents, (2) Joe's mother, who never got married, died before she told him about his father. The two boys support each other. Simon wants to help Joe find out who his father is. Joe wants Simon to experience as normal a life as possible.

（サイモンは障害を持ち、両親には愛されていないという問題、ジョーは母親が未婚で、父親のことは話してもらえなかったという問題を抱えている。二人はそれぞれの問題を乗り越えられるよう、お互いに支え合っている。）

The boys learn that the minister of their church is actually Joe's father. They are shocked at that news. Ministers are supposed to be highly moral. However, Reverend Russell and Rebecca were tempted. They had a brief affair, during which Joe was conceived.

（教会の牧師がジョーの本当の父親であることを知り、二人はショックを受ける。伝道者は道徳的であることを求められるが、ラッセル牧師とレベッカはお互いに魅かれ、ひと時の情事の際にジョーを身ごもってしまう。）

The story is about sacrifice and helping others. Simon is deeply religious. He is apparently well acquainted with the Bible. He believes that God has a purpose for creating him with his extremely small body. There are times when Simon seems to think that he is somehow reliving the life of Jesus Christ. He believes that he is destined to sacrifice his life in some heroic way.

<small>（これは犠牲と他者に対する援助の物語である。サイモンは宗教的であり、聖書に詳しい。生まれつき小さいのも、神が何か特別な目的を持っているからだと思っている。イエス・キリストの人生に続いて歩むように運命付けられていると信じている。）</small>

Frequently the boys go swimming in a lake. Simon has an unexplainable fascination with holding his breath under water. He insists on building up his lung capacity.

<small>（二人はよく湖に泳ぎに行くが、サイモンは水中で息を止めておくことに説明しがたいほどに魅せられている。肺機能を高めたいと強く望む。）</small>

At the church camp, Simon and Joe are counselors for much smaller children. On the bus returning from camp, there is an accident. The bus crashes and falls into the freezing lake. Because he is so small, Simon gains the respect of the children. He is their size. They listen to him. He helps them out of the bus and hands them to Joe. Now he understands why he always wanted to build up his stamina for holding his breath under water—he has to stay under water a long time while boosting one little boy to the surface. All of the children survive the crash. Simon, however, dies because the deep cold overwhelmed his fragile body. It becomes clear that God did have a purpose for creating Simon Birch.

<small>（教会のキャンプで、二人は年少者のカウンセラーになっている。キャンプから帰る途中で事故に会い、バスが冷たい湖に転落してしまう。体つきが小さく、子どもたちに慕われていたサイモンの言うことは子どもたちが聴き、子どもたちがバスから脱出するのを助けてジョーに渡す。サイモンは何故肺機能を高めたいと思っていたのかを悟る。子どもたちは皆助かるが、サイモンは冷たい水に耐えきれず死んでしまう。神がサイモンに命を与えた理由が明らかになる。）</small>

Bible Themes in *Simon Birch* （『サイモン・バーチ』に見られる聖書のテーマ）

1. Brotherhood ("adopting" non-DNA related people as fathers, brothers, mothers, etc.)—Rebecca acts as if she were the real mother of Simon.
2. Sacrificing one's life to save others—Simon Birch died while saving little children.
3. The importance of confessing sins—At the end of the movie, Reverend Russell confesses to Joe that he is his father.
4. Forgiveness—Joe forgives Simon for accidentally killing his mother. Joe forgives Reverend Russell for not acknowledging that he is the father earlier.

(1. 兄弟（遺伝子に関係しない、父親、兄弟、母親等の関係）：レベッカはサイモンの本当の母親であるかのようにふるまう。
2. 他者を助けるために犠牲になること：サイモンは子どもたちを救うために命を落とす。
3. 罪を告白することの大切さ：最後の場面で、ラッセル牧師は自分がジョーの本当の父親であることを告白する。
4. 赦し：ジョーは母親を殺してしまったサイモンを赦す。ジョーは、最初父親であることを認めなかったラッセル牧師を赦す。）

Bible Quotations（聖書からの引用）

1. Psalm 32: *[1]Blessed is he whose transgression is forgiven, whose sin is covered. Blessed is the man unto whom the Lord imputeth* not iniquity, and in whose spirit there is no guile.* (Probably the Reverend is reading the King James Version in this scene)

(詩編第32番1-2節：[1]いかに幸いなことでしょう　背きを赦され、罪を覆っていただいた者は。2 いかに幸いなことでしょう　主に咎を数えられず、心に欺きのない人は。)

At the beginning of the movie, Reverend Russell reads this bible passage during the church service. It is ironic that he reads this passage because he has kept a secret for more than 12 years. Although he is a married man, he had an affair with Rebecca, and they conceived Joe. Rebecca, Joe, and Simon are in the congregation as Reverend Russell reads the bible. Only Rebecca knows about Reverend Russell's sin. Joe is not aware that the father he has been looking for all of his life is standing right in front of him.

(冒頭の場面で、ラッセル牧師は聖書のこの句を朗読する。12年もの間秘密を守っていた牧師がこの句を朗読するのは皮肉なことである。彼は、妻がありながら、レベッカと不倫し、ジョーが生まれる。レベッカもジョーもサイモンも、牧師が朗読する教会に来ている。ずっと探していた自分の父親が目の前にいるということをジョーは気づいていない。)

In one of the many charming scenes in the movie, Simon is forced to sit in Reverend Russell's office. Simon had misbehaved in church. The minister takes Simon's treasured baseball card collection away as punishment. Simon protests that he should not be punished. He quotes Proverbs 17:26 to Reverend Russell:

2. Proverbs 17:26—*To impose a fine on a righteous man is not good. . .* (Probably Simon is quoting the English Standard Version of the Bible here).

(サイモンがラッセル牧師の部屋に座らされている場面が多々ある。牧師は、サイモンが大切にしている野球カードを、教会での行儀が悪いことの罰として取り上げる。サイモンは抗議し、箴言第17章26節を引用する：
2. 箴言第17章26節：[26]神に従う人に罰を科したり　高貴な人をその正しさのゆえに打つのは　いずれもよいことではない。)

It is charming that the little boy is able to challenge the minister in Bible memorization. Simon is using the Bible quotation in an attempt to convince the minister that his baseball card collection should not be taken from him. Simon does not believe that he deserves punishment.

(少年が聖書に関して牧師に挑戦するのは微笑ましい。サイモンは、野球カードを取り上げられるような罰を受ける必要はないと信じ、聖書の句を引用している。)

But Reverend Russell believes that Simon is guilty and deserves punishment. He quotes Proverbs 22: 15 to the little boy.

3. Proverbs 22: 15—*Folly is bound up in the heart of a child, but the rod of discipline drives it far from him.*

(ラッセル牧師は、サイモンが罰を受けるべきであると信じ、箴言第 22 章 15 節を引用する。
[22] 若者の心には無知がつきもの。これを遠ざけるのは諭の鞭。)

This passage specifically mentions whipping or beating a child with a "rod." That is called corporal punishment. The reverend does not physically hit Simon. He takes away something that Simon loves—the baseball card collection.

(この一節は、子どもを鞭打つこと、すなわち体罰ことを述べている。牧師は実際にはサイモンに体罰を与えることはせず、サイモンが大事にしている野球カードを取り上げる。)

Dialogue:

> Nathan: For me the funniest scene in *Simon Birch* is when Simon and the Reverend are in a Bible quoting match. Each one quotes the Bible to prove his own point.
>
> Jack: That is a cute scene. The little boy and the minister seem to be equally knowledgeable about the Bible
>
> Nathan: Did you notice that Simon quoted Psalm 32:1, 2? ***Blessed is he whose transgression is forgiven, whose sin is covered?***
>
> Jack: Yes Simon is clever. He uses Scripture to show how God forgives people who do bad things. He is saying, "God forgives me; Reverend, you had better imitate God!"
>
> Nathan: I like the words **"… whose sin is covered."** Maybe those words are the background of the modern slang expression, "Cover me!" Police on television dramas say that to each other when one of them is rushing into dangerous territory. The words mean, "Protect me!"

Blind Side
(『しあわせの隠れ場所』)

Film: *Blind Side*
Company: Warmer Brothers
Date of DVD: 2009
Honors: Sandra Bullock won the Academy Award for Best Actress as well as the Golden Globe Award for Best Actress.

(サンドラ・ブロックがアカデミー賞およびゴールデン・グローブ賞で主演女優賞を獲得。)

Characters: (主な登場人物)
Leigh Anne Tuohy
Michael Oher
Sean Tuohy
S.J. Tuohy

Plot (あら筋)

Blind Side is based on the true story of Michael Oher, American football player for the Baltimore Ravens. Before becoming a key player for the team, Oher was a homeless young man who sneaks his hand-washed wet shirt in the coin laundry dryer being used by another patron. His life is a survival game. When a Christian School considers admitting him as a special charity case, the administrators are nervous about the challenge: Michael is huge; he dwarfs all of the other students and the faculty. They note that his I.Q. is deficient, and they are unable to ascertain his exact age. He does not have the normal documents which most people would have readily available: birth certificate, a complete school record. Yet they take a chance on admitting Michael, in the hopes that he might be an asset to the school football team. Little do they realize at first that Michael's size is deceiving. Though he is large, he is non-aggressive.

(この映画は、アメリカン・フットボールのボルティモア・レイヴンズの選手である、マイケル・オハーの実話に基づいている。彼は、選手になる前は、他人の乾燥機にシャツを忍びこませるようなことをしていたホームレスであった。キリスト教系の学校が慈善で彼を受け入れようとしたとき、大男の彼が生徒や先生をこわがってしまうので、学校当局も心配する。彼の知能指数は低く、本当の年齢もわからない。出生証明書や学校の記録など、普通の人ならば持っているような書類も無い。フットボールチームの役に立つのではないかと考え、彼を受け入れる。最初は気づかないが、彼は体が大きくても他人に対して攻撃的ではないということが知られるようになる。)

The Tuohy family are wealthy white Americans. They take pity on Michael and decide to give him accommodation in their home. Leigh Anne, the mother, is particularly sympathetic to Michael, and she encourages her family to accept Michael as an "adopted" member. S.J., the precocious little boy in the family, is especially eager to welcome Michael as a big brother.

（裕福な白人一家がマイケルをかわいそうに思い、自宅に迎い入れる。母親のリー・アンは特にマイケルに同情して、彼を養子として扱うよう家族を説得する。一家の宝である少年 S.J. は、マイケルを兄として歓迎する。）

The Tuohys are football fanatics. On Thanksgiving Day, they take their elaborate meal buffet style and sit in chairs and sofas around the television. They are so involved in their love of the game that they do not follow the usual tradition of having the meal while seated at a dining table. Michael has no interest in football. He sits alone at the dining table, probably overwhelmed both by the display of food, and the beautifully furnished dining room. Leigh Anne observes Michael sitting at the table alone. She picks up the remote control and turns off the television. Her family cannot understand her move. To turn off the important football game was a big change in their family routine. She brings all of the food to the table. She makes sure everyone is seated formally. Then she signals everyone to hold hands as she says Grace—the Christian prayer before eating. Michael is deeply touched.

（トゥオヒー一家はフットボールファンで、感謝祭の日には、通常の食卓につかず、ごちそうを手に、テレビの前に陣取る。フットボールに関心がないマイケルは、ひとりでテーブルにつき、食べ物と立派なダイニングルームに圧倒されている。マイケルが一人でいることに気付いたリー・アンは、テレビを消してしまう。大切な試合の時にテレビを消してしまうのは一家の生活を大きく変えてしまうことになるが、リー・アンは食べ物を食卓に乗せ、食前の祈りを捧げる合図をする。この光景に、マイケルは感動する。）

Of course the film touches the heart: a wealthy white family accepts a homeless black young man. They provide him with all of the advantages of a son in a rich family: a private tutor, his own car, a beautiful home environment.

（裕福な白人一家が、ホームレスの黒人青年を受け入れるというこの映画は、勘当的なものである。一家は彼に、家庭教師を付け、車を持たせ、素晴らしい環境を与える。）

The problem is that Michael is a gentle giant. He does not have the necessary aggression to be a formidable football player. When Michael and S.J. go for a ride in Michael's new car, they crash. Leigh Anne rushed to the accident scene and pushed through the police, saying that she wanted to see her "children." The police were amazed that the children of this petite blonde woman were a little blond boy and a huge African American young man. Neither boy is seriously hurt, but Leigh Anne notices that Michael has a gash on his arm. He explained that he blocked the air bag from injuring S. J. She rightly observes that Michael is not normally aggressive, but he is protective. She interrupts his coaching session with the team and tells him to think of his teammates as his family. He puts his protective instincts to work, and eventually becomes a great player.

（問題は、マイケルが心優しい大男であるということである。彼は恐るべきフットボール選手として必要とされる攻撃性に欠ける。マイケルとS.J.が車で出かけたとき、事故に会う。驚いたリー・アンが駆けつけたとき、小柄なブロンドの少年と大柄な黒人青年を〈子どもたち〉と呼んで心配している姿を見て、警察も驚く。幸い二人とも重傷は負っていなかったが、リー・アンはマイケルの腕に大きな傷があることに気付く。彼は、S.J.を守ろうとしたのである。マイケルが攻撃的ではないのではなく、人を守ろうとする気持ちが強いのだということに、リー・アンは気づく。彼女はフットボールのコーチに、マイケルを家族の一員として扱ってほしいと言う。マイケルはその本能を発揮し、偉大な選手になる。）

Bible Themes （聖書のテーマ）

1. Inviting strangers to the dinner table—The Bible advises Christians to be hospitable to strangers
2. "Adopting" non-DNA family members
3. Sharing food and other necessities with the poor
4. Recognizing that God has the power to make the impossible possible.

（1. 見知らぬ人を食卓に招く：クリスチャンは見知らぬ人をももてなすよう勧めている。
2. 血縁関係のない人を養子として迎える。
3. 貧しい人と食べ物などを分かち合う。
4. 神は不可能を可能にする力を持っているということを理解する。）

Bible Quotations （聖書からの引用）

OFTEN in American films, characters quote the Bible. Often Bible passages are written on a sign in the background. In *Blind Side*, the famous words of Jesus are carved in the concrete portal of the Wingate Christian School.

（アメリカ映画ではよく聖書の言葉が引用され、場面の背景に書かれていることも多い。この映画でも、イエスの言葉がウィンゲート・キリスト教学校の入り口に刻まれている。）

Matthew 19:26 *But Jesus beheld them, and said unto them, "With men this is impossible, but with God all things are possible."*

（マタイによる福音書第19章26節：イエスは彼らを見つめて、「それは人間にできることではないが、神は何でもできる」と言われた。）

Jesus spoke these words when He explained the dangers of riches to his followers. Earlier he had said that it was easier for a camel to pass through an eye of a needle than for a rich man to enter Heaven. Of course Jesus was not denouncing rich people. He was simply warning human beings not focus all of their attention on money.

（イエスは、富が危険なものであるということを彼に従う人々に伝えるときに、この言葉を言われた。以前にも、金持ちが天国に入るよりも、ラクダが針の穴を通ることの方が易しい、とも言っている。これは、金持ちを非難している言葉ではなく、お金に執着しすぎることに対する警告である。）

So the sign at the Wingate School is especially appropriate: (1) The Tuohys are rich—but they are loving and sharing people. (2) Michael does not seem to have the background or the intelligence to do well at the school, but with God's grace, and the Tuohy's love, he overcomes his obstacles, eventually becoming a prominent professional football player.

（ウィンゲート校の入り口に刻まれた言葉は、次の点で適切なものである :(1) トゥオヒー家は裕福であるが、愛に満ち、分かち合う気持ちを持った一家であること。(2) マイケルには学校でうまくやっていく背景も知性もないが、神の恩寵とトゥオヒー家の愛とによって、障害を乗り越え、傑出したフットボール選手になったこと。）

Dialogue

Emiko: I felt inspired when I saw *Blind Side*. What a difficult life Michael Oher had before he met the Tuohy family!

Jack: It's a great example of human kindness. The Tuohys were rich people, but they shared their wealth with the homeless young man.

Emiko: Yes, the Tuohy family were very generous. But I think that the film shows the goodness of God.

Jack: You are right. There is a sign at the entrance of the school where Michael was enrolled. It comes from Matthew 19: 26. Did you notice the sign in the movie?

Emiko: I sure did, it said **"… with God, all things are possible."**[1] Those words come from Matthew 19: 26.

Jack: Two years ago, the doctor said that my days as a baseball player might be over. But I struggled to regain my strength. Now, I am playing on the team again. I know for a fact, **"… with God all things are possible."**

1) **With God, all things are possible.** （人間には不可能だが、）神にはすべてのことが可能だ。

Scripture in World Literature

（文学作品と聖書）

1. *The Chosen* .... Chaim Potok
2. *I Know This Much is True* .... Wally Lamb
3. *Life of Pi* .... Yann Martel
4. *A Prayer for Owen Meany* .... John Irving
5. *The Martyr* .... Rynosuke Akutagawa
6. *The Old Man and the Sea* .... Ernest Hemingway
7. *Anne of Green Gables* .... L M Montgomery
8. *The Sun Also Rises* .... Ernest Hemmingway
9. *Today is Friday* .... Ernest Hemmingway
10. *The Grapes of Wrath* .... John Steinbeck
11. *A Tale of Two Cities* .... Charles Dickens

The Chosen
(『選ばれし者』)

Book: *The Chosen*
Author: Chaim Potok
Publication date: 1967 (originally)　(1967 年出版)
Publishing Company: Ballantine Books, New York, 2003
Book Honors: National Book Award, Finalist; Winner of the Edward Lewis Wallant Award.

チャイム・ポトック著『選ばれし者』1967 年（初版）　2003 年ニューヨーク、バランタイン・ブックス社 ＊ナショナル・ブック・アウォード最終選考ノミネート；エドワード・ルイス・ウォラント賞受賞

Note: The background of this book is Jewish culture. Jews honor the Torah. The Christian Bible is divided into The Old Testament and The New Testament. The Torah and The Old Testament have many writings in common.

（この本の背景はユダヤ人文化である。ユダヤ人は律法（モーセ五書）を大事にしている。キリスト教の聖書は旧約聖書と新約聖書に分けられている。律法（トーラー）と旧約聖書には共通する書が多い。）

Major Characters （主な登場人物）

　　Reuven Malter （リューベン・モルター）
　　Danny Saunders （ダニー・ソーンダース）
　　Reb (Professor) Malter （モルター教授）
　　Reb (Professor) Saunders （ソーンダース教授）

Plot （あら筋）

THE story takes place in New York in the 1940s. Two teenage Jewish boys, Danny and Reuven belong to different religious sects. Danny is a member of the Hasidic group of Jews. They dress in very noticeable clothing. The men wear dark long coats, and they wear long side curls.

(1940 年代のニューヨーク。十代のユダヤ人、ダニーとリューベンは、異なる宗派に属している。ダニーはハシッド派のメンバーである。)

　Reuven belongs to the Orthodox Jewish sect, a much more modernized group. Reuven does not wear any distinctive clothing. Although both groups are Jews and are descendants of the Israelites of the Bible, they do not agree on many religious topics.

（リューベンは、近代化されたユダヤ正教に属している。リューベンは目立った服装はしていない。ユダヤ教の二つのグループは聖書に登場するイスラエルの民の子孫ではあるが、宗教上の話題に関して意見を異にすることが多い。）

The boys meet at a baseball game. Danny is a powerful player. He bats the ball and injures Reuven's eye. Reuven is convinced that Danny hates him, and that the eye injury was intended. Danny visits the hospital to say that he is sorry. He even visits Reuven at his house. But Reuven is slow to accept the apology. In the course of time, they become very close friends. It is then that Reuven learns Danny's sad story. Danny's father is the leader of the Hasidic Jews. He is very strict. He believes that he should not speak to his son more than necessary. He also believes that he should not show much affection to his son. In truth, the father loves his son very much. But Danny's father believes that his son will succeed him in the leadership of the sect. He thinks that a good spiritual leader must understand the suffering of the people of the world. By suffering the coldness of his father, he will be better able to understand people who are lonely and ignored. It is a strange concept of child rearing, but the father had good intentions.

(二人の少年は野球の試合で出会う。ダニーは強い選手で、その打球がリューベンの目を傷めてしまう。リューベンは、ダニーが自分を嫌っていて、目に受けた傷は意図的なものであると確信する。ダニーは病院を訪れ、謝る。また、リューベンの家まで訪れる。しかし、リューベンはなかなか謝罪を受け入れようとしないが、やがて非常に親しくなり、リューベンはようやくダニーの悲しい物語を知るようになる。ダニーの父はハシッド派のリーダーで、とても厳しい人で、必要以上に息子に話しかけるべきではないと信じている人である。また、実際は息子を非常に愛しているが、息子に対して愛情を示してはいけないと信じている。ダニーの父は、ダニーがいずれハシッド派のリーダーとして跡を継ぐだろうと信じている。良き精神的リーダーは、世の人々の苦しみを理解していなければならないと考えている。父親の冷酷さに苦しむことで、ダニーは孤独で忘れ去られた人々のことをよりよく理解できるようになるだろう。子供を育てる考え方としては奇妙なものだが、父親には意図するところがあるのである。)

Reuven, by contrast, has a very and loving relationship with his father. And, Danny develops a filial love for Reuven's father. Danny is very intelligent and he has a photographic memory. He can read any book in a few minutes. The problem is that his group of Hasidic Jews only focus on the religious books. Danny wants to explore a wider range of reading, and Reuven's father recommends many scholarly books to him. For a while, it seems as if Danny has stolen Reuven's father's affection.

(それに対し、リューベンは父親と良好な関係を持っている。そしてダニーはリューベンの父親に対して、父親に対するような愛を持つようになる。ダニーは理知的で、精密な記憶力を持っている。どんな本でも数分で読むことができる。問題と言えば、彼の属するハシッド派ユダヤ教徒は、宗教的な本のみを重要視していることである。ダニーは広範囲にわたる読書をしたいと望み、リューベンの父は彼に学問的な本を勧める。しばらくの間、ダニーがリューベンの父親の愛を盗んでしまったかのように思われる。)

The boys enjoy each other's constant company until Danny's father ends the friendship. He does not want the United Nations to create the modern state of Israel. Reuven's father is a Zionist; he campaigned to have the United Nations vote to create the modern state of Israel. Because their fathers disagree, the two boys cannot continue their friendship.

（ダニーの父親が二人の友情を終わらせるまで、二人は常に一緒に過ごして楽しんだ。ダニーの父親は、国連が新しいイスラエル国家を作ることは望んでいない。リューベンの父親はシオニストで、国連が新しいイスラエル国家を作るよう働きかけている。父親同士の意見が合わないため、二人の少年は友情を続けることができない。）

Finally, Danny boldly rejects his father's teaching. Eventually his father realizes that he was wrong to force his son into such a strict lifestyle. The boys resume friendship.

（とうとうダニーは父親の教えを拒絶する。父親は厳しい生活を息子に強いるのは間違っているということに気付く。二人の少年はその友情を取り戻す。）

Bible Themes in *The Chosen* （『選ばれし者』に見られる聖書のテーマ）

1. A deep brotherly friendship between two men（二人の人間の兄弟愛）
2. Forgiveness（許し）
3. The Promised Land（約束の地）
4. "God moves in mysterious ways" (The boys decide that the baseball accident was a bad thing that made their good friendship possible.)「神は不可思議な動きをなさる」（少年たちは、野球の事故はよくないことだが、二人の友情を可能にしたものであると結論付ける。）

Bible Quotations （聖書からの引用）

Page 10 (The epigram)—Proverbs 4: 3–5 (only first part is quoted in the novel):

For I was my father's son, tender and only beloved in the sight of my mother. He taught me also, and said unto me Let thine† heart retain my words; keep my commandments, and live. Get wisdom, get understanding; forget it not††; neither decline from the words of my mouth.

　† 人称代名詞2人称単数所有格の古形。／ †† 否定命令文。Cf. Don't forget it.

箴言第4章3–5節：
³わたしも父にとっては息子であり　母のもとでは、いとけない独り子であった。⁴父は私に教えて言った。「わたしの言葉をお前の心に保ち　わたしの戒めを守って、命を得よ。⁵わたしの口が言いきかせることを　忘れるな、離れ去るな。知恵を獲得せよ、分別を獲得せよ。

There are two sets of fathers and sons in *The Chosen*. Both fathers are Jewish teachers. Both fathers want to influence their sons. However, Danny does not want to listen to his father. He does not want to be the leader of the strict sect of Hasidic Jews. He develops a father-son relationship with Reuven's father. Later, he rejects the Hasidic lifestyle, but he is restored to a loving relationship with his own father.

『選ばれし者』には二組の親子が登場する。父親は二人ともユダヤ教の師で、息子たちを導こうとする。しかし、ダニーは父親の言うことを聴こうとはしない。ダニーは厳格なハシッド派ユダヤ教徒のリーダーにはなりたくないと思っている。彼はリューベンの父親と親密な〈親子関係〉を築く。後に彼はハシッド派の生活を拒むが、自分自身の父親との愛に満ちた関係を取り戻す。

Dialogue

Mariko: Reading *The Chosen* took a long time, but it was worth it. It is such a heartwarming story of the friendship of two teenage boys.

Yutaka: I know the book. I would agree it is a book about teenage friendship. But I would add that it is an excellent story of the love between a father and a son. The relationship between Reuven and his father is very touching.

Mariko: Yes, I can see your point.[1)] The book begins with an epigram. Very near the title page, we can see the words from Proverbs 4: 3– 5. Those words from the Bible describe a child who had very good parents.

Yutaka: Yes, when I become a father, I want to say to my son, **"Get wisdom, get understanding. . ."**

Mariko: You are only twenty years old, and you are already thinking about your future fatherhood.

Yutaka: Of course, proper planning is a major part of getting "wisdom and understanding."

1) **I can see your point.**　あなたのおっしゃることはわかります。

I Know This Much Is True
(『ここまでは真実であると知っている』)

Book: *I Know This Much Is True*
Author: Wally Lamb
Publication date: 1998（1998年出版）
Publishing Company: Regan Books, Harper Perennial (paperback)
Book Honors: Number One on the New York Times Bestseller List

ウォーリー・ラム著　『ここまでは真実であると知っている』1998年　リーガン・ブックス、ハーパー・ペレニアル（ニューヨーク・タイムズ紙のベストセラー第1位）

Major Characters in the Book（主な登場人物）

Dominick Birdsey（ドミニク・バージー）
Thomas Birdsey（トマス・バージー）
Ray Birdsey（レイ・バージー）
Concettina Tempesta Birdsey（コンチェッティーナ・テンペスタ・バージー）

Plot（あら筋）

THIS is a massive work. The paperback is 900 pages long covering a complicated family history that takes place over more than one hundred years, beginning in Italy and continuing in the United States. For purposes of this book on the Bible in everyday culture, it is best to focus on one aspect of the book. Dominick and Thomas Birdsey are twin brothers. Dominick is healthy. Thomas is schizophrenic.

（この長編小説は、イタリアに始まり、合衆国へと続く、100 年以上にわたるある複雑な家族の物語で、健康的なドミニクと統合失調症のトーマスは、双子の兄弟である。）

The twins were born outside of marriage. Their mother, Concettina Tempesta Birdsey had a cleft palate. It seemed that she was doomed to a life of misery. Unmarried, and with a physical deformity, she did not seem to have much promise in her life. However, a military hero, Ray Birdsey, does marry her. He does seem to care for his instant family. However, his pride is annoying. He seems to be overly proud of being a good man. He congratulates himself.

（双子の兄弟は庶子で、母親のコンコンチェッタ・テンペスタ・バージーには口蓋裂があった。みじめな人生が運命付けられているかのようであった。未婚で肉体的問題も抱えている彼女には将来の夢もないかのようであったが、軍の英雄レイ・バージーが彼女と結婚する。彼は善人であることを誇りにしているようである。）

As a university student, Thomas begins to show evidence of his mental illness. When he is about 40 years old, he shocks his community by committing a horrific act. He interpreted the words of Jesus too literally. In the famous Sermon on the Mount, Jesus taught that good people should be careful to stay away from settings that would tempt them to commit sin. The exact words of Jesus in Matthew 5:29 are: *And if thy right eye offend thee, pluck it out and cast it from thee; and if thy right hand offend thee, cut it off, for it is profitable for thee that one of thy members should perish and not that thy whole body should be cast into hell.* Of course Jesus was not recommending self-mutilation. This type of language is called <u>hyperbole</u> (or literary exaggeration).

（大学生になったトーマスは、心の病の兆しを見せ始め、40 歳の頃にイエスの言葉を文字通りに解釈して、周囲の人々を驚かせる。山上の垂訓の中で、イエスは「29 もし、右の目があなたをつまずかせる

なら、えぐり出して捨ててしまいなさい。体の一部がなくなっても、全身が地獄に投げ込まれない方がましである。30 もし、右の手があなたをつまずかせるなら、切り取って捨ててしまいなさい。体の一部がなくなっても、全身が地獄に落ちない方がましである。(マタイによる福音書第 5 章 29–30 節)」と言っているが、これは修辞学で言う「誇張法」であって、イエスが体の切断を実際に勧めているものではない。)

Jesus was only teaching that Christians must remove themselves from situations in which they would become interested in doing bad things. For instance, Jesus would caution young people today to avoid wild drinking parties. Indeed, many horrible crimes have been committed at parties where people lost control of themselves. Reading pornographic magazines could entice someone to engage in illicit sexuality. Normal people recognize that Jesus was using hyperbole to teach a lesson on good, clean living. However, occasionally, some mentally imbalanced people have interpreted the words of Jesus literally. There have been examples of such people blinding themselves, or cutting off various parts of their body. This novel opens with the schizophrenic brother, Thomas, praying loudly in the library. Shockingly, Thomas cut off his right hand.

(イエスが言っているのは、クリスチャンならば悪事を働きたいと思う気持ちが芽生えるような状況から離れなさいということである。若者の過度の飲酒や、ポルノを見ることなどが例として挙げられる。一般の人はイエスが誇張法を使っていることに気付くが、精神のバランスを欠く人は、文字通りに解釈してしまう場合がある。この小説は、図書館内で大声をあげて祈り、右手を切断してしまうトーマスが登場するところから始まっている。)

Although the beginning of the novel is shocking, the long story proceeds to unravel the complex relationship between a normal brother and his schizophrenic twin. Dominick had been forced all of his life to watch out for his sick brother. Sometimes the embarrassment of taking care of a mentally ill sibling caused Dominick frustration. Other times, Dominick realizes that he loves his brother unconditionally.

(冒頭の場面はショッキングなものであるが、双子の兄弟の複雑な関係を解く方向へと展開する。ドミニクは病に苦しむ兄弟を見守っていくことを求められ、時に欲求不満を感じてしまうこともあるが、無条件に兄弟を愛していることも理解する。)

Bible Themes in the Novel (小説における聖書のテーマ)

1. My brother's keeper (兄弟の守り手)
2. Unconditional love (無条件の愛)
3. Pride leads to destruction (自尊心が破壊へと導く)

Bible Quotations（聖書からの引用）

1. Page 5—Matthew 5: 29（マタイによる福音書第 5 章 29 節）

"And if thy† eye offend thee†, pluck it out and cast it from thee† . . . and if thy† right hand offend thee†, cut it off and cast it from thee†; For it is profitable for thee† that one of thy† members should perish and not that thy† whole body should be cast into hell."

† 人称代名詞 2 人称単数の所有格 (thy)、および目的格 (thee)。

²⁹ もし、右の目があなたをつまずかせるなら、えぐり出して捨ててしまいなさい。体の一部がなくなっても、全身が地獄に投げ込まれない方がましである。

Thomas is mentally ill. He interprets the words of Jesus literally. He cuts off his right hand in the public library.

トマスは精神病患者である。彼はイエスの言葉を文字どおりに解釈する。彼は図書館で右手を切り捨ててしまう。

2. Page 2—Matthew 6:24（マタイによる福音書第 6 章 24 節）

²⁴*"You can't worship God and money."*

²⁴「だれも、二人の主人に仕えることはできない。…」

While having lunch with his twin brother, Thomas tells a young waitress that she can't worship God and money. She is a new waitress, and she is eager to do a good job so that she can take care of herself financially. Of course, Thomas misinterprets the teachings of Jesus.

双子の兄弟と昼食を食べているとき、トマスは若いウェイトレスに、神とお金の両方を拝むことはできない、と言う。彼女は新人のウェイトレスで、良い仕事をして経済的に自立したいと思っている。もちろん、トマスはイエスの教えを誤解しているのである。

Dialogue

Miriam: It took me two weeks to finish reading *I Know This Much Is True*. I heard a discussion about it on a television show, and I organized a reading group to read the book.
Martin: I do not think I have the energy to read that book.
Miriam: Reading books does not require much physical energy.
Martin: In this case, I think a person needs energy and muscles. That book is huge. It must weigh about two pounds!
Miriam: Don't think about how many pounds the book weighs. Think about

	the great ideas in it.
Martin:	What is the most important idea?
Miriam:	A normal brother loves his schizophrenic twin. The main idea is unconditional love.
Martin:	Maybe I will read the book. But I think the author could have stated that idea in fewer than 900 pages!

The Life of Pi
(『ライフ・オブ・パイ／トラと漂流した 227 日』)

Book: *The Life of Pi* (『ライフ・オブ・パイ／トラと漂流した 227 日』)

Author: Yann Martel (ヤン・マーテル著)

Year of publication: 2001 (2001 年出版)

Publishing Company: Mariner Books of Houghton Mifflin. (ホートン・ミフリン　マリナー・ブックス)

Winner of the Booker Prize, 2001 (A very highly rated film adaptation of this book was made in 2013) (2001 年ブッカー賞受賞（2013 年映画化）)

Plot (あら筋)

Pi Patel is a young boy in India during the time of Indira Gandhi. His family owns a zoo. He grows up in a happy household. He enjoys seeing the zebras, tigers, and rhinoceroses and other large animals. His father takes care to teach Pi and his brother to respect the power of the wild animals. The wild animals are in fenced areas. But Pi has a delight in watching the animals grow. Pi is a very sensitive boy. He loves God. During the course of the story, he becomes a member of very different religious sects: Hindu, Muslim and Christian. He believes he can be a member of all of these different groups at the same time. He does not understand that people of one religious group are often prejudiced against members of the other groups.

（パイ・パテルは、インディラ・ガンジー時代のインド人少年である。一家は動物園を所有しており、幸せな生活を送っていた。パイは、シマウマやトラ、サイなどの大型動物を見るのが好きであった。父親は、野生動物の力を敬うようにパイとその弟に注意深く教えていた。野生動物は囲いに入れられており、パイは動物が成長するのを見るのが好きであった。彼は感受性の強い少年で、神を愛していた。物語が進行するにつれて、彼はヒンドゥー教、イスラム教、そしてキリスト教と、異なる宗教に属する。彼は、同時にすべての宗教の信者になりうると考えている。）

The novel quickly becomes an adventure story when Pi and his family decide to move to Canada in order to avoid the political problems in India. But the ship sinks on the way to Canada, and Pi survives in a lifeboat—alongside a dangerous Bengal tiger.

(インドでの政治問題から逃れるために一家がカナダに移住するときから、冒険物語になっていく。途中で船が沈み、パイはベンガル虎と一緒に救命ボートで助かる。)

Bible Quotations（聖書からの引用）

Page 36: *"My God, my God, why have you forsaken me?"* Matthew 27: 46.

(^{46} 三時ごろ、イエスは大声で叫ばれた。「エリ、エリ、レマ、サバクタニ。」これは、「わが神、わが神、なぜわたしをお見捨てになったのですか」という意味である。マタイによる福音書第27章46節)

These are the words of Jesus as He was dying on the Cross. Jesus was in great pain during the Crucifixion. Christians believe that Jesus was both God and Man. These words of desperation are evidence that He suffered as a human being at that hour.

(これはイエスが十字架上で死を迎えようとしていたときの言葉である。十字架上で、イエスは大きな苦しみを味わっていた。キリスト教徒は、イエスは神であり、また人であると信じている。この言葉は、イエスも人として苦しみを受けていることを示す、絶望の言葉である。)

Page 36: The Garden of Gethsemane—Matthew 26: 36.

(ゲツセマネの園。マタイによる福音書第26章36節)

Jesus knew in advance that he would be betrayed by one of His "friends," Judas. He knew that he would be arrested soon. He wanted to spend the last few hours of his life in a garden praying with His friends. But they did not understand what was going to happen. As Jesus prayed, His friends slept. There is a famous painting by Heinrich Hoffman which shows Jesus praying, *The Agony in the Garden*. That painting is copied in stained glass, and is used in many churches of the world.

(イエスは、自分の友の一人であるユダに裏切られ、まもなく逮捕されることを事前に知っていた。残された最後の時を、自分に従う友と共に、園で祈りを捧げて過ごそうと思っていた。しかし、彼に従う者たちは、何が起ころうとしているのか理解できなかった。イエスが祈りを捧げている間に、皆眠り込んでしまった。ハインリッヒ・ホフマンは、「園での苦悩」と題する、祈りを捧げるイエスの姿を描いている。この絵はステンドグラスになって、世界中の教会に用いられている。)

Page 37: Goliath—I Samuel 17.

(ゴリアテ。サムエル記上第17章)

Goliath is a famous Bible character. He was a giant who threatened the Israelite people. In the famous story, which children love especially, he challenged the young boy David to a fight. Of course, it was a mismatch. The giant towered over the boy

David. However, David was clever. He threw a rock that killed the giant. Michelangelo created the world famous sculpture of *The David*

（ゴリアテも聖書に出てくる有名な人物である。ゴリアテは、イスラエルの民を脅かす巨人であった。子どもたちも喜ぶ有名な話の中で、ゴリアテは若きダビデに戦いを挑む。賢明なダビデは、岩を投げ、巨人を倒した。ミケランジェロは、「ダヴィデ像」という有名な彫刻を残している。）

Page 25: Crown of Thorns—John 19: 2.

（茨の冠。ヨハネによる福音書第19章2節）

Jesus suffered physically and emotionally during the Crucifixion. He endured the physical pain of being nailed to the Cross. He endured the humiliation of being laughed at. The soldiers said that every "king" should have a crown. So they made a "crown" with pieces of a thorny bush. When they put the crown on Jesus, the blood ran down His Head.

（イエスは十字架刑の間、肉体的にも感情的にも苦しみを受けていた。十字架に杭打たれる肉体上の痛みに耐え、嘲笑される侮蔑にも耐えた。兵士たちは、「王たるものは冠を戴かなければならない」とし、茨の冠を作ってイエスの頭にかぶせた。すると、イエスの頭から血が流れ落ちた。）

Page 25: "Simon who is called Peter—John 1: 40–42.

（ペトロと呼ばれるシモン。ヨハネによる福音書第1章40–42節）

Peter is one of the most important people in the New Testament. He was an apostle. He is known by several different names: Simon, Cephas and Peter. The most frequently used name for this man is Peter. His name means "Rock." That is interesting because rocks are normally symbols of steadiness and strength. But when the Roman soldiers came to get Jesus, Peter apparently followed at a distance. Eventually, a young woman recognized him as a friend of Jesus. But Peter denied any connection with the Lord. Of course, Peter felt bad about the denial, and he later became one of the faithful leaders of the Christian church.

（ペトロは新約聖書中、最も重要な人物の一人である。彼はイエスの弟子で、シモン、ケファ、ペトロとも呼ばれている。この中で最もよく使われる名がペトロで、その意味は「岩」である。岩が通常安定性と力の象徴となっているのは興味深いところである。ローマ兵がイエスを捕えにやってきた時、ペトロは明らかに遠くにいた。若い女性がイエスの仲間と気がついたとき、ペトロは主との関係を否定した。後にペトロはイエスとの関係を否定したことを悔い、キリスト教の教会の最も忠実なリーダーとなった。）

Dialogue

Derrick: In *The Life of Pi*, the narrator is a zookeeper. He says that human beings are the meanest animals of all.
Makoto: That is so cynical.
Derrick: Well, he talks about some of the cruel things human beings do to animals. Once, visitors to the zoo fed glass to a giant seal named **Goliath**.
Makoto: That is terrible! I feel sorry for Goliath.
Derrick: Of course, you know that Goliath was originally the name of the giant who was killed by the boy, David, in the Bible.
Makoto: Yes, I have read I Samuel 17. In fact, people still refer to any mismatched fighters as **David and Goliath**.
Derrick: Well, Goliath in the Bible, and Goliath in *The Life of Pi* were killed by smaller opponents. But I am sorry that Goliath, the seal in the novel, suffered such cruelty.

A Prayer for Owen Meany
（オーウェン・ミーニーのための祈り）

Book: *A Prayer for Owen Meany* 『オーウェン・ミーニーのための祈り』
Author: John Irving　ジョン・アーヴィング著
Publishing Company: Ballantine Books, New York　ニューヨーク バランタイン・ブックス社
Date of Publication: 1989（1989年出版）

Major Characters（主な登場人物）

Owen Meany　オーウェン・ミーニー
John Wheelwright　ジョン・ウィールライト
Tabitha Wheelwright　タビサ・ウィールライト

Note: There is a very good film adaptation of this bestseller. The movie title is *Simon Birch*. However, the movie only adheres to a very small part of the storyline. The character names are changed in the movie as well.

（このベストセラー小説には、素晴らしい脚色で映画化され、そのタイトルは「サイモン・バーチ」となっている。物語全体のほんのわずかしか保たれておらず、登場人物の名前も変えられている。）

Plot （あら筋）

A severely deformed little boy insists that God created him for a particular purpose. The problem is that the boy grows up to be a very intelligent young man who only discovers his purpose <u>at the end</u> of his young life. Owen Meany was born an extremely small baby. Surprisingly, he survived, and had a best friend, John Wheelwright. Both boys depend on each other's support. John is normal sized, but he was born to an unmarried mother. Although his mother is very loving, John's dream is to find his father. The mother refused to tell him the father's name.

（ひどく奇形に生まれた少年は、神が特別な目的のために自分を造られたと主張する。問題は、少年が非常に賢い若者に成長し、青年期の末期になって自分の目的を発見したということである。オーウェン・ミーニーは非常に小柄に生まれつき、驚くことに生き延びて、親友ジョン・ウィールライトを得たのである。ジョンは普通の体型に生まれたが、母は未婚の女性であった。母親は愛情豊かな人であったが、ジョンの夢は父親を捜し出すことである。母親は、ジョンに父親の名前を教えることを拒んだ。）

In addition to being so physically handicapped, Owen has uncaring parents. Basically they only supply food and water. They show no love toward him.

（肉体的にハンディに加え、オーウェンの両親は面倒見が悪い人たちである。両親は彼に食べ物と水を与えるだけで、愛のかけらも示そうとはしない。）

Owen develops a special love for John's mother, Tabitha. She is so kind and loving. She treats Owen as if he were her second son. However, the happy relationship between Owen and John is disrupted briefly. Owen and John were members of a Little League baseball team. John's mother was just arriving at the ballpark when tiny Owen was preparing to bat. He batted a foul ball that hit Tabitha Wheelwright in the head, instantly killing her.

（オーウェンはジョンの母親に特別な愛情を抱く。彼女は親切で愛情にあふれ、オーウェンを二番目の息子であるかのように扱う。しかし、オーウェンとジョンの幸せな関係は一時的に途絶えてしまう。オーウェンとジョンはリトル・リーグの野球チームのメンバーで、ジョンの母親が野球場に着いたとき、ちょうどオーウェンが打席に立とうとしていた。オーウェンの打ったファウルがタビサの頭を直撃し、タビサは即死してしまう。）

Owen is deeply grieved. He killed the one adult that he loved most. And, he killed his best friend's mother. The story develops as the two boys resume their great friendship, and as they attempt to find out John's true father. The story ends as Owen, now a military man, meets John at the Phoenix, Arizona airport. Owen sees some Catholic nuns leading a group of newly arrived Vietnamese orphans. The children are coming to live in America. One of the nuns asks Owen if he would escort some little boys to the bathroom. While in the restroom, a bomb goes off. Owen loses his life while he and John rescue the children. John survives, and he spends the rest of his life mourning the death of his best friend.

（オーウェンは、彼が最も愛した大人、しかも親友の母親を殺してしまい、嘆き悲しむ。物語は、二人の少年が友情を取り戻し、ジョンの本当の父親を捜そうとする場面へと移って行く。今や軍人となったオーウェンが、アリゾナ州フェニックスの空港でジョンに会うところで終っている。オーウェンは、カトリックの修道女たちが、到着したばかりのベトナムの孤児たちを率いているのを目撃する。一人の修道女が、男の子をトイレに連れて行ってくれないかとオーウェンに頼む。トイレにいる間に爆弾が破裂し、ジョンと一緒に子どもたちを助けている時に、オーウェンは命を失ってしまう。ジョンは生き延び、親友の死を悼みながら生涯をすごす。）

Bible Themes in *A Prayer for Owen Meany*
（『オーウェン・ミーニーのための祈り』に見られる聖書のテーマ）

1. Deep Friendship（深い友情）
2. Adopting others as "brothers," "sisters," and "mothers."（兄弟、姉妹、母親として他人を選ぶこと）
3. A Sacrificial Death（犠牲的死）
4. Forgiveness（赦し）

Bible Quotations （聖書からの引用）

1. Philippians 4: 6—*⁶Have no anxiety about anything, but in everything by prayer and supplication with thanksgiving let your requests be made known to God.* (The Revised Standard Bible translation is used as the epigram, or introduction, to the entire novel).

   （フィリピの信徒への手紙第4章6節：どんなことでも、思い煩うのはやめなさい。何事につけ、感謝をこめて祈りと願いをささげ、求めているものを神に打ち明けなさい。（小説全体のエピグラム、導入部として、改訂標準訳聖書が使われている。）

   Both Owen Meany and John Wheelwright have a request to make to God. Owen wants to know the purpose of his life. John wants to know who is his father. By the end of the novel, both young men receive their answers.

   （オーウェン・ミーニーもジョン・ウィールライトも、神に求めようとするものを持っている。オーウェンは自身の人生の目的を知りたがり、ジョンは自分の父が誰であるのかを知りたがっている。小説の終わりに、二人ともその答えを教えられる。）

2. Page 112—Isaiah 6: 5 *"Woe to me!" I cried. "I am ruined! For I am a man of unclean lips, and I live among a people of unclean lips, and my eyes have seen the King, the LORD Almighty."*

(イザヤ書第6章5節：わたしは言った。「災いだ。わたしは滅ぼされる。わたしは汚れた唇の者。汚れた唇の民の中に住む者。しかも、わたしの目は　王なる万軍の主を仰ぎ見た。」)

Although Owen is very religious, he also is very human. Sometimes he uses angry and vulgar language. He knows that God chose a man who had similar problems to be a great teacher in the Old Testament.

(オーウェンは非常に宗教的ではあるが、また人間的でもある。時に怒りに満ちた野卑な言葉を使う。神は旧約聖書において、大いなる師になるために同じような問題を抱えていた人を選ばれた、ということを彼は知っている。)

3. Page 111—Ephesians 6:13–15 *Wherefore take unto you the whole armor of God that ye[†] may be able to withstand in the evil day, and having done all to sand. Stand therefore, having your loins girt about with truth, and having put on the breastplate of righteousness; and your feet shod with the preparation of the gospel of peace.* (This is the King James translation—only the beginning of the famous passage is actually quoted in the novel.)

[†] 人称代名詞2人称複数主格。

(エフェソの信徒への手紙第6章13-15節：13 だから、邪悪な日によく抵抗し、すべてを成し遂げて、しっかりと立つことができるように、神の武具を身に着けなさい。14 立って、真理を帯びとして腰に締め、正義を胸当てとして着け、15 平和の福音を告げる準備を履物としなさい。(これは欽定英語訳聖書の表現で、小説ではこの有名なくだりの初めの部分だけが引用されている。))

The Scriptures 2, and 3 above are words that Owen and John heard often in their church. They were bored with the preacher who was always quoting these words. But later, when the boys grow up, they must make a decision. They must decide whether or not to enter the military and fight in the Vietnam war. John chooses to escape to Canada. Owen puts on the military uniform. He joins the army because he believes that maybe he can do something heroic as a military man.

(上記2と3の聖書の言葉は、オーウェンとジョンが教会でよく聞いた言葉である。二人とも、牧師がいつもこうした言葉を引用するのに、飽き飽きしていた。しかし、二人が成長した後に、二人とも決心しなければならないことになる。軍隊に入ってベトナム戦争で戦うかどうかを選択しなければならない。ジョンはカナダに逃れることを選ぶ。オーウェンは軍服を着ることを選ぶ。オーウェンは、軍人として何か英雄的なことができるのではないかと思い、軍隊に入る。)

Dialogue

Trevor: I saw the movie, *Simon Birch*. I think that is the first time I have cried in a movie theater.

Dane: I agree it is a powerful film. I must admit that I had tears in my eyes at the end. Although the movie is great, it does not have the artistry

	of the book.
Trevor:	Oh, was there a book?
Dane:	Yes, the movie is an adaptation of John Irving's bestseller, *A Prayer for Owen Meany*.
Trevor:	I don't remember a character by that name in the movie.
Dane:	No, the film changed the names of the characters and re-arranged many of the details from the book. But the basic idea is the same in the book and in the movie. The main character sacrifices his life in order to save other people. I recommend the book, but you should be prepared to read over 600 pages.

The Martyr
(『殉教者』)

Book: *The Martyr* (included in *Rashomon and Other Stories*) 『殉教者』(『羅生門』他)
Author: Ryunosuke Akutagawa　芥川龍之介著
Publication date: Originally published in 1918（1918年出版）
Publisher: Tuttle and Company, 1952

Plot（あら筋）

The Martyr is a long, short story reflecting Akutagawa's interest in Christianity. It is a story about an orphan who shows up at a Jesuit Christian monastery in Japan. The child is named Lorenzo. He is loved by the community of monks. He is particularly religious and pious. However, as he grows into young adulthood, a Japanese girl falls in love with him. He tries to discourage her romantic approaches. Monks in the Roman Catholic tradition must be celibate. They cannot get married. But the girl writes a love note to him. The note is discovered by the superior of the monastery. Lorenzo is questioned about the relationship. He insists that he has done nothing improper. However, the girl becomes pregnant, and Lorenzo is put out of the monastery. He lives in shame and poverty on the streets near the monastery. A fire breaks out at the house where the girl lives with her baby and her father. The girl and her father escape the fire, but the baby is left behind. The girl screams for help. A strong monk attempts to walk into the burning house, but the fire overwhelms him. Finally, seemingly from nowhere, Lorenzo walks into the burning house. He emerges with the baby. He throws the baby into the arms of the waiting mother. She confesses that Lorenzo is not the father. The father is another boy in the neighborhood.

(『殉教者』は、芥川のキリスト教に対する関心を反映する長い、短編小説で、日本のイエズス会修道院に現れたみなし子の物語である。ロレンゾと名付けられたその子は、修道士にかわいがられた。ロレンゾは非常に宗教的で敬虔な人物である。青年になる頃、少女が彼に恋してしまう。ロレンゾは少女の恋心を諦めさせようとする。ローマ・カトリック教会の伝統では、修道士は独身でなければならないことになっており、二人は結婚などできない。少女はロレンゾに恋文を書き送るが、修道院長に見つかってしまう。ロレンゾは二人の関係について尋問されるが、何もやましいことはしていないと主張する。しかし、少女は妊娠し、ロレンゾは修道院を追放される。彼は修道院の近くの路上で、不名誉と貧困のうちに暮らしている。少女と赤ん坊が少女の父親と暮らしている家が火事になってしまう。少女と父親は逃げることができたが、赤ん坊は中に取り残されてしまう。少女は助けを求めて叫び、屈強な修道士が燃え盛る火の中に入ろうとするが、火の勢いに圧倒されてしまう。どこからともなくロレンゾが現れ、燃え盛る火の中に入って赤ん坊を助け出す。助けを求めて待っていた少女の手に赤ん坊を渡すと、少女は赤ん坊の父親はロレンゾではなく、近所の別の青年であることを告白する。)

Meanwhile, Lorenzo is on fire. His clothes are burned off of him. The monks and the superior rush to him. They are sorry that they did not believe him. When the burning clothes fall away from Lorenzo, everyone notices that Lorenzo is a female. She had lived in disguise as a male all of those years. She gave up her life so that she could rescue the baby of her "enemy" (the girl that had told a lie about her).

(ロレンゾは炎に包まれ、衣服が燃え落ちてしまう。修道士たちはロレンゾの元に駆けつけ、彼を信じなかったことを悔いる。ロレンゾの衣服がすっかり燃え落ちてしまうと、女性の姿が顕わになる。ロレンゾはずっと、男性の姿で生きてきたのである。ロレンゾは、嘘の証言をした「敵」の赤ん坊を救うため、自らの命を犠牲にしようとしたのである。)

Bible Themes in the Story（物語における聖書のテーマ）

1. A person sacrifices his life for another（他者のために犠牲となる者）
2. Silent suffering（沈黙のうちの受難）
3. Forgiving our enemies（敵を赦すということ）

Bible Quotations（聖書からの引用）

1. Luke 23: 34—*"Lord, forgive them, for they know not what they do."* Jesus said this when He was being Crucified. Lorenzo, in *The Martyr*, uses similar words when a fellow monk strikes him on the head.

(ルカによる福音書第23章34節:「『父よ、彼らをお赦しください。自分が何をしているのか知らないのです。』」これはイエスが十字架の刑に処せられた時の言葉である。『殉教者』のロレンゾも、仲間の修道士が頭を殴った時に同様の言葉を使っている。)

2. Philippians 2: 7–8—*⁷But made himself of no reputation, and took upon himself the form of a servant, and was made in the likeness of men. And being found in the fashion as a man, ⁸he humbled himself, and became obedient unto death, even the death of the cross.* Lorenzo in *The Martyr* lived as a beggar on the streets. He could have easily maintained his innocence if he had revealed his true identity.

（フィリピの信徒への手紙第2章7–8節：「⁷かえって自分を無にして、僕の身分になり、人間と同じ者になられました。人間の姿で現れ、⁸へりくだって、死に至るまで、それも十字架の死に至るまで従順でした。」『殉教者』のロレンゾは路上で乞食の生活をしていた。自分の真の姿を現わしていたならば、自分の無実を簡単に証明できたであろうに。）

Dialogue:

Emiko: Our teacher assigned Akutagawa's short story, *The Martyr* to us, and I am really confused about it.

Stephan: I read that story two years ago. What confused you about it?

Emiko: Well, the main character, Lorenzo, was wrongly accused of being a father. The situation could have been easily cleared up if Lorenzo had made it plain that he was actually a female in disguise.[1]

Stephan: But I think you miss the whole point of the story. Lorenzo suffered quietly. She was a character who had the qualities of Jesus Christ.

Emiko: But the most shocking part of the story was that she entered the burning house and rescued the baby. Of course, in the end, Lorenzo died because of the fire. Do you think many people would die for somebody else?

Stephan: Well, maybe it doesn't happen often, but there are some unselfish people in the world.

1) **in disguise** 変装した

The Old Man and the Sea
（『老人と海』）

Author: Ernest Hemingway（アーネスト・ヘミングウェイ著）
Original Year of Publication: 1952（1952年出版）
Publisher: Scribner（スクリブナー社）

Characters:(主な登場人物)
　　Santiago(サンチャゴ)
　　Manolin(マノリン)
　　Village of Fishermen(漁師たち)

Plot(あら筋)

SANTIAGO is an old fisherman. At the beginning of the book, he has gone without catching a fish for 84 days. The local fishermen are afraid to have any contact with him, fearing that bad luck is contagious. The only person who readily keeps company with Santiago is the young boy, Manolin. By some scholarly accounts, Manolin is probably only ten years old. Amazingly, he shows a very mature attitude. He says loving things such as "You'll not fish without eating while I am alive." (Hemingway, p. 19.) In that quotation, the little boy expresses his determination to show love and care for an old man who is really not a relative.

(サンチャゴは年老いた漁師で、84日間も魚が獲れないでいた。漁師たちは、不運が伝染することを恐れ、彼に近づかないようにしていた。唯一サンチャゴとすすんで接していたのは、おそらく10歳くらいの少年マノリンである。その年齢にも関わらず、マノリンは成熟した態度を示す。彼は「私が生きている間は、食事をとらないと魚は獲れないよ」と、気の利いたことを言う*。少年は、身内でもない老人に対する愛情を示しているのである。
*19ページ

The story has two main ideas:

1. The unconditional love which Santiago and Manolin have for each other
2. Santiago's determination to catch the great fish (not necessarily for fame or for money, but for the discipline of the experience)

(この物語には2つの大きなテーマがある：
1. サンチャゴとマノリンの間に見られる無条件の愛
2. (名誉やお金のためにではなく、経験を求めて)大きな魚を捕まえようとするサンチャゴの決意)

The Charm of the Child(子どもが引き付けるもの)

IT is a very charming part of the story that Manolin defies his parents and expresses his love for the old man. Although not DNA related, they are like grandfather and grandson. Manolin brings food to Santiago. The boy even brings beer to him. Apparently he pays for some of the food and beer with money he earns as a helper to another man on another boat. Other times he gets "credit" (Hemingway, p. 27.) at a store of a kindly bodega owner. The child's great care of the older man (a care that is lovingly reciprocated), reminds readers of the "adoption" which Jesus encouraged in the Gospel of John (19: 26 and 27). While on the Cross, Jesus instructed His friend, John, and His mother, Mary, to "adopt" each other. The names of Jesus and Mary appear many times throughout the novel, in fact Santiago recites the famous Roman Catholic Prayer, *Hail Mary* (Ibid, p. 65.) (Of course the words of the prayer have inspired two famous compositions of the *Ave Maria*, one by Gounod; one by Shubert). That prayer is a blend of several verses from the Bible, principally Luke 1: 28:

Hail, thou[†] *that art*[††] *highly favoured, the*
Lord is with thee[†]*; blessed art*[††] *thou*[†]
Among women . . .

  [†] 人称代名詞 2 人称単数主格 (thou)、目的格 (thee)。／[††]BE 動詞 2 人称単数現在形。

(少年マノリンが両親に反抗し、老人に対する愛を示すのは、この物語の素晴らしいい部分である。遺伝子では結ばれていないが、二人は本当の祖父と孫のようなものである。マノリンは食べ物やビールをサンチャゴのもとに運ぶが、そのお金は自分で稼いだものである。時に親切な食糧雑貨店の店主から「つけ」*で売ってもらう。老人に対する愛は、ヨハネによる福音書の中でイエスが述べている「用紙縁組」を思い起こさせる。十字架上で、イエスは母マリアと友ヨハネに養子縁組を指示する。イエスとマリアの名前は、小説中に幾度となく現れ、サンチャゴはローマ・カトリック教会の祈り「マリアに幸いあれ」** を唱える。(この祈りの言葉はグノーとシューベルト作曲による 2 つの「アベ・マリア」を生み出した。)この祈りはルカによる福音書を中心とした聖書に見られる節を混ぜ合わせたものである。)
  *27 ページ
  **65 ページ

Although Sanitago recites the prayer, he claims not to be such a serious Christian. His greatly beloved deceased wife was a devoted Catholic. While enduring the pain of the fishing ordeal alone on the wide ocean, he prays to Mary and to God. He thinks that his wife would be pleased by the acknowledgement of the Divine.

(サンチャゴは祈りを唱えるが、自分は敬虔なクリスチャンではないと言う。亡き妻は敬虔なカトリック教徒であった。大海で一人で漁をしているとき、サンチャゴはマリアと神に祈り、亡き妻が喜んでくれるだろうと思う。)

Santiago launches his little skiff far out into the ocean, going where no other fishermen dare. Ordinary fishermen are satisfied to catch the smaller fish which are available closer inland. Santiago even chooses the time of the roughest water (September) to make his attempt to catch the great marlin. He distinguishes himself from other men who prefer the easiest life. He says, "Anyone can be a fisherman in May." (Hemingway, p. 18.) Clearly, Santiago is not interested in doing what is easy. He is interested in challenging the difficult. Readers are reminded of Jesus who advises his followers use the narrow and unpopular path:

Enter ye† at the strait (narrow) gate: for
Wide is the gate, and broad is the way
That leadeth†† to destruction. . . (Matthew 7: 13)

† 人称代名詞 2 人称複数主格。／††lead の 3 人称単数現在形。

（サンチャゴは他の漁師が行こうともしない沖合にスキフを漕ぎ出す。大きなマカジキを捕まえようとして、荒れる 9 月の海に出る。彼は「5 月ならば誰にでも漁はできる」*と言い、楽なことをしようとはしないのである。イエスが弟子たちに「狭い道を進むよう」に言う場面を思い出す人も多いだろう。）
*18 ページ

Simply put, Jesus encourages people to discipline themselves. Human beings should build their characters by challenging themselves to avoid the attraction of the easy and the popular.

（イエスは、「自分を律しなさい」と言っている。人間は、簡単で楽な道を選ぶのではなく、挑戦する気持ちを持って自分を磨かなければならない。）

Santiago is Obviously Similar to Jesus （サンチャゴとイエスの類似点）

1. Jesus suffered the discomfort of the "Crown of Thorns." The Roman soldiers made a crown out of a plant that had sharp stickers, and placed it on Jesus' head for a joke. (John 19:2)

   （1. ローマ兵が茨の冠を作り、イエスの頭にかぶせる。）

   Santiago suffered the discomfort of the old straw hat. He had only this old hat to protect him from the sun on the ocean. When he pulled it down hard, it cut his forehead. (Hemingway, p. 46)

   （サンチャゴは、古い麦わら帽子しか持っていない。その帽子を無理やり脱ごうとしたとき、額に傷がついてしまう。）

2. Jesus was whipped and tortured. There were "stripes" or bruises on his body.

   （2. イエスは鞭打たれ、体中に傷がつく。）

   Santiago had wounds on his hands and his back. He has marks on his back which were made by the rope he used to haul in the great fish. These bruises are like the "stripes" on Jesus' back.

   （サンチャゴの手と背中には、大きな魚を手繰ろうとした時に付いた傷跡がある。）

3. Jesus is associated with fish. His earliest followers were fishermen. And Jesus famously told them that He would make them fishers of men. (Matthew 4: 19.)

(3. イエスは魚と縁がある。イエスの最初の弟子は漁師で、彼らに「人を獲る者にしよう」と言っている。)

4. Santiago has dedicated his life to fishing. And, Manolin praises the old man: "And the best fisherman is you." (Hemingway, p. 23.)

(4. サンチャゴは漁に人生を捧げ、マノリンは「あなたこそ最も優れた漁師だ」と言って讃える。)

Dialogue:

Mrs. Clark:	Mark, thank you for reading *The Old Man and the Sea* to me. I am blind, but I can just "see" everything as you read. Of course I like the part where Santiago says the *Hail Mary* prayer on the boat.
Mark:	That is a very touching part. The fisherman, Santiago, said that he wasn't as good a Christian as his deceased wife had been. But he said the prayer because he knew she would want him to pray.
Mrs. Clark:	That prayer uses words from the Bible. It comes from Luke 1: 28, ***"Hail, thou that art highly favored, The Lord is with thee: blessed art thou among women."***
Mark:	Yes, I know the prayer very well. I often recite the *Hail Mary* in Church.

Anne of Green Gables
(『赤毛のアン』)

Author: L M Montgomery (L. M. モンゴメリー著)
Original Year of Publication: 1908 (1908年初版出版)
Original Publishing Company: Harrap (ハラップ社)
Special Centennial Paperback Edition: Puffin Books (2008) (百周年記念ペーパーバック版 パフィン・ブックス (2008))

Plot (あら筋)

It is particularly appropriate that we should include a study of *Anne of Green Gables* in this book. NHK in Japan is celebrating the hundredth anniversary of the publication of this Canadian novel (in actuality, the book is slightly over 100 years old) by televising a series about the first Japanese translator of the book. At first glance, *Anne of Green Gables* is a highly sentimental book written in a style that would appeal to young readers, especially young, sub-teen girl readers. A closer scrutiny could support idea of the book as a thoughtful work which has sufficient elements of feminism and 19th century social commentary to warrant more adult, even scholarly, attention. Things that are a departure from the usual sentimental literature for children include:

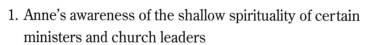

1. Anne's awareness of the shallow spirituality of certain ministers and church leaders
2. Classism of the 19th century Canadian culture—references are made to "stupid … French boys."
3. Anne's refusal to swoon over the handsome boy who has overwhelmed the hearts of other girls.

> (『赤毛のアン』は本書にとってもふさわしいものと言える。NHKも出版百周年記念に、最初の日本語訳者に関するシリーズを放送した。『赤毛のアン』は、十代初めの少女が興味を抱くような作品に思われるが、よく読むと、フェミニズムの要素や19世紀の社会的評釈を含み、学術的研究にも十分に値するものである。単なる子どもの情緒的な作品とは異なる点は、
> 1. 牧師や教会のリーダーたちの薄っぺらい精神性にアンが気づいていること
> 2. 19世紀カナダの階級敵偏見：「馬鹿なフランス小僧」が言及されていること
> 3. 他の女の子たちがうっとりするようなハンサムな男の子に、アンは恍惚とならないこと
> である。)

Anne is an orphan whose great imagination and assertiveness are defense mechanisms allowing her to cope with several major disappointments in her young life. Born into an educated family (her father and mother had both been high school teachers), Anne suffered a series of heartaches. Both parents died; she was assigned to the foster care of people who only wanted to use her as an unpaid maid and nanny for their several children. Had her parents lived, it is certain that she would have had a happier life than she had in the temporary care of different families. The two different foster families never showed love to the orphan, Anne. Both of those families suffered the loss of the father, and (in the words of the one of the foster mothers) were at their wit's end in deciding what to do with this child who was not really related to them.

> (みなし子のアンは、その想像力と自己主張でもって、幼い頃の悲しい出来事に対応している。高校教師の子として生まれたアンだが、両親が亡くなり、彼女をただ働きの女中、子どもの世話係として働かせようとする家に預けられる。彼女が預けられた2つの家族共、アンに対する愛のかけらも示さなかっ

た。養父が亡くなったとき、養母が血のつながりもないアンをどうしてよいのか〈途方に暮れ〉てしまう。)

Bible References（聖書への言及）

1. The care of widows and orphans
2. Jesus' love for little children
3. Daniel and the Lion's Den

(1. 未亡人と孤児
2. 幼い子どもたちに対するイエスの愛
3. ダニエルとライオンの巣穴)

Major Bible Ideas（聖書に見られる考え方）

Care of Widows and Orphans（未亡人と孤児への気づかい）

The major idea of *Anne of Green Gables* is a meditation upon James 1:27:

"Pure religion and undefiled before God and the Father is this, To visit the fatherless and widows in their affliction, and to keep himself unspotted from the world." (KJV)

(『赤毛のアン』のメインテーマは、「ヤコブの手紙」第1章27節の黙想である。
27 みなしごや、やもめが困っているときに世話をし、世の汚れに染まらないように自分を守ること、これこそ父である神の御前に気良く汚れのない信心です。)

That simply means that God prefers that people protect one another—we should be especially protective of the weakest among us: orphans and widows. It means nothing to God if we give a lot of money to the church, or if we pray many hours in a day without being generous to the people who are suffering.

(これは、神が互いに守りあうこと、特に孤児や寡婦のような弱者を守ることを望んでおられるということを意味している。教会に多額の寄付をしたり、苦しむ人に対して親切にしないで何時間も祈りを捧げることなどは、神にとって何の意味もない。)

Anne of Green Gables is an 11 year old girl who has been mistreated by a series of people. When an couple send for her (they are brother and sister, not husband and wife), they are disappointed that she is a girl. They had hoped the orphanage would send them a boy to work on their farm. Gradually, Anne wins their hearts, and Marilla and Matthew learn the meaning of James 1:27.

(11歳の赤毛のアンは多くの人からひどい扱いを受ける。ある兄妹が農場の働き手が欲しくて孤児院に依頼したとき、やって来たのが女の子であるとわかってがっかりした。やがてアンは二人の心を掴み、兄妹はヤコブの手紙の意味を悟る。)

Jesus Loves Little Children（イエスは幼い子を愛する）

Anne notices a painting of Jesus surrounded by little children, but one little girl stands off, feeling shy, perhaps. Anne identifies with the little girl in the painting. (Montgomery, p. 69.) The reference is to the famous scene in Matthew 19:14:

"Suffer (be patient with) little children and forbid them not[†], to come unto to me: for of such is the kingdom of heaven." (KJV)

[†] 否定命令文。Cf. Don't forbid them.

(アンは幼い子どもたちに囲まれているイエスの絵を見、一人の女の子が離れた所に立っていることに気付く。それはマタイによる福音書第19章14節の有名な場面である。
[14] しかし、イエスは言われた。「子供たちを来させなさい。わたしのところに来るのを妨げてはならない。天の国はこのような者たちのものである。」)

*69 ページ

Probably the painting that Anne is looking at is Gar Van Vogelstein's *Christ and the Children* (1890). Anne is probably a better Christian than several adults in the story who are so proud of themselves. She has the spirit of sincerity and honesty that are virtues which the Bible recommends.

(アンが見た絵は、恐らくヴォーゲルシュタインの「キリストと子どもたち」であろう。アンは、作中の高慢な大人たちよりも、ずっとクリスチャンらしい。彼女には、聖書が説いている誠実さと正直さが備わっている。)

Daniel and the Lion's Den (The Book of Daniel, Chapter VI)
（ダニエルとライオンの巣穴（ダニエル書第6章））

Often in the story, Anne is seen as more "spiritual" than some of the adults in the church. She complains about the repetitious and apparently insincere prayers of one of the church leaders. When a new minister is assigned to the church, Anne has a higher estimation of him and his wife than she has of the previous minister. When the wife allowed children to ask questions about the service that morning, Anne is disappointed that one of her classmates asked a question that had nothing to do with the Bible chapter that the new minister had presented: *Daniel and the Lion's Den.* (Ibid., p. 209.) This is one of the most loved Bible stories, especially by children. The story tells of a young foreign man who was taken into captivity by the Persians. Daniel was very likable, and he became a favorite of the Persian King. Jealous members of the King's court decided to harm Daniel. They encouraged the King to sign a law stating that no one could pray to any God (except the King) for 30 days. But Daniel knelt down and prayed to God. The King was forced to punish Daniel. He put Daniel in a den of hungry lions. The king went home very sorrowful. He did not want Daniel to die. In the morning, the king went to the Den and called to Daniel. The young man answered happily that God had sent an angel to close the mouths of the lions. The King was very happy.

（物語の中で、アンは教会に来る大人たちよりも「精神的」であると見なされている。長老たちが繰り返す〈不誠実〉な祈りに不満を持つ。新しい牧師が赴任したとき、アンは前任者よりも期待する。礼拝の後で牧師の妻が子どもたちに質問を聞いたとき、説教の「ダニエルとライオンの巣穴」とは全く関係のない質問が出て、アンはがっかりしてしまう。子どもたちが大好きな聖書の物語は、ペルシャの囚われの身となった若い異国の男性の話である。ダニエルは誰にも好かれる人で、ペルシャ王のお気に入りとなる。彼に嫉妬した宮廷の人々が、「王を除き、30日間誰も、どの神にも祈ってはならない」という法律に署名するよう王を説得する。ダニエルは膝まづいて神に祈り、王は彼を罰せざるをえなくなる。空腹のライオンの巣穴にダニエルを入れ、悲しい気持ちで戻った王は、翌朝巣穴に行ってダニエルに声をかけると、「神が天使を遣わし、ライオンの口をふさいだ」というダニエルの返事が聞こえた。）

*209 ページ

Of course the implication is that God protected the obedient young man Daniel in the Old Testament, and God protects the innocent and goodhearted Anne in the novel.

（この話が示しているのは、旧約聖書では神が従順なダニエルを守り、小説では無垢で良心的なアンを守るということである。）

Dialogue

Derrick: If you ask me, *Anne of Green Gables* is overly sentimental.

Jack: Sure. Any story about orphans struggling to survive in society will be sentimental. Charles Dickens wrote several stories about sad little orphans. Did you read *Oliver Twist*?

Derrick: Yes, but Dickens' books seem to be a higher level of literature.

Jack: Maybe so, but I like Anne's reaction to the minister's sermon about **Daniel in the Lions' Den**.[1] She was just a little girl, but she understood the message of that Bible story.

Derrick: Remind me of the message of that Bible story.

Jack: The Persians put young, innocent Daniel in the den of lions. They expected the lions to tear the boy's body apart. But the Great God of

> the Hebrews cast a spell on the lions. They did not harm Daniel.
>
> Derrick: I see, so Anne thinks that God will protect her, too. That is a good story. I guess many people survive frightening situations. Perhaps we can say that all of us have been in **"The Lions' Den"** at some point in our lives.
>
> Jack: I agree. I think *Anne of Green Gables* is a sentimental book. But I also think it has some realistic elements.

1) **Daniel in the Lions' Den** 非常に危険な状態

The Sun Also Rises
(『陽はまた昇る』)

Author: Ernest Hemingway (アーネスト・ヘミングウェイ著)

Publication date: 1926 (originally) (1926年初版出版)

Publication Company: Charles Scribner's Sons, 1954, New York (ニューヨーク、チャールズ・スクリブナーズ・サンズ、1954年)

Note: The reference to the Bible begins with the very title. The title comes from Ecclesiastes 1: 4–11. Hemingway, like Ryunosuke Akutagawa, had a fascination with the Bible, and particularly with the character of Jesus Christ. Neither man seemed particularly interested in committing to a long term church membership.

(このタイトルは、「コヘレトの言葉（伝道の書）」第1章4-11節から出ている。ヘミングウェイは、芥川龍之介と同様、聖書に魅せられ、特にイエス・キリストの性格に魅せられている。ヘミングウェイも芥川も、教会に長く関わることには関心がなかったようである。)

Major Characters: (主な登場人物)
Jake Barnes (ジェイク・バーンズ)
Robert Cohn (ロバート・コーン)
Lady Brett Ashley (ブレット・アシュリー夫人)
Pedro Romero (ペドロ・ロメロ)

Plot (あら筋)

It might be a good idea <u>not</u> to read this famous Hemingway novel if you are easily depressed. The story is about a man, Jake Barnes, an expatriate living in Paris. In actuality, many American artists, writers, dancers and singers lived a free style life in Paris in the early 1920s. In this story, Barnes is a very sad man. He is in love with a divorcee, Lady Brett Ashley. Unfortunately, Jake was injured in the war. His wound makes him impotent. He can no longer have a physical relationship with the beautiful and charming Lady Brett. She is apparently unsympathetic to his situation. At various times during the story she comes into Jake's presence with a series of boyfriends. She is a new style woman (for the 1920s); she cuts her hair very short, she talks freely about sex, and she even seduces a 19 year-old Spanish bullfighter, Pedro Romero. To make matters worse, one of Jake's good friends, Robert Cohn, has an affair with Lady Brett. The theme of the novel is frustration.

（簡単に落ち込んでしまう人は、この小説は読まない方が良い。これは、国を捨てたジェイク・バーンズという男の物語である。1920年代には、多くのアメリカ人芸術家が、自由を求めてパリで生活していた。バーンズは離婚したブレット・アシュリーと恋に落ちるが、戦争で負傷し、不能になってしまう。ブレットは当時としては〈新しい人〉で、髪を短くし、自由に性を語り、19歳のスペイン人闘牛士ペドロ・ロメロを誘惑し、さらにはジェイクの親友ロバート・コーンと肉体関係を持つ。これは〈欲求不満〉の小説である。）

Perhaps one of the harshest of life's experiences is to be in the very presence of something that you can't have. Brett seems to enjoy taunting Jake. Futility is expressed in many different ways in the novel. Many of the artists are bored. They are in the great city of Paris, but they spend their time getting drunk, gambling, and going to cafes. In one of the sad scenes of the novel, Jake returns to his hotel alone. He cries himself to sleep. Suddenly, Brett arrives drunken at his hotel. She makes a lot of noise entering his room. She tells Jake that a rich old man is waiting for her in his car. She thinks it would be fun if Jake joined her and the rich old man for a drive. Of course, what Jake would really like is to be alone with Brett. In her mind, however, she is the victim. She makes Jake feel guilty because he cannot physically express his love for her.

（人生の中で最も過酷なことは、どうしても手に入れられないものが目の前に置かれている状態である。ブレットはジェイクをあざけるのを楽しんでいるように見える。こうした空しさが小説の中で何度も表されている。ある日ジェイクは一人でホテルに戻り、泣きながら寝入ってしまう。そこに酔っぱらったブレットがやって来てわめきたてる。金持ちの老人が車で待っているので、一緒にドライブに行こうと言う。ジェイクは、ブレットと二人きりになりたいのにである。一方ブレットは、ジェイクが彼女に対する愛を肉体で表すことができないので、自分の方が被害者だと思っている。）

Although this book might not be for everyone's taste, it is considered one of the important works in American literature, and it has won the acclaim of several intellectuals.

（全ての読者の好みには合わないかもしれないが、この小説はアメリカ文学の中で重要な作品であり、専門家の間では大いに称賛されている。）

Bible Themes in *The Sun Also Rises*
(『陽はまた昇る』の中に見られる聖書のテーマ)

1. The need to find a purpose for our lives
2. The sadness of selfishness

 (1. 人生の目的を見いだす必要性
 2. 自分本位の悲しさ)

The story really does not have a satisfying ending. It is about boredom and frustration. Interestingly, that is the overall theme of the Book of Ecclesiastes in the Bible. Both the novel and the Bible depict rich people who have "everything," but who are nevertheless depressed. Of course, the implication in the Bible is that if we focus on God and on helping other people, we will have satisfaction in our lives.

(これはハッピーエンドになる小説ではない。退屈さと欲求不満の物語である。このテーマは、『コヘレトの言葉(伝道の書)』に流れるテーマでもある。どちらも、全て持っている裕福な者が打ちひしがれている様を描いている。聖書が意味しているのはもちろんのこと、〈神のみに焦点を当て、他者を助けることに徹するならば、満足が得られる〉というものである。)

Bible Quotations (聖書からの引用)

Hemingway quoted a fairly long section of Ecclesiastes, (1: 4–11) using it as the very epigram of his novel.

(ヘミングウェイは『コヘレトの言葉』の長い節を引用し、この小説の警句としている。)

One generation passeth[†] away, and another generation cometh[†]; but the earth abideth[†] for ever. The sun also riseth[†], and the sun also goeth[†] down, and hasteth[†] to his place where he arose. The wind goeth[†] toward the south, and turneth[†] about unto the north; it whirleth[†] about continually, and the wind returneth[†] again according to his circuits. All the rivers run into the sea; yet the sea is not full; unto the place from when[††] the rivers come, thither[†††] they return again. (It seems Hemingway used the King James Version of the Bible, but some of his spellings vary from the original.)

[†] 動詞 (pass, come, abide, rise, go, hasten, go, turn, whirl, return) の3人称単数現在形。／ [††]from when = whence = from where ／ [†††] = there

(4 一代過ぎればまた一代が起こり　永遠に耐えるのは大地。5 日は昇り、日は沈み　あえぎ戻り、また昇る。6 風は南に向かい北へ巡り、めぐり巡って吹き　風はただ巡りつつ、吹き続ける。7 川はみな海にそそぐが海は満ちることなく　どの川も、繰り返しその道程を流れる。(ヘミングウェイはKJVを使っているように思われるが、原典とは綴り方が異なっているものもある。))

The Bible passage talks about the repetition of life. Some people, sadly, have lives where each day is the same. Even rich people are sometimes bored with all of the grand things they have: gorgeous houses, expensive furniture, servants, etc. However, there are some poor people who manage to find adventure and excitement in each new day. The difference is attitude. Some poor people find joy in helping people who are even poorer.

> （聖書のこの一節は、人生における繰り返しについて述べている。毎日が同じことの繰り返しでうんざりしてしまう人もいれば、新しい冒険と興奮に満ちた日々を送っている人もいる。その違いは人生に対する姿勢である。）

The writer of Ecclesiastes does offer a remedy for boredom: "Fear God and keep His commandments." The word <u>fear</u> in the King James English does not mean the fear we might have when we see a dangerous animal or monster. "Fear God" means "respect God." If we keep God's commandments we will find opportunities to love other people and develop the talents that we have. Several movies have this idea. In *Music of the Heart*, the great American actress Meryl Streep plays a woman, Roberta, whose husband has deserted her for another woman. Roberta, is extremely depressed until she finds a job in a school in a poor neighborhood. She is a violin teacher, and manages to get the children their own instruments. Finally she prepares them for a big concert. She found happiness in focusing on others.

> （『コヘレトの言葉』の著者は、退屈さを逃れる方法を与えている。それは「神を畏れ、その命令に従え」である。KJVの「神を畏れる」とは、「神を敬う」ことで、神の戒めを守れば、他者を愛する機会が見つかり、自分の才能を伸ばすことができる。『心の調べ』のロバータは、夫の裏切りに会い、沈み込んでしまうが、貧しい地区の学校でバイオリンの教師の仕事を得、生徒たちのためのコンサートを開く。）

Dialogue:

Jack: Hemingway sure could create some depressing stories. *The Sun Also Rises* is really a "downer."

Anne: Life cannot always be bright and happy. Some people have great challenges in their life.

Jack: Jake Barnes really does. He is the main character. He was injured during World War I. He is impotent. And, his girlfriend is not nice. She always comes around him with her new boyfriends. Women can be so mean.

Anne: Of course, Hemingway was alluding to the sadness and boredom of the speaker of Ecclesiastes 1: 4–11. In that Bible story, a rich man is bored and cannot find any reason to live.

> Jack: Well, how does Ecclesiastes end?
> Anne: Basically, the narrator concludes that we must trust that God will make everything all right in the future. I guess that is the meaning of the phrase, "the sun also rises." There is always a tomorrow. I hope I am not like the woman in the novel.
> Jack: Oh, no! You are the sweetest person in the world! I was just expressing my immediate reaction to the novel.

Today Is Friday
(『今日は金曜日』)

(included in *Ernest Hemingway—The Collected Stories*)
Author: Ernest Hemingway（アーネスト・ヘミングウェイ著）
Publication date: 1926 (Originally)(1926 年初版出版)
Publication Company: Everyman's Library (1995, London)（エブリマンズ・ライブラリー（ロンドン、1995 年）

Note: Ernest Hemingway admired men who were physically and mentally strong. He frequently wrote about men who suffered silently. His heroes are typically men who accept their pain stoically (uncomplainingly). His characters are often alone or abandoned. Jesus Christ fit Hemingway's idea of a heroic man. This short story is really a very short drama. Hemingway rewrites the Bible story of the killing of Jesus. He sets the story in a modern setting. The characters are the Roman soldiers who carried out the execution, but the language seems to be the language of a big American city.

（ヘミングウェイは肉体的、精神的に強い人を讃えていた。静かに苦しむ人を描き、その主人公はストイックに痛みを受け入れるのが典型である。イエスはヘミングウェイの描く像に合う。ヘミングウェイはイエスの死を現代の場面にして描いている。）

Main Characters:（主な登場人物）
First Roman Soldier
Second Roman Soldier
Third Roman Soldier
The Wine Seller (or bartender)

Plot （あら筋）

SOME of the details of the real Bible story are intact in this very short story or drama. In the Bible, Jesus was nailed to the Cross. He died on a Friday. He was rather silent (speaking just a few words). In Mark 15:30, there was a crowd of witnesses to the horror of the Crucifixion. These people made fun of Jesus, saying "If you are God, come down from the cross. Save yourself." At the torturing of Jesus while he was on the Cross, one of the soldiers stuck a spear into the side of Jesus (John 19 :34). The Bible suggests that several of the women followers of Jesus witnessed the killing. All of these things are mentioned or implied in the Hemingway story.

（聖書に描かれている詳細がこの短編の中にもそのまま表されている。イエスが十字架に杭ではりつけにされたこと、金曜日に亡くなったこと、言葉少なかったことなどである。十字架刑の場に居合わせた人々は「神ならば、十字架から降りて来い」などと言い、ローマ兵は槍でイエスを突いた。ヘミングウェイの小説には、こうした場面が言及され、暗示されている。）

Hemingway's Imagination （ヘミングウェイの想像）

HOWEVER, Hemingway used his imagination and added things that are not in the Bible. The soldiers in this story meet in a bar after the death of Jesus. They get drunk, and they admire the manner in which Jesus died. They marvel that He seemed to accept the pain with minimal complaint. The Third Soldier is feeling rather ill after witnessing the killing. Perhaps he is more tenderhearted than the other two Roman soldiers. Typical of many soldiers, they are interested in talking about sex. They indicate that Jesus' girlfriend was present at the Crucifixion (There is no Bible indication that Jesus ever had a girlfriend or got married). The men make a dirty joke about the girlfriend.

（ヘミングウェイはその想像力を駆使し、聖書には見られないことも付け加えている。小説中の兵士はイエスの死後酒場で酔っ払い、イエスの死に様を称賛する。第三の兵士は優しい気持ちからか、イエスの死を目撃して具合が悪くなってしまう。兵士には典型的なことであるが、性について語ることが好きで、イエスのガールフレンドが刑場にいたと言っている。（聖書では、イエスにガールフレンドがいたとか、結婚していたとかは何も書かれていない。））

Bible Theme in *Today is Friday*—
（『今日は金曜日』に見られる聖書のテーマ）

Jesus accepted His suffering and death on the Cross
　　（イエスは十字架上での苦しみと死を受け入れる。）

Dialogue:

Stephan: Do you think that artists have the right to add extra details to a historical event?

Martin: I am not sure what you mean. Can you elaborate on your thoughts?

Stephan: Well, take Michelangelo's painting *The Creation*. It shows God wearing a long white robe with a flowing beard. I don't think that the Bible gives such a description of God.

Martin: I see what you mean. Painters and writers often change details and add certain dramatic effects to a real event. I read Hemingway's short story based on the Crucifixion. It is called *Today Is Friday*. At first I was shocked at how he included a scene of Roman soldiers at a bar, just after the death of Jesus.

Stephan: Yes, that is a great example of what I am talking about. Do you think Hemingway was right in distorting the sacred story?

Martin: I don't know if he was right in doing so. But I think intelligent people should keep in mind that art is different from reality.

Stephan: Good point. Intelligent people should be appreciative of art. And they should study the actual event which inspired the art.

The Grapes of Wrath
(『怒りの葡萄』)

Book: *The Grapes of Wrath*

Author: John Steinbeck (ジョン・スタインベック著)

Original Year of Publication: 1939 (1939年初版出版)

Original Publishing Company: Viking Press (バイキング・プレス社)

Year of Centennial Publication: 2002 (one hundred years after the birth of Steinbeck) (生誕百周年記念版：2002年)

Centennial Edition Publisher: Puffin Paperback Books (百周年記念版出版社：パフィン・ペーパーバック・ブックス)

Plot (あら筋)

THE main idea of the novel is rich people exploit poor people. Steinbeck's novel has the same criticism of cruel businessmen as the Book of Amos in the Bible. God is angry when unkind people take advantage of the poor.

(この小説のメイン・テーマは、金持ちが貧しい人々から搾取するということである。これは『アモス書』でも扱われていることである。)

The time period is the 1930s. Because of years of drought, the earth in Oklahoma becomes unsuitable for farming. Many farms go out of business. Some poor people are sharecroppers—farmers who do not own land; they only work on the land and receive a small portion of the crops as salary. However, the situation becomes desperate, and the Joad family (like many others), decides to move to California. They hear that California is like heaven; it has good weather, and fruits grow very well on the West Coast. The Joads see advertisements for farm workers to come to California. They think all of their troubles will be over if they can only get to California. Meanwhile, Tom Joad, an older son of the family, has been newly released from prison. He had killed a man in a bar fight. It is not fully explained why he is released from prison, but he surprises his family by showing up at the old house just as they are about to depart for California—all of the members pile into (and onto) a broken down car.

(時代は1930年代。干ばつのため、オクラホマの土地は農地に適さなくなり、農場がつぶれてしまう。貧しい小作人は望みを持てなくなり、ジョード一家はカリフォルニアに移住する決心をする。おんぼろ車に乗り込んでカリフォルニアに出発しようとしていた時、出獄したばかりの息子トムが現れる。)

The basic story is a road trip. The impoverished family has several hardships as they travel toward California. The car breaks down, the old grandfather dies on the way, the poor travelers from Oklahoma experience discrimination. Nobody seems to want to let the poor "Okies" come into their state.

(物語の中心はカリフォルニアに向かい道中の出来事である。車が故障し、祖父が亡くなり、オクラホマからやってきた一家は差別を受ける。誰もオクラホマの田舎者が自分たちのところに入ってくるのを望んでいない。)

When they arrive in California, they are disappointed that the jobs are not as plentiful as they were lead to believe. The salaries are very low. They have very little food. Tom Joad, and his friend Jim Casy begin to think about protesting the discrimination and exploitation of poor people in California.

(カリフォルニアに着いてみると、言われていたほど仕事が豊富ではなく、給料も安く、食料も少ないので、がっかりしてしまう。トムと友人のジム・ケイシーは、カリフォルニアでの差別と搾取に抗議しようとする。)

Interestingly, Jim Casy is a former Christian preacher. However, he does not have the formal education that most Christian ministers have. None of the main characters of the story have a good education. They speak with very bad English grammar, and apparently their experience with Christian religion seems to have been the highly emotional and irrational variety. Nevertheless, they are good people who are cruelly treated by the wealthy people of American society.

（ジム・ケイシーは以前牧師をしていたが、他の登場人物と同様、正式な教育は受けていなかった。英語の文法もひどく、宗教的にも感情的で非合理的なものであったが、彼らは善人で、アメリカ社会の富裕層からひどい扱いを受けている人々である。）

Steinbeck was interested in the social movements of the 1930s which attempted to liberate the poor.

（スタインベックは、貧しい人々を解放しようとした1930年代の社会運動に興味を持っていた。）

Bible Influence （聖書の影響）

THERE are only a very few direct references to the Bible in this story. But there are <u>many</u> indirect references. Many of the character names come from the Bible. One of the main characters, Jim Casy (the man who gave up his Christian preaching) has the initials of Jesus Christ. And the irony is that Jim Casy had been a bad preacher (he used his authority to seduce women. He became disgusted with himself and left the ministry). However, after abandoning the church, Jim Casy became a better human being. He developed a deep concern for protecting poor people.

（この物語では、聖書への直接的な言及は少ないが、間接的な言及は多く見られる。登場人物の名前は聖書に由来するものが多い。例えば、ジム・ケイシーのイニシャルはJ.C.で、これはイエス・キリストと同じである。彼は女性を誘惑するのに牧師という立場を利用し、その後悔から牧師職を捨てる。教会を去った後で善人になった彼は、貧しい人々を助けることに関心を向ける。）

Let's look at the names of some main characters which suggest Bible personalities:

（聖書に出てくる人物の名前を見てみよう。）

Jim Casy—His initials suggest Jesus Christ; and he offers himself in place of his friend, Tom Joad to the police—an action suggestive of the sacrifice of Jesus Christ on behalf of humanity.

（ジム・ケイシー：イニシャルはイエス・キリストを指すJ.C.で、友人の身代わりとなって警察に出頭する。これは人間の身代わりとなったイエス・キリストを暗示している。）

Rosasharn—This is a countrified contraction of *Rose of Sharon*, one of the beautiful nicknames for Jesus Christ in the Bible. In the novel, this is the name of Tom Joad's sister. She is pregnant, but she is not getting enough good food to nourish her baby.

(ロサシャーン：イエス・キリストを表す Rose of Sharon の田舎訛の形である。物語の中ではトムの妹の名前になっている。妊娠している彼女は、子どものために十分な食べ物を得られずにいる。)

Tom (for Thomas)—Possibly Tom Joad's name is meant to suggest Thomas the friend of Jesus who did not believe, at first, that Jesus had returned from the dead. The character of Tom Joad is that he is suspicious of religion. At the end of the novel, Tom runs away from the police. Before his departure, he makes the famous speech in which he tells his mother that he will dedicate his life to liberating the poor.

(トム：死者の中から復活したイエスを最初信じることができなかったトマスを表している。トム・ジョードは宗教に対して懐疑的である。小説の最後で、トムは警察から逃げるが、その前に、母親に対して「貧しい人々を解放するために人生を捧げる」と告げる。)

Ruthie—This is a variation of Ruth, one of the major Old Testament characters. Ruth was a foreign woman who relocated to Israel with her Israelite mother-in-law. In *The Grapes of Wrath*, Ruthie is the little girl who moves to California with her hungry parents.

(ルーシー：旧約聖書に登場する人物ルツの変形である。ルツはイスラエル人の義母と共にイスラエルに移り住んだ異国の女性である。『怒りの葡萄』では、お腹を空かせた両親と共にカリフォルニアに移住する少女として描かれている。)

Noah—The older brother of Tom Joad. Noah in the Bible (Old Testament), is the famous character who gathered all of the animals into the ark before the Great Flood destroyed life on earth. In the novel, Noah is a silent but hard worker. Perhaps his ability to do physical work is similar to Bible Noah's talent at building the huge ark.

(ノア：トムの兄。旧約聖書では、全人類を滅ぼす大洪水の前に全ての動物を箱舟に乗せた人物である。小説中のノアは、物静かだが一生懸命に働く人である。彼の肉体労働の能力は大きな箱舟を造ったノアの才能に似ている。)

Bible Themes (聖書のテーマ)

1. The Exodus—The Joads leave their home and move to California. In the Old Testament, The Hebrews leave Egypt where they were slaves and try to find their way back to their home country.

   (1. 出エジプト記：ジョード家は家を出てカリフォルニアに移る。旧約聖書では、ヘブライ人がどれとなっていたエジプトを出て、故郷に向かおうとする。)

2. The Special Sin of Cheating Poor People—*The book of Amos* shows God's anger at merchants who looked forward to market days when they could cheat poor people by using inaccurate scales:

Saying, When will the new moon be gone, that we may sell corn? And the Sabbath, that we may set forth wheat, making the ephaph small, and shekel great, and falsifying the balances* by deceit. Amos 8: 5

* Balances means scales for weighing vegetables and other goods in market places.

Just as the bad businessmen in the Old Testament enjoyed cheating poor people, so, too, did the California farm bosses enjoy cheating the poor Oklahoma farm migrants.

(貧しい人々をだます罪：アモス書では、市の日に不正確なはかりを使って貧しい人々をだまそうとする商人に対して神が怒りを向ける。
⁵お前たちは言う。「新月祭はいつ終わるのか、穀物を売りたいものだ。
安息日はいつ終わるのか、麦を売り尽くしたいものだ。
エファ升は小さくし、分銅は重くし、偽りの天秤を使ってごまかそう。(アモス書第8章5節))

　＊天秤とは、市場で野菜などの商品の重さをはかる秤である。

3. A Savior—Jesus Christ took the place of humanity and suffered in our place. Jim Casy took the place of Tom Joad and allowed himself to be arrested.

(救い主：イエス・キリストは、人類の身代わりとなった。ジム・ケーシーはトム・ジョードの身代わりとなって、逮捕された。)

Dialogue:

Caitlynn: Reading *The Grapes of Wrath* makes me angry!

Kelly: Calm down. It is only a novel.

Caitlynn: Yes, but it is based on historical fact—poor people did leave Oklahoma during the "Dust Bowl"[1] years. They thought that their life would be so much better in California.

Kelly: I know. I read about that in my high school history text. Many of the migrants were badly treated by rich people

Caitlynn: Doesn't it make you angry that rich people cheat poor people?

Kelly: Of course it does. But I believe that there are good people in every place. And good people can be either rich or poor.

Caitlynn: You always think positively.

1) **Dust Bowl** ダスト・ボウル (アメリカで1930年代に起こった砂嵐)

A Tale of Two Cities
(『二都物語』)

Author: Charles Dickens（チャールズ・ディケンズ著）
Year of Publication: 1859（1859年出版）
Publishing Company: Pocket Book Classics (1996 is a good paperback edition)
ポケット・ブック・クラシックス (1996年版はお奨めのペーパーブックである。)

Plot（あら筋）

This is a very long British novel of the Victorian period. There are numerous editions of the book, and there are even "Graded Readers Editions" (shortened for second language learners). Basically, the story is about an amazing love triangle. Two men, who look exactly alike, fall in love with the same woman. Sydney Carton is an alcoholic law clerk. Charles Darnay is a wealthy French gentleman. Lucie Mannette, thinks kindly of both of them. But she marries Charles. Sydney is heartbroken, but he promises her that he will do any favor that she asks of him. When Charles is captured by the French peasants during the French Revolution of the 1700s, he is scheduled to have his head cut off. Without being asked by Lucie, Sydney decides he must rescue Charles from prison. He manages to enter the prison, drug Charles, and change clothes with him. He arranged for friends to help remove Charles from the prison. Sydney is prepared to die in place of Charles. Because they look alike, the executioners will never know that they have killed the wrong man.

（『二都物語』は、ヴィクトリア朝時代の長編小説で、様々な版がある。基本的には、この物語は二人のそっくりな男性が同じ女性に恋をしてしまう、愛の三角関係の話である。シドニー・カートンはアルコール依存症の弁護士助手で、シャルル・ダルネイは裕福なフランス紳士である。ルシー・マネットは二人ともよく思っていたが、シャルルと結婚することにした。シドニーは打ちひしがれたが、ルシーが望むことなら彼女のために何でもすると約束する。1700年代のフランス革命の際、シャルルはフランスの農民の囚われの身となり、斬首刑の処せられることになった。ルシーに頼まれるまでもなく、シドニーはシャルルを牢獄から救わなければならないと決心する。彼はなんとか牢獄に入りこみ、シャルルに薬を飲ませて衣服を取りかえる。彼は友人と、シャルルを牢獄から救い出すことを取り決めていた。シドニーはシャルルの代わりに死ぬ覚悟でいる。シドニーとシャルルは瓜二つなので、死刑執行人は、別人を殺してしまったことに気がつくことはない。)

The entire novel includes several important Bible themes:
1. Great friendship
2. A person dying in place of another person
3. Resurrection, or coming back to life.

(この小説全体には、幾つかの聖書のテーマが見られる。
1. 良き友としての関係
2. 他者の身代わりとなって死ぬ人
3. 復活、蘇り)

Wine as a Symbol of the Blood of Jesus Christ
(イエス・キリストの血の象徴としてのワイン)

DICKENS was obviously a great Bible reader. Many of the scenes in the book suggest Bible scenes. For example, there is a scene of a wagon full of wine barrels. The barrels fall off of the truck. The poor people were amazed at wine flowing in the streets. They gather cups or use their hands to get some wine to drink. In the Bible, wine represents the blood of Jesus Christ. Christians sometimes sing songs in Church about the blood of Jesus flowing down from the Cross. They drink a tiny bit of wine or grape juice in Christian services to remember that Jesus bled and died so that human beings could be forgiven of their sins.

(ディケンズは聖書を良く読んでいる人である。『二都物語』の中にも聖書の場面を暗示する場面が多く見られ、その一例が、ワインの樽を満載した荷馬車の場面である。樽が落ち、ワインが道路に流れ出ているのを見て、貧しい人たちは驚き、カップや手を使ってワインを飲もうとする。聖書ではワインはイエス・キリストの血を表している。キリスト教信者は、十字架から流れ落ちるイエスの血について、教会で讃美歌を歌う。人間がその罪を赦されるようにと、イエスが血を流し、死んだということを思い出すため、信者は礼拝の際に少しワインかグレープジュースを飲むのである。)

Bible Quotations (聖書からの引用)

THE novel quotes John 11:25 at the very end. When Sydney prepares himself to die, he cites the famous Bible passage.

(小説の終わりにヨハネによる福音書第11章25節の言葉が引用されている。シドニーは死の準備をし、有名な聖書の一節を引用する。)

The Bible passage that Sydney quotes is the scene of Jesus' arrival at the tomb of his dead friend. Jesus was a particular friend of Lazarus and his two sisters. They had called to Jesus to come to their house when their brother was sick. However, Jesus was slow in arriving at the house. It seemed that Jesus was too late. One of the sisters complains that Jesus was not "on time." Of course, Jesus had a plan. It seems that Jesus waited until He knew that Lazarus was dead. When he arrived, he asked to be taken to the tomb. Jesus called Lazarus to return to life. Lazarus got up. It is one of the favorite Bible stories of many people.

（シドニーが引用するのは、イエスが亡き友の墓に到着した場面である。イエスはラザロとその二人の姉妹と特に親しい間柄であった。二人の姉妹は、兄が病気の時、イエスを呼びにやったのである。しかし、イエスが到着するのは遅すぎた。姉妹の一人が、イエスが「間に合わなかった」と嘆いた。もちろん、イエスにはある計画があった。イエスは、ラザロが死んだことを知るまで待っていたようである。ラザロの家に到着すると、イエスは墓に連れて行くようにと頼んだ。イエスはラザロに生き返るように呼びかけ、ラザロは起き上がった。この話は多くの人が好む話である。）

Page 469 (*A Tale of Two Cities*): John 11: 25–26—*I am the resurrection, and the life, saith*[†] *the Lord: he that believeth*[†] *in me, though he were dead, yet shall he live: and whosoever believeth*[†] *in me shall never die.* (KJV)

[†] 動詞（say、believe）の3人称単数現在形。

(²⁵イエスは言われた。「わたしは復活であり、命である。わたしを信じる者は、死んでも生きる。²⁶生きていて私を信じる者はだれも、決して死ぬことはない。このことを信じるか。」)

Sydney Carton recites these words as he awaits death. As a British citizen, he would not have been harmed in Paris. However, he is posing as the French gentleman so that he can die in Charles' place. Sydney's sacrifice is motivated by two kinds of love: (1) Of course he still has romantic love for Lucie, and (2) He has brotherly love for Charles. He wants Lucie and Charles to be happy. He wants them to raise their little daughter in happiness and love.

（シドニー・カートンは、死を待つ間、この言葉を唱えている。英国国民として、彼はパリで処刑されることはなかったのに。しかし、彼はシャルルの身代わりとなって死ぬため、フランス紳士のふりをしているのである。シドニーが払った犠牲は、二種類の愛によって動かされている。すなわち、(1) ルシーに対する失うことなく持ち続けているロマンチックな愛と、(2) シャルルに対する兄弟愛である。彼はルシーとシャルルに幸福になってほしいと願っている。二人の間の幼き娘を幸福と愛のうちに育ててほしいと願っているのである。）

Dialogue

Yu: It amazes me that Charles Dickens was so religious. *A Tale of Two Cities* has so many references to the Bible. In fact, the major theme of the novel is John 11:25—**"I am the resurrection and the life..."**
Emiko: Why should that surprise you?
Yu: Well, Dickens was married and had 10 children, yet he left his wife and fell in love with a very young actress.
Emiko: Unfortunately, many good people commit sins. The Bible teaches us that no one is completely without sin.
Yu: You are right. Perhaps Dickens was thinking about God's forgiveness when he repeated John 11:25 several times in *A Tale of Two Cities*: **"I am the resurrection and the life; he that believeth in me, though**

> **he were dead, yet shall he live."**
>
> Emiko: Exactly. Maybe Dickens hoped that he would be allowed to live in Heaven after his death.

Appendix

Books of the Bible

Old Testament（旧約聖書）

Book Name	本の名前	Theme/Topic	English Expressions
Genesis	創世記	The Book of Beginnings	More than I can bear (4:9-15)
			A fig leaf (3:6-7)
			By the sweat of his brow (3:16-19)
			Old as Methuselah (5:27)
			A flood of Biblical proportion (7:20-22)
Exodus	出エジプト記	Israel Out of Bondage	(Nothing is) written in stone. (31:18)
			Manna from Heaven (16)
Leviticus	レビ記	The Jewish Priests' Law	Scapegoat (16:6-10)
			Stumblingblock (19:14)
Numbers	民数記	Counting the People	
Deuteronomy	申命記	The Law of Moses	Apple of the [his] eye (32:10)
Joshua	ヨシュア記	Into the Promised Land	Get your feet wet (3:15-16)
Judges	士師記	Jewish Leadership	
Ruth	ルツ記	A Poor Woman's Story	
I Samuel	サムエル記上	Making a Kingdom	Man after my own heart (13:13-14)
II Samuel	サムエル記下	Passing on the Crown	How the mighty have fallen (1:17-27)
I Kings	列王記上	First Kings of Israel	
II Kings	列王記下	Last Kings of Israel	
I Chronicles	歴代誌上	History of Israel, Part 1	Fall on his own sword (10:4-6)
II Chronicles	歴代誌下	History of Israel, Part 2	
Ezra	エズラ記	Coming Back Strong	
Nehemiah	ネヘミヤ記	Restoring the Homeland	
Esther	エステル記	Beauty Contest Winner	
Job	ヨブ記	Bad Things Happen to Good Men	By the skin of our teeth (19:13-20)
			Laughingstock (12:4-5)
Psalms	詩編	Poems and Songs of praise to God	Broken heart (34:18)
			Wit's end (107:23-27)
			Bite [lick] the dust (72:9)
			An upright man (37:37)
			My cup runneth over. (23:5)
			Fire and brimstone (11:5-7)
			Out of the mouths of babes and sucklings (8:1-2)
Proverbs	箴言	Wise Sayings worth Remembering	A baptism of fire (17:3)
Ecclesiastes	コヘレトの言葉（伝道の書）	Wisdom To Live By	Eat, drink and be merry. (8:14-15)
			There is nothing new under the sun. (1:9)
			To everything there is a season. (3:1-8)

Book Name	本の名前	Theme/Topic	English Expressions
			A little bird told me (10:20)
			A fly in the ointment (10:1)
			Two are better than one. (4:9-12)
The Song of Solomon	雅歌	A Love Song	
Isaiah	イザヤ書	Someone Is Coming	Eat, drink and be merry. (22:12-13)
			See eye to eye (52:8)
			A drop in the bucket (40:12-15)
Jeremiah	エレミヤ書	The Weeping Prophet	
Lamentations	哀歌	Tears for Israel	
Ezekiel	エゼキエル書	God is in Control	
Daniel	ダニエル書	Visions of a Visionary	The handwriting on the wall (5:1-16)
			Feet of clay (2:32-33)
			Your number is up! (5:24-28)
Hosea	ホセア書	Loving the Unfaithful	
Joel	ヨエル書	Repent and Live	
Amos	アモス書	Seek Good and not Evil	
Obadiah	オバデヤ書	Pride will lead to a Fall	
Jonah	ヨナ書	Jonah is Always Running	
Micah	ミカ書	Prophet of Destruction	
Nahum	ナホム書	Judgement on Nineveh	
Habakkuk	ハバクク書	Injustice and Suffering	
Zephaniah	ゼファニヤ書	Judgement is Coming!	
Haggai	ハガイ書	Consequences of Disobedience	
Zechariah	ゼカリヤ書	Keep up the Good Work	
Malachi	マラキ書	The Great King to Come	

New Testament（新約聖書）

Book Name	本の名前	Theme/Topic	English Expressions
Matthew	マタイによる福音書	The teachings of Christ	An eye for an eye (5:38-42)
			Salt of the Earth (5:13-16)
			The blind leading the blind (15:10-14)
			The second mile (5:40-42)
			Wolves in sheep's clothing (7:15-20)
			A baptism of fire (3:11)
			Kiss of death (26:47-50)
			Man does not live by bread alone. (4:1-4)
			Strait [straight] and narrow (7:13-14)
			The spirit is willing, but the flesh is weak. (26:41)
			The bitter cup (27:34)
			Prophet without honor in own country (13:53-58)
			Jot and tittle (5:17-18)

Book	Japanese	Theme	Notable phrases
Mark	マルコによる福音書	The actions of Christ	
Luke	ルカによる福音書	The story of Christ	Broken heart (4:18)
			Good Samritan (10:33-35)
			Prodigal (15:11-32)
John	ヨハネによる福音書	Jesus is the Christ of God!	Cast the first stone (8:7)
			Doubting Thomas (20:24-25)
The Acts	使徒言行録	History of the Early Church	It is better to give than to receive. (20:35)
			A baptism of fire (2:1-4)
Romans	ローマの信徒への手紙	Paul's Gospel	
I Corinthians	コリントの信徒への手紙一	Christian Love	
II Corinthians	コリントの信徒への手紙二	Living for Christ	Thorn in the flesh (12:7)
Galatians	ガラテヤの信徒への手紙	Grace Over Law	As you sow, so shall you reap. (6:7)
			Fall from grace (5:4)
Ephesians	エフェソの信徒への手紙	Christ and the Church	
Philippians	フィリピの信徒への手紙	Live in Joy!	
Colossians	コロサイの信徒への手紙	Christ is God	
I Thessalonians	テサロニケの信徒への手紙一	Resurrection is Real!	
II Thessalonians	テサロニケの信徒への手紙二	No Work, No Eat!	
I Timothy	テモテへの手紙一	Keep on Truckin', Tim	You can't take it with you. (6:6-10)
			Fight the good fight (6:12)
			Old wives' tale (4:7)
II Timothy	テモテへの手紙二	Guard & Preach the Gospel	Fight the good fight (2:3-4)
Titus	テトスへの手紙	Encouraging a Young Preacher	
Philemon	フィレモンへの手紙	Accept my Brother, Brother	
Hebrews	ヘブライ人への手紙	Jesus is Supreme	Labor of love (6:10)
			A two-edged sword (4:12)
James	ヤコブの手紙	Faith and Works	
I Peter	ペトロの手紙一	Christian Life and Duties	
II Peter	ペトロの手紙二	Facing False Teachers	
I John	ヨハネの手紙一	God's Love among Men	
II John	ヨハネの手紙二	Selective Christian Faith	
III John	ヨハネの手紙三	Two Types of Leaders	
Jude	ユダの手紙	Contend for the Faith	
Revelation	ヨハネの黙示録	He is Coming Again!	

著者紹介

Jim D. Batten（ジム D. バットン）
  担当箇所：第1章
  専門分野：異文化間コミュニケーション
  茨城キリスト教大学教授

Harris G. Ives（ハリス G. アイヴス）
  担当箇所：第2章、第3章
  専門分野：アメリカ文学
  茨城キリスト教大学教授

髙橋　教雄（たかはし　のりお）
  担当箇所：日本語訳・要約および KJV 脚注（第1章、第2章、第3章）
  専門分野：英語学
  茨城キリスト教大学教授

上野　尚美（うえの　なおみ）
  担当箇所：はしがき、脚注（第2章、第3章）
  専門分野：英語教育学
  茨城キリスト教大学教授

英語における聖書の言葉
英語学習者のために
Bible Words in Everyday English

2015年3月20日　初版発行

著　者　Jim D. Batten
　　　　Harris G. Ives
　　　　髙橋教雄
　　　　上野尚美

発行者　山口隆史
印　刷　株式会社太平印刷社
製　本　株式会社太平印刷社

発行所　株式会社音羽書房鶴見書店
〒113-0033 東京都文京区本郷 4-1-14
TEL 03-3814-0491
FAX 03-3814-9250
URL: http://www.otowatsurumi.com
e-mail: info@otowatsurumi.com

Printed in Japan
ISBN978-4-7553-0283-1 C3098
組版・ほんのしろ／装幀・熊谷有紗（オセロ）